THE SOE'S BROTHERS OF VENGEANCE

T0322492

About the Author

The idea for *The Twins* came to Peter Jacobs when he bought Alfred Newton's medals, although he was already a keen military historian. He served in the Royal Air Force for thirty-seven years as an air defence navigator on the F4 Phantom and Tornado F3, after which he completed staff tours at HQ 11 Group, HQ Strike Command, the Ministry of Defence and the RAF College Cranwell. Jacobs has written several books, including the highly successful *The RAF in 100 Objects* (The History Press, 2017). Married with five children, he is now retired and lives in Lincoln.

THE SOE'S BROTHERS OF VENGEANCE

PETER JACOBS

Front cover illustrations: (left) Lieutenant Henry Newton (TNA HS 9/1097/1) and *(right)* Lieutenant Alfred Newton (TNA HS 9/1096/8).

First published 2020, as *The Twins: The SOE's Brothers of Vengeance*
This paperback edition first published 2024

The History Press
97 St George's Place, Cheltenham,
Gloucestershire, GL50 3QB
www.thehistorypress.co.uk

British Library Cataloguing in Publication Data.
A catalogue record for this book is available from the British Library.

ISBN 978 1 80399 695 0

Typesetting and origination by The History Press
Printed and bound in Great Britain by TJ Books Limited, Padstow, Cornwall

Trees for LYfe

CONTENTS

ACKNOWLEDGEMENTS

When I first started out on this journey, I hoped there would be people out there who were prepared to help me, because without the assistance of others this story could not be fully told. I need not have worried – there were. And so, I would now like to thank them all, whether they helped me during my research at a national institution, answered one of my many emails, provided me with an image for the book or gave up their valuable time during my visits to France and Germany, showing me around and sharing their knowledge.

First, I would like to thank the staff at the National Archives, Kew, and the Imperial War Museum in London. Books like this would not be possible without the help and support of these marvellous national institutions. We are so lucky to have them.

In addition, more websites and chat forums have become available online over the years. There are far too many of them to mention here but, run by enthusiasts, they provide a wealth of information. I have learned so much from websites and associated SOE forums.

Most of all, I would like to thank all those who helped me put the detail of this story together. In no particular order, they are: Chris Trigg (for his help with tracing details of the Newton family); Maria Choules (Commonwealth War Graves Commission); Marcus Bateman and Patrick Yarnold (Puttenham & Wanborough History Society); Kristina Lawson, Trudie Rawlings and Angela Muchmore (Tun Abdul Razak Research Centre, Brickendonbury); Mandy Pover (Stoke City Central Library); Cherif Boussoufa (Hôtel Château Perrache, Lyon); Adrien Allier (Mémorial National Prison de Montluc, Lyon); Stephane Bogner (No. 84 Avenue Foch, Paris); Wendy Santerre (Mémorial de l'internement et de la déportation Camp de Royallieu, Compiègne); and Sandra Siegmund and Rikola-Gunnar Lüttgenau (Buchenwald and Mittelbau-Dora Memorials Foundation).

I must also thank my wife, Claire, for willingly following me around the streets of Lyon and Paris, which included spending our valuable time together in former Gestapo headquarters and a prison, and for putting up with me spending endless hours in the study; even now in my retirement. Thank you to my daughter, Rebecca, for accompanying me during the long drive and visits to Compiègne and Buchenwald.

I would also like to acknowledge the other authors who have written about the SOE over the years. They have all helped to keep the story alive. In the case of this particular story, I must first single out Jack Thomas for his book, *No Banners*, published by W.H. Allen in 1955. Through this book, the Twins – Alfred and Henry Newton – were able to tell their gripping wartime story in their own words. It is a must-read and, while some of the events have inevitably been included here, I believe their personal accounts are best left told in their own words in *No Banners*.

There are other publications that proved to be valuable sources of information, particularly those written by agents who served alongside the Twins. Sydney Hudson, for example, went through preliminary training at Wanborough Manor with them, and so his memoires in *Undercover Operator* provide a good cross-reference for that period. Similarly, Peter Churchill's *Duel of Wits* describes in detail the preparation for the Sainte-Assise mission that never happened.

In *Who Lived to See the Day*, Philippe de Vomécourt, for whom the Twins first worked in the field, provides a valuable insight into the troubles in France at the time. And Christopher Burney, who suffered the hardships of captivity with the Twins, gives his account of life at Fresnes Prison and the concentration camp at Buchenwald in his books, *Solitary Confinement* and *The Dungeon Democracy*.

These are just a few of the many publications relating to this story, all of which are included in the bibliography. As for the images used in this book, they have come from my own collection unless otherwise stated.

Finally, I wish to pay tribute to all the men and women of the SOE, who bravely went into the field. Courage comes in many different forms, especially during wartime, but all those who went into Nazi-occupied France displayed courage in abundance. They came from all walks of life and were there for varying reasons, but they all went into the field knowing they would probably receive no recognition for their actions and their lives could be cut short in a most miserable way. Without their courage there would be no books such as this.

My personal thanks also go to the management and staff at The History Press, particularly Chrissy McMorris and Jezz Palmer for their work behind the scenes in order for this story to be told.

INTRODUCTION

Nearly eighty years have now passed since the sinking of SS *Avoceta*, a 3,442-ton steam passenger liner belonging to the Yeoward Line, which was sunk by a German U-boat, *U-203*, during the last minutes of 25 September 1941 while on her return passage from Gibraltar to her home port of Liverpool. The wreck, records tell me, lies at the bottom of the North Atlantic at a position of 47°57'N and 24°05'W, some 700 nautical miles off the south-west tip of Ireland.

While the loss of the *Avoceta* represents a minute part of the immense slaughter that took place in the North Atlantic during the Second World War, its position is important for this story because it marks the grave of seven members of the Newton family, and the consequences of what happened that night would be felt elsewhere for the rest of the war. For, having been told of the loss of their family – their parents, their wives and three children – two brothers, Alfred and Henry Newton, were from that moment on consumed with a passion for revenge. Their hatred of the Nazis was implacable.

I first came across the story of Alfred and Henry Newton a few years ago when I bought Alfred's medals. I knew very little about him at that stage, other than he had served with the Special Operations Executive, the SOE, during the Second World War. But with the medals came other bits and pieces, including the book *No Banners* by Jack Thomas, published in 1955 and written with the benefit of the brothers still being alive at the time.

Fascinated by what I had read about the Newton brothers – or 'the Twins', as they were known within the SOE, even though they had been born more than ten years apart – I simply wanted to know more. My research naturally took me to the Imperial War Museum and the National Archives where the Twins' private papers and official files are held, having been made available to the public in recent years.

From these sources, we now know far more about the Twins and their family. They had a sister, Lola, who had married before the war to become a Vivet and remained in the Paris suburb of Gentilly throughout the Nazi occupation. She heard nothing of them from 1943 and assumed her brothers must long be dead, but she never gave up hope and kept writing to the Red Cross until she eventually received news at the end of the war that they had both survived. We also know there was an uncle and auntie, Mr and Mrs James Boorn, living in London during the war. And from other sources we now know the true identities of the agents who had worked so closely with the Twins in

France, and we know far more about what happened that fateful night in September 1941 out in the depths of the North Atlantic.

And so, we can add substance to the story told in *No Banners* and put the Twins' story into context. Way back in 1955 the book was unable to reveal certain things, either because of the sensitivities at the time, the Official Secrets Act or simply because Alfred and Henry did not know all the facts.

To understand their story better, I decided to follow the path trodden by the Twins all those years ago. My travels took me to France – Lyon, Paris and Compiègne – and ultimately to Buchenwald in central Germany. It was a humbling experience and I was extremely fortunate to meet many people along the way who were prepared to help (their names are included in the acknowledgements).

However, when I set off on my journey I never imagined that in Lyon I would have breakfast in the room that had once been Klaus Barbie's office, nor had I ever imagined that I would be given a tour inside the notorious No. 84 Avenue Foch in Paris. The importance of both these places will become evident later, but I am sure there will not be many modern-day historians who have had such a privilege.

Inevitably, though, I came across some inconsistencies between what I had discovered and the story told in *No Banners* that, in places, is colourfully and dramatically told. For example, the book describes an uncomfortable moment in a café in Lyon during July 1942, involving the Twins and four Germans. In the book, the Twins claim that one of the Germans, wearing a trench coat and

accompanied by a large Alsatian dog, was the notorious
Klaus Barbie. This is unlikely to have been the case. Barbie,
the 'Butcher of Lyon', did not arrive in the city until the
Germans occupied southern France later that year, some
four months after the Twins claimed to have seen him,
although they would meet Barbie all too soon.

There are also inconsistencies between published
sources – an example being when trying to establish how
many were on the same preliminary training course at
Wanborough Manor as the Twins. In *No Banners* it is suggested there were eleven on the course. Sydney Hudson,
meanwhile, who is known to have been on the same
course as the Twins, refers in *Undercover Operator* to being
in a group of some twenty. John Starr, who is also known
to have been on the same course, refers in Jean Overton
Fuller's book, *The Starr Affair,* to there being about four-
teen, while in Patrick Yarnold's *Wanborough Manor: School
for Secret Agents*, the course is said to initially have had eight
members, which then increased to twelve. When trying
to determine if the Twins met up with Brian Stonehouse
after the three had been dropped into France together, the
Twins' mission report clearly states they had twice met up
with him in France. Yet, according to Tom Bower in his
book, *Klaus Barbie: Butcher of Lyons*, published some forty
years after the war, Stonehouse is quite emphatic that
he never met the Newton brothers after their insertion
into France.

Such inconsistencies do not affect the overall story of
the Twins. The point of highlighting some of them here
is to show the difficulty we now face when trying to piece
together a sequence of events that happened nearly eighty
years ago.

Where discrepancies do exist, I have chosen to go with the version that is either the most consistent or that I consider most likely to be correct. However, if there are any errors, then I can only apologise in advance. And, it is imperative that we do not fall into the trap of making accusations or questioning today the decisions made by individuals at the time. We are seldom in possession of all the facts. Only those who were there know what really happened.

However, we must start somewhere, and using the official files, records and private papers of Alfred and Henry, all backed up by the personal accounts of those who served with them, there is more than enough to be able to tell this remarkable story, although there is only limited space to tell it. Please note that I use Alfred and Henry when referring to them individually throughout the book, but collectively as 'the brothers' before they joined the SOE, after which they become 'the Twins', although to the French they were Auguste and Artus and to the Germans, '*die Zwillinge*'.

Finally, as this book is about the Twins and their time with the SOE, the story concludes at the end of the Second World War, but rather than leave you wondering what happened next, it is worth briefly summarising the rest of their lives here, as both Alfred and Henry recovered to some extent from their ordeal.

They initially ran the Red Tape club in Hanley, Stoke-on-Trent, in partnership with their wartime colleague, John Starr. After running the club, Alfred worked for the British Overseas Airways Corporation in London, planning flights for businessmen and celebrities, while living in a tiny Chelsea flat. He married Doris in 1952 and the couple settled in Staines, from where they ran a printing business.

Henry, meanwhile, had been granted a full disability pension after the war and was unable to work again. He lived a quiet life in Walthamstow, then part of Essex, where he enjoyed breeding terriers and making rugs in his workshop. In 1954 he married Margaret and the couple settled in Walthamstow.

In 1959 the Twins' story was serialised in the *Empire News and Sunday Chronicle* under the title 'Twins Against the Gestapo', in which they were described as 'Britain's toughest secret agents'. They were also amongst half a dozen former SOE agents who returned to Paris and Lyon in 1966, filmed by National Broadcasting Company cameras for viewers in the United States.

Their time in captivity had crippled them and they were both compensated under the terms of an Anglo-German agreement, made in 1964, in respect of UK nationals who were victims of Nazi persecution during the Second World War. Alfred's numerous medical problems were mounting and so he and Doris spent time living in New Zealand and Spain before returning to Middlesex in the mid-1970s, where he became something of a recluse in his suburban home, venturing no further than his garden. Alfred died in a nursing home in Ashford on 6 July 1978 at the age of 64.

Henry had also suffered the mental scars of his wartime ordeal and was left in a nervous state. His deteriorating health also meant a move. He and Margaret moved to Herne Bay in Kent and then to Alicante in Spain where, on 16 January 1980, Henry died at his home at the age of 76.

And now, sixty-five years after *No Banners* first appeared, and with the benefit of now having access to new and more in-depth material, it is time to retell the story of Alfred and Henry Newton, and to set it into a more meaningful context that we can better understand. It is a remarkable story of courage based on a burning desire for revenge. I hope you enjoy the book.

Peter Jacobs

1

TROUBLE IN STORE

With the Allied convoy sighted once more, *U-203* slipped quietly out of its submarine pen at Saint-Nazaire. The harbour on the north bank of the River Loire estuary had changed enormously from a quiet fishing village and since its more recent pre-war days as a transatlantic port. Now, the docks and buildings once belonging to the magnificent French line Compagnie Générale Transatlantique had given way to the huge submarine pens under construction.

It was 20 September 1941; a Saturday, not that it made any difference to the crew of *U-203* – it was war, after all. Memories of quiet and enjoyable weekends spent relaxing with family and friends had already faded into the distant past. Besides, it had been seven weeks since their last patrol and everyone seemed eager to head back out into the Atlantic once again. Reports of an Allied convoy bound for England had added to the excitement and anticipation on board. Now, several U-boats, including *U-203*, were being directed into position to mount an attack.

For 28-year-old Kapitänleutnant Rolf Mützelburg, it was good to be back at sea after the time spent ashore. It had been far too long. The son of a naval officer, he was always going to spend his life at sea. He had enlisted into the Reichsmarine at the age of 19 and by the outbreak of the Second World War was in command of a minesweeper flotilla. But it was submarines he had always wanted and, having volunteered for U-boats, he was now in command of *U-203*, one of the Kriegsmarine's newest boats.

Alongside him in the conning tower was Hans Gilardone, a commander in training of the same rank who had joined the crew for the patrol, and the boat's *Wachoffizier* (watch officer), Oberfähnrich zur See Hans-Jürgen Haupt, an experienced former merchant navy officer and *U-203*'s second in command. Shadowing their every move was the young second *Wachoffizier*, Leutnant zur See Heinz-Dieter Mohs. He would mark his twenty-second birthday during the patrol, but any celebrations would have to wait until they were safely back ashore.

Although this was to be just their third operational patrol, Mützelburg was quietly pleased with how well his forty-five-man crew were shaping up. Since leaving Kiel for their maiden combat patrol a little over three months before, five Allied ships, totalling 15,000 tonnes, had been sent to the bottom of the Atlantic. It had been a good start and after a well-earned rest it was now time to go hunting again.

Once clear of the estuary, Mützelburg set *U-203* onto a west-north-westerly course; his plan being to intercept the convoy somewhere to the south-west of Ireland.

Because of minefields in the southern part of the Irish Sea and the neutrality of Eire, he knew the Allied convoys were forced to pass to the west of Ireland before finally heading for their destination. The weather was good and, all being well, *U-203* would be in position ready to attack in a little over seventy-two hours. Joining them would be two other U-boats that happened to be in the vicinity having just attacked another convoy, while a fourth was on its way. Together, they would penetrate the convoy's perimeter before simultaneously making their attack in a salvo of torpedoes. It would be a classic and devastating U-boat attack.

As *U-203* headed out into the Atlantic, Convoy HG.73 – twenty-five Allied merchantmen and their Royal Navy escorts – continued its passage northwards bound for England. Flying his flag in the British steam passenger-cargo ship SS *Avoceta*, the Convoy Commodore, Rear Admiral Kenelm Creighton, knew all too well that it would not be long before they came under attack.

The recent introduction of the convoy system had seen a change in U-boat tactics in the Atlantic. Where once the U-boats had operated alone, the compact convoys now made it difficult to pick off an isolated ship and so they had started operating in groups, known as 'wolf packs'. Only a matter of days before, a convoy outbound from Liverpool had the dubious distinction of being the first to be attacked by a wolf pack, which at its peak involved eight U-boats and resulted in the sinking of ten Allied ships with the loss of 400 lives. Creighton knew that HG.73 had been lucky so far, but as they were now just a few days from their destination they would soon come under the protection of RAF Coastal Command bases in south-west England,

and if the U-boats waited any longer they ran the risk of coming under attack themselves.

It was now a matter of waiting to see what happened next. It was certain, though, that the convoy would come under attack. Only bad weather could come to its rescue, and there was no sign of that. Creighton knew how threatening the situation had become. It was time to bring the children up from the cabins below to the smoking room directly beneath the bridge. Should the *Avoceta* be hit, then hopefully they had some chance of making it into a lifeboat.

As darkness fell, the passengers settled down for another night at sea. All they could do now was to pray for a quiet and safe following day.

★★★

Miles away, in the Dordogne in south-western France, 37-year-old Henry Newton and his younger brother, Alfred, were contemplating what they should do next. It was the end of another fine, late summer's day, but with the rest of their family on their way to England they had a feeling of emptiness neither enjoyed.

France had long been their home. Their father, Ernest, was a former horse-racing jockey from Rochdale in Lancashire. When his age eventually forced him out of the saddle, he met and married a cabaret artist, Matilda Elvira Boorn, after which the couple spent many years working their way around Europe. They had married in Italy, raised their family in Spain and since 1924 had settled in France, with the family home in Chantilly in the northern suburbs of Paris where Ernest had found work as a trainer in a racing stable.

Alfred, born in Valencia on 19 February 1914, was more than ten years younger than Henry, who had been born in Jerez on 10 October 1903, but the brothers had always been extremely close. From an early age they had followed in their mother's footsteps to become cabaret artists. Known as the Boorn Brothers, after her maiden name, they had thrilled audiences for a decade at music halls across Europe and South America with their crazy comedy and tap-dancing act.

The brothers were in no way tall – each stood at around 5ft 8in – but at first glance their physical and rugged appearance, with their short brown hair, gave the impression of tough, hard-boiled individuals – and they were. However, beneath the surface they were both gentle and kind, with Henry being the quieter of the two, and they were both fluent in French, Spanish and English.

Much had happened in the two years since Europe had been at war, and fond memories of the last days of peace had long faded into the distant past. It was hard to believe that only a couple of years ago the brothers had been the headline act at the new Casino Municipal in the coastal resort of Saint-Jean-de-Luz, where fishing boats clustered around the harbour and a row of white houses topped with red roofs stretched along the beach of fine golden sand. Against the blue sea and cloudless sky, it presented a most tranquil scene.

Then came the voice of the French Prime Minister, Édouard Daladier, shattering any hopes of a lasting peace in Europe. Further broadcasts and posters called men to arms. Audiences thinned as men disappeared for service until there were only the elderly and young boys left. And when the casino's doors were finally closed, the brothers were left with no other option than to pack their bags and board the train for Paris.

By then, the family had moved to Gentilly in the southern suburbs of Paris. Alfred and Henry included, there were nine living in the family home. There was Henry's wife, the dark and vivacious Marcelle. She was from Bordeaux, a couple of years younger than him and spoke fluent English at a rate faster than anyone else. They had married in Paris in the summer of 1929. Then there was Alfred's wife, Theodosia, known as Thea. She was a pretty and petite, blonde German-born dancer from Berlin and the same age as Alfred. They had married in 1932, also in Paris, and she was an excellent mother to their three young boys: Henry, known as 'Gigi', Jimmy and little baby Ernest, affectionately known as 'Coco'. There were also the brothers' parents, whom the children called Nanny and Patter.

On the outbreak of war, Alfred and Henry went to the British Consul in Paris and asked if they should evacuate their family to England, and themselves join the British Army, but the consul told them to do nothing and to wait and see how things developed. Then, a few weeks later, the brothers were summoned to the local town hall at Gentilly and although British subjects, they were enrolled as dispatch riders in the Front Passive, a French equivalent to Britain's ARP (Air Raid Precautions).

Alfred and Henry remained convinced it was only a matter of time before they were called for armed service, even though they had no real ties with Britain, their last visit to England having been a few years before while appearing at the Vaudeville Theatre in London. But with France facing an uncertain future, they decided it would be best to get their family well away from Paris, and so the Newtons hired a small cottage in the hamlet of Pézou near Vendôme, 100 miles to the south-west of the capital in the department of Loire. And as soon as the family had settled, the brothers returned to Paris to await the call to arms.

But the call to arms never came. The phoney war dragged on until May 1940, when Hitler suddenly struck. As the Germans approached Paris, Alfred and Henry headed south. With France in full retreat, the roads were so congested that it took them several days to reach Pézou and, as there was no knowing just how far the Germans would advance, the Newtons decided to head even further south.

All they had for transport was an old René-Gillet motorcycle and sidecar, once the property of a Paris fire station, which the brothers had earlier commandeered. With Nanny, Marcelle and the three children crammed into the sidecar with one of the family's two dogs and a cat, and Thea sat astride its nose, Alfred took up his position in the riding seat with Patter behind and their Alsatian dog wedged in between. It might have been overcrowded, but it worked. There was no room for Henry, though. He had to follow behind on a bicycle and catch up every now and then.

The Newtons decided to head for the port of Bordeaux, from where they hoped to escape France and either get to England or, perhaps, the safety of Spain or Portugal. Slowly they all pressed on south, through the ancient city of Blois in central France but, having arrived in Périgueux, they heard that Bordeaux was in German hands.

France had fallen after a campaign lasting just six weeks, leaving the country's proud military reputation in ruins and its government divided. It was left to a First World War hero, Marshal Philippe Pétain, to sign a humiliating armistice with Germany.

However, while Hitler would always be suspicious of the French, the total occupation of France was an unnecessary liability and, given that France had delivered a government that was willing to co-operate, dividing the country seemed an ideal solution and allowed him to concentrate his efforts on the invasion of Britain as a necessary preliminary to his attack on Russia.

The legitimacy of Pétain's leadership was immediately challenged by the exiled, and at that time little known, French officer, Brigadier General Charles de Gaulle. From London, de Gaulle claimed to represent the legitimacy and continuity of the French nation and used the BBC to broadcast his message to the French people at home to continue to resist the Nazi occupation. But however shameful the French might have considered the armistice to be, its terms seemed curiously mild and somewhat sympathetic in their regard for the French.

France was left with an unoccupied zone, called the *Zone Libre* (translated as the 'free zone'), in the south of the country and inland from the Atlantic coast, which was administered from the spa town of Vichy, while the Germans occupied and governed the northern zone, the *Zone Occupée* (occupied zone), from Paris. A demarcation line dividing the zones ran just to the north of the River Cher, crossed the Loire to the south of Nevers and then cut across country to the Swiss border. There was no fence or barbed wire indicating the boundary of each zone, but the line did follow obvious features, such as a road or a river, and was closely patrolled by the Germans on the occupied side. The only way of legitimately travelling between the two zones was with a valid permit, but these were severely restricted and so most who wanted to make the crossing had to do so by some other way.

The demarcation line had given those living in the south a certain feeling of independence and freedom, and it was in the south where the reconstruction of France would begin. However, just because the south was unoccupied, it did not mean resisters had total freedom to operate in the region; far from it. The Vichy Police guarded its integrity, and it did mean there were fewer Germans about, but although the armistice agreement had forbidden German military forces from operating in the unoccupied zone, the ruling was blatantly ignored by the Nazis.

The Gestapo (*Geheime Staatspolizei*, Germany's secret police) operated in the unoccupied zone from the start, wearing civilian clothing and often using false identities and papers provided by the Vichy Government. Gestapo agents were as omnipresent in unoccupied France as they were in the occupied areas of Europe. They operated without any restriction by civil authority, and agents could not be tried for their actions. Whatever they undertook, no consequences would arise. And by carrying out the orders of the Vichy regime, Pétain's police were working for the Germans, whether they recognised the fact or not.

The more Alfred and Henry found out, the more they concluded there was little sense in trying to move on

anywhere else. The safest place for the family was to be
tucked up somewhere in southern France. Any thoughts
of trying to hit back at the enemy were put on hold, for
the time being at least. Their immediate priority was to
find somewhere for the family to live, and after making
a few enquiries at the *Comité d'Accueil* (a committee that
helped find refugees somewhere to live), the Newtons
were sent to a barn in the isolated hamlet of Cendrieux,
20 miles further south, which they shared with a group of
refugees from Paris.

Cendrieux was a small community of just 500 people
and so refugees were not always made to feel welcome.
Gradually, though, many of the refugees filtered out into
neighbouring villages and towns in search of work and
better amenities. The Newtons, however, stayed and were
even able to rent a small house on the edge of the hamlet.
The locals soon warmed to them, referring to the family as
'*nos Anglais*' – 'our English'.

Having settled into the community, Alfred and Henry
were keen to do something to disrupt the enemy's war
effort. They began observing those around them. Most
villagers seemed neither convicted Vichyites nor Gaullists,
and so the brothers decided the best they could initially
do was stop them falling for the constant pro-German
propaganda, fuelled by the Vichy-controlled radio and
newspapers. But, while some were ready to do anything to
upset the enemy, there was a small and dangerous group of
others who seemingly hated the British and were likely to
become collaborators.

Realistically, there was little the brothers could do, but
they started off by spreading news of what was going on
in the war to counter the pro-German propaganda. Using

a hidden receiver to pick up the BBC Home Service, they passed on its news twice a day to a trusted group, who then hurried away on bicycles to nearby villages to spread the word. Those receiving the information would, in turn, spread the news further still.

The bush telegraph worked well. One courier, for example, a girl called Flavie, the daughter of a local farmer, André Perdioux, would happily cycle 25 miles a day to collect and deliver the news. Word was soon spread over 100 miles, but through their expanding network the brothers were saddened to hear that their family home in Chantilly had been ransacked. Furniture and belongings had been removed, presumably to grace some German officer's quarters somewhere else.

The weeks passed. Europe had been at war for a year. Gradually, the 'Nuisance Committee', as the Newton brothers called them, grew both in size and ideas. They met at Perdioux's farm to plan their next move, but at that stage their activities were restricted. At best, they could only ever cause minor disruption, such as putting sugar into the petrol tank of a Vichy official's car or spoiling an officer's uniform, but their ideas soon became more ambitious. They discussed how to gather and store weapons and explosives and came up with plots aimed at preventing the forwarding of enemy goods and raw materials.

Unfortunately for Alfred and Henry, though, their late-night bicycle rides and early morning fishing trips had come to the attention of the authorities. They were summoned to Périgueux and questioned by Vichy officials, the outcome being the brothers were allowed home but only on what was called 'forced residence'. Every morning they were required to report to an official who was responsible for their behaviour, while the gendarmes at nearby Vergt were to ensure the brothers did not stray more than a couple of miles from their home.

This latest incident merely reinforced what the brothers had been thinking for some time. Neither had any intention of staying in Cendrieux for the rest of the war. Their family was safe, and they had formed the nucleus of what could prove to be a useful resistance group for the future, and so it was now time to make their way to England.

But then, out of nowhere, came a letter from the American Consul General in Marseille and any thoughts the brothers had of escaping France were suddenly put on hold. The letter urged all British civilians residing in unoccupied France to leave the country as soon as could be arranged. Negotiations had taken place with Vichy officials for the safe repatriation of British subjects, both under and over military age, via the French hospital ship *Djenne*. The letter went on to emphasise that those who elected to remain in France did so at their own risk as the American Consul would no longer be able to protect British interests.

The arrival of the letter was like a bomb going off. The Newtons had thought their days of travelling were over. They were faced with a most difficult decision, and whatever they chose to do there was huge risk attached. If the family travelled to England by sea, as was being proposed, there was the risk the ship might strike a mine or even come under attack, even though it was a hospital ship. Alternatively, if they ignored the advice and remained in France there was the risk the Nazis would eventually occupy the whole of the country, and they were under no illusions as to what that would mean.

In the end, the family decided that Marcelle, Thea, the three children and Nanny and Patter would all travel to England on the *Djenne*, while Alfred and Henry would follow on behind at the earliest opportunity. However, nothing more was heard as to when the family were required to leave. Christmas came and there was still no news and so the family put everything into making it special as they had no idea when they might get the chance to enjoy the festive season together again.

Then came spring. There had been further letters from the American Consul, but nothing as to when the repatriation would take place. Negotiations with Vichy officials seemed to have broken down. Finally, the plan to use the *Djenne* was cancelled. Instead, the family must make their own way to Lisbon in Portugal, via Spain, from where the matter would be in the hands of the American authorities.

Meanwhile, Vichy officials had been stamping down harder on subversive activities. Alfred and Henry were again summoned to Périgueux, this time to appear in front of a military tribunal, the outcome being they were sent for disciplinary labour at Chancelade, just a few miles down the road, and given a final warning there could be no further trouble in the future.

Chancelade was not a prison, it was a labour camp, albeit a secure one. Alfred and Henry spent the nights there and during the daylight hours they were sent out to work. Chancelade was run in a relatively easy way and so the brothers were able to serve their sentence without any real hardship. There was just one roll call in the morning, otherwise things were quite relaxed.

It was now the summer of 1941, but it would shortly be time for their family to leave for England. Only the children were looking forward to the adventure with great excitement, while Thea and Marcelle feared what might lie ahead; Nanny and Patter too. But they never let their fear show, certainly not in front of the children.

With the summer all but over, it was finally time for the family to leave. Alfred and Henry were given time off from Chancelade to go and say goodbye.

The final hours together were difficult. Alfred watched his three young boys, all of them fast growing up, getting ready to depart. Gigi was now 8 years old and, although rather shy, he was the oldest of the three with a responsible head on his young shoulders. Jimmy was two years younger and altogether different. A stocky young boy with long, black lashes and mischievous blue eyes, which the local young girls all loved, there was no doubt that he would grow up to be a handsome chap. And then there was little Coco. He was now nearly 3 years old and no longer a baby but a smart little boy, brawny and sun-tanned.

With their bags packed, the family spent their last morning together having breakfast. Watching them during that last time together, Alfred would have given his soul to have kept them with him for ever. They had already said their goodbyes to friends and neighbours and were chatting happily together, just as they had always done when going on a trip. They even spoke about shopping in Lisbon; the shops would no doubt be full of wonderful things to buy.

When it was time to leave, they all piled into a van. A friend had come to take them the 6 miles to the railway station at La Gélie, from where they intended to catch the Bergerac train. From there they would continue across the border into Spain and eventually on to Portugal.

When the train pulled in there was hardly time to say goodbye. Perhaps it was better that way. Alfred and Henry had dreaded the moment. Then, with the blow of a whistle and the waving of a green flag, the train slowly pulled away in a cloud of steam. The family had gone.

Alfred felt lost and sick. His heart was frozen. He sat down on a luggage trolley and, without shame, burst into tears.

2

CONVOY HG.73

It had been a pleasant, if rather quiet stay in Gibraltar for Kenelm Creighton. Now aged 58, he had been called from retirement on the outbreak of the Second World War and appointed Commodore of Ocean Convoys with the rank of rear admiral. It was all quite different to the four years he had spent with Admiral Beatty's battlecruiser squadron during the First World War.

Rather than use his normal room at a busy hotel overlooking the straits to North Africa, Creighton had instead enjoyed the calm and tranquil setting of the Mount, the official residence of the Royal Navy's most senior officer in Gibraltar, courtesy of his old naval friend, Frederick Edward-Collins. Some forty years earlier the two had spent their early naval days together, serving as young lieutenants on the China station. Now a vice admiral, Sir Frederick had been appointed Commander-in-Chief North Atlantic with responsibility for the administration of the naval base at Gibraltar, used by convoy escorts operating in the North Atlantic.

Fortunately for Creighton, the outbound passage from Liverpool, Convoy OG.72 (outbound to Gibraltar and the 72nd convoy of the year), had passed relatively quietly; unlike the previous convoy, OG.71, which had left Liverpool just six days earlier and had been the first to be attacked by a U-boat wolf pack. Amongst those lost on that day was its Convoy Commodore, Vice Admiral Pat Parker.

Now, after nearly two weeks in Gibraltar, it was time for Creighton to lead the hazardous journey back to England at the head of Convoy HG.73 (homeward from Gibraltar), flying his flag on the British steam passenger-cargo ship, SS *Avoceta*.

Built in 1923 for the Liverpool-based Yeoward Line, the 3,442-ton *Avoceta* had spent her pre-war years running the trade route from Liverpool to Lisbon, Casablanca and the Canary Islands, but more recently she had been running the familiar, but now hostile, waters between Liverpool, Lisbon and Gibraltar. She was capable of 13 knots, and in addition to carrying 3,000 tonnes of cargo she could carry up to 150 passengers, all accommodated in cabins spread over three decks.

The *Avoceta* had just returned from the round trip up the Iberian Peninsula to Lisbon to pick up her passengers. On board were dozens of refugees from German-occupied Europe, many of whom were British citizens, mostly women and children, including the seven members of the Newton family. There were other families on board, too, such as the Barker family – mum Ida with her seven children ranging from 15-year-old Kathleen to little baby Alan. Then there was Rosalie Cassels and her three children, all girls aged under 12, and the Goddard family, Russel and Muriel and their three children under the age of 6.

Creighton was all too aware of the dangers that would be faced during the passage home. He had not wanted to take so many civilians on board, particularly the children, but he had been left with no choice as the *Avoceta* was the only ship in the convoy capable of carrying passengers. Also joining the ship in Gibraltar were survivors from the *Aguila*, the *Avoceta*'s sister ship, which had been one of the ten vessels lost in OG.71, with only sixteen of the 168 on board having survived. And at least there were four naval gunners to man *Avoceta*'s defensive guns. These would provide some form of defence against surfaced submarines or while under attack from the air.

On board the *Avoceta*, the ship's master, Harold Martin, and his crew were now making the final preparations for the journey back to Liverpool. It was a busy scene. Peter Murphy, the ship's boatswain, was overseeing the final loading of cargo – cork, mail and diplomatic bags – while the first radio officer, Harold Quinn, checked the communications equipment.

Below deck, the chief engineer, Thomas Williams, and his three officers were getting the engine under way. Thomas Barnett, the chief cook, was preparing the meals for the day, while the chief steward, Edward Slater, was organising his team looking after the passengers on board. With just a few hours to go, everyone was doing something, including 16-year-old Cadet William Marsden from Cheshire, the youngest member of the crew. Including Creighton and *Avoceta*'s crew of fifty-one, there were 166 on board.

During the afternoon of 17 September 1941, the *Avoceta* slipped its moorings and headed out to sea. The twenty-five merchantmen of Convoy HG.73 were carrying a mix of cargoes such as iron ore, potash, cocoa beans and scrap metal, and after the tragedy of OG.71 they had assembled the heaviest escort that could be made available – sixteen naval warships, including anti-submarine corvettes and destroyers. Some would escort the convoy all the way back to England while others would be replaced during the days ahead.

Once out at sea, Creighton set course to the westward and formed the convoy into five columns, with *Avoceta* leading the central column. It was impossible for any convoy to leave Gibraltar unobserved and it was to be no different for HG.73. Petty Officer Stanford, one of Creighton's longest-serving and most trusted staff, soon reported that the ship's wireless operator, Norman Larson, had already intercepted a stream of wireless messages coming from a group of Spanish trawlers as they passed Tangier. Although Larson did not know what the signals had said, Creighton knew they would almost certainly contain details of the convoy.

The following day, HG.73 continued heading west. It was only a matter of time before an enemy reconnaissance aircraft appeared, and at just 7 knots convoy speed Creighton knew there would be little the merchantmen could do. He would have to rely solely on his escorts to provide the best protection they could. Having headed out as far west as possible, the convoy swung north to run the gauntlet of the North Atlantic.

High above the headland of Cape St Vincent in southern Portugal, once the scene of one of the opening battles of the Anglo-Spanish War, a Focke-Wulf 200 Condor of KG 40, the Luftwaffe's primary unit dedicated to supporting U-boat operations in the Atlantic, was conducting another lengthy patrol. From their vantage point above the cape, the crew had found the convoy easy to spot and after first reporting its position the Condor descended to 2,000ft to circle HG.73 from a safe distance a couple of miles to its beam.

The big four-engine Condor had once been an airliner and so was easy to spot from the ships in the convoy off the starboard bow. The escorts opened fire, while on board the British fighter catapult ship HMS *Springbank* the order was given to launch its Fairey Fulmar.

Any thoughts the Condor's crew might have had about attacking HG.73 quickly disappeared once the Fulmar was seen. Besides, they had succeeded in enticing the convoy's only fighter aircraft into the sky. Last seen turning away and descending to wave-top height, the Condor disappeared. So, too, did the Fulmar as it set course back to Gibraltar. While it might have done its bit, and for now HG.73 could proceed unscathed, the convoy had lost the only air cover it had.

As a token effort to counter the Condor's report, Creighton ordered the ships to port to take the convoy further out into the Atlantic, but he knew that the combination of the convoy's slow speed and the good visibility in the area meant this manoeuvre would almost certainly be in vain. And to make matters worse, he had received the ominous news from his escort commander that two U-boats were reported to be in the area.

The following day a Condor again appeared over the convoy. It was quite possibly the same one. Keeping safely outside the range of the escorts' guns, it freely circled above the ships, no doubt sending endless reports and homing signals to help the U-boats take up position. It was now only a matter of time. One thing was for certain, the convoy would at sometime soon come under attack.

On board the *Avoceta*, Creighton decided to bring the children up from the cabins below to the smoking room directly beneath the bridge. Should the ship be hit then hopefully the children might have some chance of making it into a lifeboat. It is impossible to say for certain whether the Newtons were separated at this point. Gigi, Jimmy and Coco would certainly have been amongst the children brought up to the smoking room from the decks below. As their mother, Thea would most likely have been allowed to stay with them, and possibly Marcelle, while Nanny and Patter would have almost certainly have been required to remain below.

While the *Avoceta*'s crew did everything possible to keep the passengers at ease, this latest move would have left everyone on board in no doubt as to what might happen next. If the dangers of their passage had not been evident before, then they certainly were now. For the Newtons, and all the other civilians on board, these would have been moments of uncertainty and terror.

But no attack came. People relaxed a little. Some of the younger children even started to play, although the older ones picked up on the fear of the adults. And for a while, that was how things stayed. For now, HG.73 pressed on northwards. It was the end of their fourth day at sea, but Creighton knew they were riding their luck.

Meanwhile, on board the Italian submarine *Leonardo da Vinci*, Capitano di Corvetta Ferdinando Calda was keeping a plot of the reports. At the time HG.73 was first spotted, the *Leonardo da Vinci* had been loitering to the west of Gibraltar with two other Italian submarines, *Morosini* and *Luigi Torelli*, and as the closest Axis submarines to the convoy they had been ordered in pursuit.

The *Morosini* had been the first to find the convoy, but as it manoeuvred to shadow the ships it suffered an engine problem and was forced to head for home, leaving the other two Italian submarines in pursuit. Finally, it was Capitano di Corvetta Antonio de Giacomo commanding the *Luigi Torelli* who was given the order to attack, but because it would take time to take up a suitable position, he planned to carry this out under the cover of darkness the following night. However, as they were closing on their intended target, the *Luigi Torelli* was detected by two of the convoy's escorting destroyers, which unleashed their depth charges with great effect. Beneath the waves, the *Luigi Torelli* suffered the full force of the attack and with his submarine badly damaged, de Giacomo was forced to head for safety, his crew lucky to have escaped with their lives.

For the next twenty-four hours, HG.73 carried on unscathed with only Calda's *Leonardo da Vinci* in pursuit, but further to the north, Rolf Mützelburg was finalising *U-203*'s position to attack. Now joined in the area by *U-201* and *U-124* and with *U-205* on its way, the U-boats were all closing on Convoy HG.73 and with a final homing signal provided by a Condor, they were ready to attack.

It was now the early morning of 25 September. The plan was for the U-boats to penetrate the convoy's perimeter, slightly ahead of the ships. From there, they would wait until the naval escorts had passed, after which they could then slip inside the cordon to strike; the ideal position being to attack the convoy broadside with the merchantmen's angle to bow being as near to 90 degrees as possible. The ships would be attacked as close together as possible, with each U-boat firing a salvo of four torpedoes; the furthest target would be fired at first so that the torpedoes would arrive at around the same time to maximise the element of surprise. It would be a classic U-boat attack.

First to reach the convoy was *U-124* and within minutes the British merchantman *Empire Stream*, heading for the Scottish port of Dundee with its cargo of potash, was on its way to the bottom of the Atlantic. Later that same day, *U-203* would also be in position to attack. For now, though, Mützelburg held off, deciding instead to make his move under the cover of darkness. There was no rush. Besides, attacking while on the surface gave him the advantage of speed. When surfaced the U-boat could manage 18 knots, twice what it could manage beneath the waves, and a surfaced U-boat was highly manoeuvrable, faster than the merchantmen and a match for the convoy's escorts. Furthermore, they were undetectable to the escort's sonar, which was an underwater detection device.

Even though the earlier and seemingly isolated attack on the *Empire Stream* had not been followed up, Creighton knew there would be more U-boats in the area, and his prediction that the main attack would come that night, just after the moon had set, proved to be right. By 11.30 p.m. (British time), Mützelburg had manoeuvred *U-203* into position to attack. With some of the escorts giving chase elsewhere, he had spotted a momentary gap in the convoy's protective screen and within minutes had penetrated its perimeter. Then, using the position of the moon to silhouette the ships, it was just a matter of picking his targets.

From his vantage point in the conning tower, Mützelburg picked on two high-tonnage ships in the middle of the convoy that were crossing ahead from the right, now less than 1,000 yards away and comfortably within firing range. Choosing the lead ship of the column

immediately ahead and the second merchantman following close behind, he ordered the firing of four torpedoes at
the two ships. But there was no time to wait and observe
the result of their attack. They had been spotted by one
of the escorts, HMS *Larkspur*, and as *U-203* dived to make
its escape its first torpedo struck.

On board the *Avoceta*, a violent tremor passed through
the ship, followed by the sound of an explosion coming
from the engine room where the torpedo had hit. There
was complete pandemonium on board as the thunderous
bangs and crashes of furniture and cargo being hurled about
below decks mingled with the vicious scream of escaping
steam and the terrifying shrieks of people waking to their
deaths. The *Avoceta* staggered like a stumbling horse and
shuddered to a lurching halt, the creaking sounds signalling a ship about to meet its end.

Distress rockets were fired and those who could manage
to stumbled for safety. But there was very little time. The
doomed *Avoceta* sat back in the water, her bows rising ever
steeper in the cold night air. As the bows went higher, so
did the shrieks and screams as the torrent of water swept
through the smoking room, carrying children into the
darkness below.

It took less than four minutes for the *Avoceta* to sink.
There was not even time to lower any of the lifeboats.
Of the 166 people on board, 123 died. Forty-three were
from the ship's crew, including Thomas Barnett, Peter
Murphy, Harold Quinn, Edward Slater, Thomas Williams
and 16-year-old Cadet William Marsden. Eight were
members of Creighton's staff, including Norman Larson.
Seventy-two were passengers, including thirty-two
women and twenty children. The youngest victims were

four babies, all just a year old. All eight of the Barker family died together, as did Rosalie Cassels and her three young daughters, and the five members of the Goddard family.

Amongst those who perished were all seven members of the Newton family. The Commonwealth War Graves Commission lists the family with their ages in brackets, although not all the ages correspond with other sources: Ernest William Newton (aged 68) and Elvira Newton (62); Marcelle Marie Yvonne Newton (36); Theodosia Anneliese Johanna Newton (29) and her three children – Henry Seth Ernest (8), James Jack Theodore (6) and Ernest Alfred William (2).

Whether any of the Newtons even made it off the *Avoceta* will never be known. Most of those who survived had been on the deck or on the bridge at the time, giving them a few brief moments to abandon ship. The majority, though, had stood no chance. The combination of the dark night, an icy cold sea and the sheer terror of what was happening meant a frightening and horrible death.

Rolf Mützelburg would later state that he had misidentified the *Avoceta* to be a 12,000-ton petrol tanker – a different shape altogether and nearly four times the size of the steam passenger ship that he had, in fact, sent to the bottom. Did he really believe that? If so, how could such a misidentification have occurred? Or did he say that after he found out that his actions that night had resulted in the deaths of so many innocent civilians and children? We shall never know. Such is the fog of war.

The Battle of the Atlantic was a maelstrom of death. For the record, the second ship caught by *U-203*'s salvo of torpedoes was the Norwegian steam merchantman *Varangberg*, which went to the bottom as quickly as *Avoceta* with the loss of all but six of the twenty-seven crew. Between them, the U-boats accounted for ten of the convoy's twenty-five merchant ships in a devastatingly short period of time, resulting in the loss of 26,000 tonnes of precious cargo and 310 lives. Although HMS *Larkspur* dropped twenty-six depth charges following *U-203*'s attack, none caused any damage and after sinking a third merchantman that night, the *Lapwing*, with the loss of a further twenty-four lives, *U-203* arrived safely at its new home of Brest.

A Court of Enquiry was later held in Liverpool, not particularly looking to apportion blame on the commanding officers of the naval escorts of Convoy HG.73 but more to identify why the enemy had achieved so much success without a single U-boat being sunk. Sadly, any lessons learned were too late to save the Newton family.

The consequences of what happened that night would soon be heavily felt elsewhere.

3

THE EXIT

Having seen the family off at the railway station at La Gélie, Alfred and Henry returned to Chancelade. For a while depression set in, but they knew they had to get on. Conversation was mostly about the war and how they were going to escape France, rather than about the family for fear of bringing on more tears. It was impossible to know when they would hear from them next. They were on their way to England and that was that.

Having picked themselves up, it was time to think about making their break for England. But how they were going to get there was another matter. The obvious way was to cross the Pyrenees into Spain, but the mountain range extends from the Bay of Biscay to the Mediterranean, some 300 miles, and reaches a height of more than 11,000ft (3,400m) at the peak of Aneto.

While Alfred was happy with the idea of crossing the Pyrenees without any help, Henry wanted a guide, insisting that it was too dangerous to wander around the mountains on their own. In the end, Alfred gave in. They agreed that an organised escape line would be their best chance of getting out of France, and that meant contacting someone they had heard about in the Mediterranean port of Marseille.

Alfred and Henry were still discussing the idea when they were told their case was being forwarded to a Vichy official the following week, after which a decision would be made as to what was going to happen to them next. With that, the brothers decided it was now time to leave for England. Otherwise, they faced being banged up for the rest of the war.

Their plan was for Alfred to go to Marseille to organise their escape. He would go over the wall that night, just as soon as it was dark, so that he could be back at Chancelade the following night before anyone noticed that he had gone. It meant Henry covering for him at the morning roll call, assuming there was to be one the following day.

It all sounded simple enough, but Marseille was nearly 400 miles away and that meant a long train journey through the night. Nonetheless, by the following morning Alfred was in Marseille. He had easily got over the wall and had quickly made his way to the Gare de Périgueux, where he had jumped on the overnight train.

At first glance, little had changed since Alfred was last in Marseille. More than a year had passed since the French surrender, but life in the city seemed to be going on as normal. With no time to hang around, Alfred made his way straight to the British Seamen's Mission near the old Vieux Port where he met with the Reverend Donald Caskie. Caskie had been a minister in Paris before the war but following the German occupation had fled south to

Marseille rather than return to Britain and had now set up a refuge for stranded Britons. With the help of Pat O'Leary and others, he helped as many as 500 Allied servicemen to flee France along what became known as the Pat Line.

Having listened to what Alfred had in mind, Caskie suggested he go and see a Madame Gardner at a hotel on Rue Bernard du Bois. He then gave him an address and the room number.

With renewed energy, it did not take Alfred long to walk to the hotel. He had been told not to ask for Madame Gardner at the reception, but instead to go straight up to room 21 on the second floor. Having knocked, the door opened, and a woman invited him inside. It was Madame Gardner.

Once inside her room, Alfred could observe Madame Gardner more closely. Her brown hair and make-up were somewhat untidy, her blue-grey dress was shabby and her necklace of white beads cheap. He later described her as more resembling a schoolteacher than the agent she was.

Their discussion was kept brief. It had to be. But having established who Alfred was and what he was trying to do, Madame Gardner told him that a guide was leaving for the Pyrenees the following night and suggested that he go with him and get out of France while he could. She went on to explain that of the four guides she had worked with until recently, one had been caught and another had betrayed those he had been escorting, handing them over to the frontier guards while taking off with the money. Of the two guides who were left, one was getting cold feet and was about to pack it in. This left the fourth, who was leaving with two downed aircrew the following night.

While grateful for the offer of immediate help, Alfred had no intention of leaving Henry behind. Madame Gardner thought he was mad and even offered to contact Henry and get him out later, but she gave in to Alfred's wish for the brothers to go out together on the next trip.

Fortunately, the journey back to Chancelade was as uneventful as the one to Marseille had been and there had been no roll call earlier that day. After discussing all that had happened in Marseille, Alfred and Henry spent the rest of the day on hard labour, digging a new road under the watchful eyes of their Algerian guards. It was a blazing hot day. There was little in the way of food and barely any water. Conversation was not allowed and there had hardly been a break all day. As they climbed back into the lorry for the hour-long journey back to Chancelade, they were close to passing out. They knew that unless they did something about it, they would be in for the same the following day. Enough was enough. It was time to get out. They would go over the wall that night.

Back at camp, they were shocked to see that barbed wire now decorated every wall. Perhaps word had got out that someone had recently been over the top. Alfred's route out of only a couple of nights before was no longer an option.

It was Henry who came up with another idea. He would steal a couple of leave passes from the orderly room. He knew the layout well and only needed the office orderly to be distracted for a moment so that he could steal the passes from the desk drawer.

The moment soon came. Alfred and Henry had gone to the orderly room when they knew only a young and rather naive French junior officer would be there. They had used the cover of wanting to talk to him about conditions inside the camp and decided they would keep confronting him until they could create a moment for Henry to make his move.

As it happened, though, they did not need to cause a distraction. A rather timely phone call, which the officer answered in his own office, temporarily left the adjoining orderly room unmanned. Henry did not need long to rifle through the drawer. Quickly grabbing two passes, he applied the rubber stamp giving the authority required, folded the sheets and slipped them into his pocket.

The young officer had not been on the phone long, but it was enough. By the time he returned to the orderly room Henry had moved away from the desk and now stood innocently where he had been standing before. Coincidentally, the officer explained the telephone call had been to inform him that a Vichy officer would be arriving at Chancelade the following day to speak to the brothers about what was to happen to them next. There seemed little point in continuing the conversation. The brothers now had a way out. All that was needed was a signature on the leave passes, a simple task for a forger as good as Henry Newton.

The brothers could not risk spending another day at Chancelade. They had to get out that evening.

Just a few hours later, they made their way down to the main gate, their leave pass complete with a convincing signature in one hand and their other hand holding a rock inside a pocket, ready to strike should things not work out.

But they need not have worried. The guard on the main gate summed up the mood of most of the French guards. It was late in the day and he was half asleep. He really did not seem to be at all interested in checking their passes in any detail. Alfred and Henry were on their way to England.

By the following morning they were in Marseille. They headed straight to the hotel on Rue Bernard du Bois and while Henry stayed outside on lookout, Alfred made his way up to the second floor. He knocked on the door of room 21 as before, but this time no one was there.

Having gone back outside, Alfred discussed with Henry what they should do next. A little old man had been watching on from across the street and now came across to speak to them. The woman they were looking for, he said, had been taken ill. He went on to say that it had suddenly become a very unhealthy street and suggested they should quickly move on before they were also taken ill.

The brothers were unsure of what they should do. They discussed going on to cross the Pyrenees without any help, but Henry was against the idea. Alfred remembered Madame Gardner mentioning that an American bar in Perpignan was being used as a relay station for the guides and so, he suggested, they should head there next – at least it was on their way.

★★★

Perpignan is the southernmost city in France. With the mighty Pyrenees as a backdrop and just inland from the Mediterranean Sea, it is a quaint and most pleasant location. Back in the Second World War it was far from the sound of guns, but Perpignan had become a hive of activity as one of the main jumping-off points for anyone wanting to cross into Spain. Mountain guides looking for an opportunity to make a few francs roamed the streets and frequented the bars, while informers and Gestapo agents prowled the same turf in search of victims.

Getting to Perpignan was easy, although the route along France's Mediterranean coast through Montpellier was a busy one. The stations were crowded, and the trains packed. No one seemed to question anyone else about who they were or where they were going. People just went about their business.

But finding the American bar was another matter. Alfred and Henry did find an American bar, which might have been the one they were looking for, but there was something about the people hanging around it that left the brothers feeling uncomfortable. They decided to give the bar a miss and instead pressed on towards the village of Cerbère, on the French side of the border. However, as there would certainly be border guards there, they agreed it would not be the best place to try and cross into Spain.

By now, Henry had reluctantly accepted they would have to cross the Pyrenees without a guide. He was not at all happy with the idea and, for the first time since leaving Chancelade, Alfred's patience was tested to the full. Henry could be unbearable at times and it was as much as the brothers could do not to take it out on each other in the normal way – with their fists.

Short of Cerbère, they left the road to the frontier and started their climb up through the thick brushland at the foot of the mountains. Using a small pocket compass, they were able to keep heading roughly in a southerly direction and for the first couple of hours they avoided the regular pathways and tracks, using the shadows and darkness to conceal their position. Armed patrols were known to be out there – Vichyites, who would stop at nothing to trade in their fellow countrymen for a few francs.

The brightness of the moon provided enough light for them to keep moving. Neither said a word. It was as much as they could do just to keep going. The hours passed. Their every action had become automatic, placing one foot in front of the other without thinking and their minds elsewhere. Every now and then they stopped, either to take a break or because they had spotted torches or heard voices in the distance. At one point they spotted torches nearby and ended up taking cover in one of the many tunnels cutting through the mountains.

As the sun began to rise, they collapsed exhausted under the cover of a thicket. They stayed there all day, their ragged and torn clothes drying in the sun. Then, as soon as it was dark, they made off once more.

Their second night in the mountains was misty and it started to rain. Once again, they were soaked to the skin. The compass was proving useless and the night sky was covered by cloud, making it impossible to know for certain in which direction they were heading. Rather than risk going around in circles or, worse still, doubling back on themselves, they agreed to wait until dawn before carrying on.

They were woken by rain. It rained all morning and still they pressed on. Then, in the afternoon the sun came out and it became very warm.

A shot was heard. They laid low for a while. Eventually, concluding that it was probably a hunter somewhere in the distance, they decided to make a move. The sound of more shots cracked somewhere in the distance. Now they were wriggling forward on all fours, using the cover of the scrub and the contours of the land to conceal their position.

Any concerns about being pursued eventually disappeared, but there was still the summit to come. Alfred and

Henry pressed on through the hot afternoon and out into open country. They spotted a man and a woman working on a cultivated patch. Henry went over to speak to them, hoping they were friendly, while Alfred watched on. Alfred saw Henry waving and pointing at a large white boulder on top of the ridge. Spain was on the other side.

They could now enjoy the scenery around them. It was an area still untouched by the modern world. It had been only three years since around half a million Spanish refugees had made the same crossing, but in the opposite direction, to escape the Spanish Civil War. And for the next three years of the Second World War, thousands more risked their lives crossing the Pyrenees into Spain.

The brothers were soon deep into Spanish territory. Whatever happened to them from here on, they could not be handed over to the Germans or Vichy authorities. Their plan now was to go to the British Consul in Barcelona and once there they would arrange their onward journey to England to join up with the rest of their family. But Barcelona was 100 miles away and without official papers or any Spanish money, it was going to be difficult for them to get very far. They would just have to accept whatever was in store.

As it turned out, Alfred and Henry were not to get much further. Having reached the village of Espolla, they were stopped by a member of the Guardia Civil, the oldest law enforcement agency in Spain. But other than enter the country illegally, they knew they had done nothing else wrong, at least as far as the Spanish authorities were concerned.

They had long worked out their cover story for having to flee France, their wine importation business had collapsed because of the war. The brothers were first taken to the police station in the village, where they were searched and put in a cell with two others. And so they spent their first night in Spain in a cell. It was 10 October 1941, Henry's thirty-eighth birthday.

The following morning, they were manacled and put aboard a single-deck bus packed to the capacity with all kinds of criminals. They were driven to Girona, 40 miles to the south, where they were taken to the *Palacio de Justicia*. As the trials were already over for the day, they were put in a cell with a French Jew. Conditions inside the cell did not seem that bad and at least they were given a decent meal.

The following afternoon they were on the move again. Still manacled, ragged and unshaven, the brothers were taken to a large building, where they appeared in front of a Spanish official. Sat behind a large desk and knowing no different, the middle-aged man seemed to accept their explanation for being in Spain and understood their reason for wanting to go to England. Nonetheless, he said, they had entered the country illegally and so they were required to serve fifteen days in prison, after which they would be sent to a concentration camp at Miranda de Ebro until their future was decided by the British authorities in Spain. And with that they were dismissed.

For the first two days, Alfred and Henry were held at the old *Carrer Ferran el Catòlic*, a former convent transformed under the Franco regime into a fortress prison, after which they were transferred to Barcelona's *Cárcel Modelo*, the city's old prison, where they spent the next two days in a cell with three others. The prison was overcrowded, mostly with Spanish political opponents or petty criminals, although there were many other nationalities as well. There were British, Polish, Czechs, Dutch, Danes, Belgians, Norwegians, French, Greeks, and even Arabs and a Jamaican, although it was difficult to tell anyone apart – with shaved heads and dark grey uniforms, everyone looked the same.

The brothers were transported by train with two other prisoners to Saragossa, nearly 200 miles inland. As evening fell, the train stopped in a small town where the four prisoners were due to be handed over to more *carabinieri* for the rest of the journey to Saragossa. But their new escorts were nowhere to be seen and so they ended up at the *ayuntamiento*, an official building in the town, or town hall, where there was an empty cell in the back yard that was usually used for locking up drunks.

The cell was grubby and small, with barely enough room for them all to sit. But the police chief was friendly enough and he even agreed to Alfred's request to call the nearest British Consul. It was the first chance they had to speak to a British official and it lifted their spirits no end. At last someone in authority knew who the brothers were and where they were being kept.

For the next four days, Alfred and Henry lived in relative style. The police chief ensured they were at least well fed even though they were still under lock and key. Eventually, though, they had to leave, and Saragossa was every bit as bad as they had heard. They were put in a cell with six others and again the prison was overcrowded, while the food was insufficient and nauseating.

With their fifteen days of imprisonment up, Alfred and Henry were finally taken to the Miranda Concentration Camp, 100 miles away in northern Spain. Miranda was, in fact, a civilian and military internment camp and one of 200 such camps created during the Spanish Civil War. Since the early months of the Second World War it had become Spain's central camp for all foreign prisoners and although Miranda was essentially run by the Spanish Army, there was little in the way of discipline. Everything was much better there than before. Morale was boosted by a well-stocked canteen and every fortnight a lorry from the British Embassy in Madrid brought in extra rations for the Allies being held there. Sometimes there were individual food parcels and even mail.

The fortnightly visits came and went, but there was never any mail for Alfred and Henry. As the weeks passed by the initial disappointment turned to worry. Christmas Eve came without further word.

The internees wanted to make sure that the festivities passed in the best possible way. A stage was rigged up in one of the huts and a variety programme full of international flavour was planned, while on the menu there was salmon, bully beef, baked beans and cheese. Being former entertainers, Alfred and Henry were to play their part, with a humorous act that was most uncomplimentary to their Spanish captors.

Then the senior British prisoner being held at the camp entered the hut waving a piece of paper. It was a list containing the names of those who were to be released as a special gesture of festive goodwill. On that list were the names of Alfred and Henry Newton. At last they were free.

A lorry was waiting outside to take the lucky few to Madrid. It was a journey of more than 200 miles and so it was past midnight by the time the lorry finally pulled up at the British Embassy. Then, after a hearty meal, they were all driven to a comfortable hotel.

The brothers woke early the following morning. It was Christmas Day. Thoughts immediately turned to their family and fond memories of their wonderful times together; the children opening presents and playing while the adults looked on. That night, the embassy staff threw a party for those who had escaped war-torn France, but Alfred and Henry were not in the mood for partying; their thoughts were still elsewhere.

They decided to spend Boxing Day shopping, buying presents for their family. But then the telephone rang. It was someone at the embassy. They were told the military attaché wished to see them and a car would shortly be outside the hotel. There were no further details, but it could only be news of the family or details of their onward passage to England. While Henry was excited, Alfred suddenly became concerned.

At the embassy, the military attaché stood behind his desk in uniform, hands behind his back and his eyes full of pain. He had bad news, he said, 'I'm afraid there were no survivors.'

It was the heaviest of hammer blows. Alfred felt cold and sick, his legs trembling. He opened his mouth, but no words came out. The silence that followed was broken by Henry questioning the military attaché, who went on to explain that the ship had gone down very quickly, in a matter of seconds. No one had stood a chance.

The days that followed were nothing but a blur. Alfred refused to believe what he had been told. There must have been some mistake. He walked around like a zombie, his eyes vacant and his inner thoughts clinging to the past. Disbelief then turned into anger. The storm that raged within him would never be appeased.

While stoically enduring his own private hell, Henry tenderly looked after his younger brother. He never left his side. The embassy staff, too, did all they could, taking the brothers on trips around the city and to afternoon tea. But their efforts met little success. Alfred would not go anywhere there might be Germans for fear of losing control of himself. He ached with the primitive urge for vengeance. He knew that he and Henry would never find peace until they had avenged their family.

Gradually the violent windy storm that raged within was replaced in the hearts of both brothers by a cold hate for everything German and a huge desire for revenge that renewed with every rising sun.

4

THE FIRM

Just as soon as they could, the staff at the British Embassy set Alfred and Henry on their way to England. The train journey south to Gibraltar took all day and was noisy with the singing and laughter of those going home, but the brothers did not feel like joining in. Nothing seemed to matter anymore. Others respectfully left them alone.

Their days in Gibraltar were spent at the transit depot and passed in a haze, even though they were there for three weeks. Alfred and Henry met with an intelligence officer, Colonel Medlam, but any slender hope they might have had about the news being a mistake soon disappeared. Further information merely confirmed the sad truth of what they had been told before. The convoy had been hit in exactly the way the military attaché in Madrid had described.

When asked about where they would go and what they planned to do next, their only answer was to go to London where they had an uncle and auntie living in Islington.

Perhaps they would be able to stay there until they could become commandos so they could get to grips with the Germans as soon as possible.

In what seemed like no time at all, the brothers were aboard HMS *Hesperus*, a destroyer bound for England to undergo extensive repairs after attacking and then ramming a U-boat off Cape St Vincent just over a week before. Since returning to Gibraltar, she had been patched up sufficiently for the voyage home but, rather than sail alone, she was to escort the troop ship SS *Almanzora* back to England.

The voyage passed without incident and *Hesperus* docked in Liverpool on 1 February 1942, a cold and very wet Sunday. As Alfred and Henry walked down the gangplank an army lorry pulled up in front of them and a man in military uniform offered them a lift to Lime Street railway station.

As it was pouring with rain the brothers accepted what seemed like an opportune offer of kindness, but at the station they were approached by a small man wearing a suit and a grey trilby hat. He invited the brothers into a small office and proceeded to ask them a series of questions.

The incident took Alfred and Henry by surprise. They had absolutely no idea what any of the questioning was about. It was all rather strange. They were still wondering what was happening when the man in military uniform who had just given them a lift to the station walked into the office. He introduced himself as Sergeant Green of the Field Security Police and explained that he had been instructed to accompany the brothers to London.

They were soon on the night train to London. Alfred and Henry still had no idea of what was going on or where they were going, and Green could offer little in the way of information. He had simply been told to escort the brothers to the War Office and knew nothing more than that.

The streets of London were covered in a blanket of snow. It was bitterly cold. Having arrived at Euston Station, they walked to a house in Coram Street in Holborn where the brothers were told to get some rest as they were not due to be seen at the War Office until after lunch.

Early that afternoon, the three walked through the slushy snow to Whitehall and, after leading the brothers inside the War Office to reception, Green was dismissed, leaving Alfred and Henry still wondering what all this was about.

They were not left wondering for long. A messenger soon appeared and guided the brothers through the labyrinth of corridors to an office where they were to wait to be seen. Understandably, Alfred and Henry were feeling a little uncomfortable. After a short wait, a dark-haired man wearing a blue lounge suit arrived. He introduced himself as Captain Johnson.

They all sat down. Johnson first expressed his sympathies at their loss and then asked the brothers what they had in mind next. Henry's answer, as usual, was quite bullish, telling Johnson all they needed was a couple of Tommy guns and a bunch of grenades, with which they knew damn well what they were going to do next.

While sympathetic, Johnson explained that letting the brothers loose with a handful of weapons and grenades was not going to happen. He was, however, extremely interested when the brothers went on to tell him about the Nuisance Committee, which they had set up in France, and about some of the activities they had been up to. He became even more interested when the brothers told him that, in one way or another, they were both determined to go back to France and fight.

After they had finished, Johnson told them he might be able to help and would arrange for someone else to see them in a couple of days. He gave them an address to go to and a name to ask for. In the meantime, they were to stay at the London Transit Camp in Marylebone. And with that, he bid them good day.

★★★

The captain was an intelligence officer working for Britain's security service. As soon as the story of Alfred and Henry Newton had become known to the staff at the British Embassy in Madrid, their details had been passed to British Intelligence in Gibraltar and Colonel Medlam had then passed the information on to MI5 in London. Finally, news of the Newton brothers had been passed on to the Special Operations Executive.

The SOE had been formed in July 1940 after the British Prime Minister, Winston Churchill, had given the order to 'Set Europe ablaze'. Churchill wanted to hit back at the enemy in Nazi-occupied Europe in whatever way he could. SOE operations would, he believed, divert vital enemy resources in order to counter their actions, and any act of defiance, no matter how small, would raise the morale of those under occupation.

In the words of its founding charter, the SOE was to 'co-ordinate all action, by way of subversion and sabotage, against the enemy overseas'. It was an unorthodox organisation set up to fight the Nazis, but to fight a successful clandestine operation required huge support from elsewhere. However, although the SOE as an organisation sat alongside Britain's armed forces, it gained little support during its early days from within Whitehall and was kept separate from existing military and intelligence organisations.

The SOE's main headquarters was established in a greyish five-storey building at 64 Baker Street, and for a long time its very existence remained unknown. Those attached to the organisation from other departments were discouraged from referring to it as 'the SOE' and so they tended to refer to it as simply 'the Org', 'the Racket' or 'the Firm'. And if the organisation had to be referred to in any official correspondence then the designation Inter-Services Research Bureau, or ISRB, was adopted to allay unwelcome curiosity. Furthermore, people were rarely invited to Baker Street and meetings were held elsewhere, typically in a flat somewhere in Marylebone, Bayswater or South Kensington, as there was no need to know where their employer was based.

In one way, at least, the SOE was like a club, for membership was by invitation only. There was no recruiting system as such, but every potential member was carefully scrutinised before anyone considered suitable was invited to join. The principal recruiting difficulty, security apart, was the need for such a wide variety of characters and skills, and so there would never be a typical SOE type.

As it grew, the SOE spread its operations far and wide but, for several reasons, France always offered the best opportunities to foster sabotage and subversion. It was just across the Channel and could be supplied and resupplied with relative ease. There was no shortage of places where agents could be dropped off or picked up and the terrain in many parts of the country, particularly areas of rolling hills and dense woodland, proved ideal for conducting guerrilla warfare. Furthermore, French-speaking agents could be found without too much difficulty and, once on the ground, they could blend into the local population with credibility and ease.

The main body for organising French subversion was F Section ('F' for French), which worked closely with the many resistance movements in France. By the time Alfred and Henry Newton arrived on the scene in early 1942, F Section was being run by a handful of staff led by Maurice Buckmaster, a former reporter with a French newspaper and a past senior manager of the French branch of the Ford Motor Company.

Buckmaster saw his section's role as not that of spies, but active and belligerent planners of operations to be carried out in advance of the Allied landings in Europe, as and when they came. F Section was still very much in its infancy. Its missions were exploratory, and it had still been less than a year since the first agents were inserted into France. They had been left battling against an enemy that seemingly held all the trump cards. There had, so far, been little in the way of sabotage, apart from some damage to the railway network and the odd train wrecked here and there, and a period at the end of 1941 had seen London cut off from France completely. There was clearly much to do.

While F Section's agents were struggling across the Channel, those back in London were busy formulating a plan for the construction of circuits (or networks) in France. During the next few months the number of agents in the field increased to around fifty, and this figure would more than double in the year after that, reaching around

200 by the beginning of 1944, with circuits spread far and wide across France. While Europe was not yet ablaze, it was beginning to smoulder, and so men like Alfred and Henry Newton were just what the SOE was looking for.

***

It had now been three days since Alfred and Henry arrived in England. Exactly on time, they turned up at Orchard Court in Portman Square. From the outside, the tall building appeared little different to any other in the square, but the residential flats within had since been taken over by F Section for many purposes, including interviewing potential recruits.

The brothers were met by an elderly porter wearing a dark suit and tie, known as Park. He had worked in the Paris branch of the Westminster Bank before the war and was now working for Buckmaster, and it was his job to make sure that visitors were taken to the right room. Park also ensured that visitors did not see anyone else when inside the building as this could prove awkward in the field.

Having asked for Major Gielgud as instructed, Alfred and Henry were ushered across the hall and up two flights of stairs to Flat 6, where they were welcomed by Lewis Gielgud, F Section's chief recruiting officer. They were soon all sitting and chatting at ease. Gielgud asked the brothers the same question they had been asked before – what did they have in mind now they were in England? And, as before, Henry was quick to repeat what he had said to Johnson just a few days before. Gielgud again pointed out that they would not be let loose with guns and grenades. As he said, the brothers were too precious for that. What would they have gained by killing a handful of Germans before being cut down themselves? No, Gielgud explained, the brothers could achieve far more than that.

During the conversation that followed, Gielgud talked about the SOE and how his organisation wanted the brothers to go back into France to continue the excellent work they had begun. They would be able to turn passive resistance into armed aggression by paralysing the enemy's movements, disrupting lines of communication and sabotaging factories to ultimately help pave the way for the liberation of France. But, as Gielgud went on to explain, it would be dangerous work. The enemy was no fool. Those captured could expect to be dealt with ruthlessly. Even so, when the Nazi war machine crumbled, as it surely would one day, the brothers would feel as if they had achieved something special that they could be proud of for the rest of their lives.

The brothers listened intently to what had been said. Henry's eyes lit up at the thought of being able to get revenge on the Nazis, whereas Alfred was thinking more of the dangers involved. But as far as Gielgud was concerned, the brothers were just the types he was looking for. He had found two men who would shirk no task, however difficult or dangerous. They were ideal for training. He later wrote on each of their reports, 'ultimately to be employed in France as agent or thug'.

As they left the building, Alfred and Henry talked about what might lie ahead. One thing they both agreed on – once the war was over their services would no longer be required and their contribution forgotten. That is, assuming they survived the war. However, if they failed in their task, they would almost certainly face a shabby death in some forgotten place. It was time to go for a drink.

***

A week later, Alfred and Henry were back in Gielgud's office, where they were introduced to six other members of their group. They were all about to embark on a journey into the unknown. They were not adventurers nor highly trained thugs, nor were they characters dreamt up by cloak-and-dagger novelists. But from that moment, their true identities were lost to the past as each took on a new name – in the case of Alfred and Henry Newton, they were to be Arthur and Hubert Norman.

Whereas most of F Section's agents had, thus far, come from within the armed forces, the Newton brothers were amongst the first to be directly enrolled by the SOE, and although other brothers would work for the SOE, Alfred and Henry were to be the only ones allowed to work together as a team. In work such as theirs, where implicit trust played an important part, allowing them to work together made perfect sense. They were regarded within F Section as a single unbreakable team and, despite their age difference, from now on they became known to everyone as 'the Twins'.

The eight, including the Twins, left the building in pairs several minutes apart to board a bus waiting around the corner, their bags already loaded. They were driven through the south-west suburbs of London and out into the Surrey countryside, along the narrow, elongated ridge of the North Downs known as the Hog's Back. The bus then turned off the main road into the ancient rural hamlet of Wanborough, which lies at the foot of the northern side of the ridge, and finally pulled up outside a rather impressive looking Elizabethan manor.

They had arrived at Wanborough Manor. Although its exterior remains unchanged, the manor house has long since been divided into three privately owned dwellings. During the Second World War it was requisitioned from its owners, the Perkins family, and used by the SOE. Given the official title of Special Training School No. 5, abbreviated as STS 5, Wanborough Manor became home to students undergoing their preliminary training.

The eight new arrivals were designated Party 27M (27 indicating F Section and M being the next course in alphabetical order). It was now 11 February 1942 and theirs was to be the last course of two weeks' duration, after which the length of preliminary training would double.

The Twins had been in England less than two weeks and so much had happened in such a short period of time. Not that they had arrived in England with a plan, but it was all quite different to how they had thought things might turn out.

***

Addressing the new arrivals on their first day, the school's commandant, Major Roger de Wesselow, a middle-aged officer of the Coldstream Guards, was keen to point out they were to be given intensive instruction during their time at the manor. They would be worked very hard and, he warned, their reactions and progress during the course would be carefully noted. There was no limit to the number of candidates accepted for the tough and solitary life of the organisation for which they had volunteered, but the requirements of physical endurance, patience, technical knowledge and security were high. Not only would their own lives depend on these qualifications, but also the lives of their comrades. Finally, de Wesselow said, he could not stress enough the importance of security. Nobody outside of the school knew what went on there, and it had to stay that way.

The eight members of Party 27M were soon joined by four others to become a course of twelve. Each was given a number and a false identity for use during training, after which those who successfully completed the course would be given a code name for use in the field and a pseudonym, complete with a cover story and documentation in order to establish a false identity.

The students were instructed to say little about their personal histories but, from what is now known, the course members came from a wide variety of backgrounds. One was 23-year-old Adolphe Rabinovitch, who was born in Moscow to Russian parents. He later went into France with the code name Arnaud. Then there was 25-year-old Alan Jickell, a half-French Cardiff-born shipping clerk, who would be known in France as Gustave, and a commercial artist called John Starr, aged 31 from Lancashire, soon to become known as Bob. Others were already commissioned army officers, one being 22-year-old Brian Rafferty (later code-named Dominique) and another was Sydney Hudson (later Albin), aged 31, born in Kent and educated bilingually in Switzerland, who had been commissioned into the Royal Fusiliers.

Even though the students were undergoing basic military training, the atmosphere at Wanborough resembled more the country manor than a military establishment. There was much to learn and so most days started early with reveille at 6 a.m., followed by physical training on the lawn in front of the manor.

Wearing just PT kit in the freezing cold was not the way most would choose to start the day. Facing the instructor in two lines, they were put through their paces with various exercises – and all before breakfast. The rest of the day was spent in class, during which the students were taught skills such as weapons training. They were introduced to all known types of revolver, automatic and light weapons, including French and German. There were navigation exercises, fieldcraft and leadership tests. There was also signalling, wireless operating and coding, and an introduction to demolition techniques with live training carried out at a chalk quarry on the Hog's Back.

The day was broken up for lunch, and then again for afternoon tea, after which there was another hour of lessons before dinner. Both English and French were spoken during the course as students were required to have a firm grasp of both. At the dining table, though, only French was spoken, with fluency being an important factor when determining a student's suitability for further training.

Behaviour was also closely monitored throughout the course to see how observant the student was in everyday occurrences, when under the influence of alcohol or while asleep in their room at night. It was important to know that if they talked in their sleep, in what language they talked. No stone was left unturned.

Everyone undergoing preliminary training had been selected because of their potential to work for the SOE, but just because they might have interviewed well during the selection process it did not mean they would be reliable or careful when out in the field. It was only when they were put under pressure during training that it could be determined how best to employ them in the field; deciding whether they should become a circuit organiser, or a wireless operator or a saboteur, or whether they should even be employed at all.

The SOE demanded a combination of qualities far beyond the requirements of the ordinary fighting man – abnegation and moral courage, a level head and steady nerves. Ordinary people were going to be asked to do quite extraordinary things.

While potential saboteurs such as the Twins could be swift and brutal, they were seldom patient, careful or methodical enough to undertake the grinding task of organising and training members of an underground resistance circuit. Nor were they necessarily technically minded or suited to the often dull but extremely dangerous work of a wireless operator in the field. All this would have to be taught in the weeks ahead, as well as learning how to 'remove' inconvenient people. It was no use trying to do things by the book. There was no book. Those who could not think for themselves or were found unsuitable for specialist training were simply weeded out; not by the staff at Wanborough, but by those back in London, as it was ultimately F Section that decided who went on to further training and who did not.

At the end of preliminary training there was an exercise known as a 'scheme', when the students were required to put into practice what they had been taught on the course. In the case of Party 27M, they were first taken to the south coast by train before being split up, after which they were required to make their way back to the manor on foot, without a map and without being caught by the Field Security Police playing the enemy. For the Twins, this kind of exercise was child's play and the scenario was made even more realistic by the increased security bolstered by the Home Guard and Canadian troops based in the area following a report that two German agents had landed in the same area where the exercise was taking place. A genuine alarm had been raised, but the Twins succeeded in getting back to the manor, although they were disappointed to find that two others had beaten them back.

Alfred and Henry were doing well. An early staff report, written by Sergeant Searle, one of the school's instructors, described Henry as 'athletic and very keen, very good natured and friendly, and full of common sense'. Writing about Alfred, Searle reported that he was 'more apt to learn than his brother and had a greater knowledge of English'. Searle also stated that Alfred had 'come across as very keen on the course, was very security minded, and had been especially attracted to Morse, but all he wanted was action and that raid work appealed to him'. Searle also noted that both brothers were counting the hours to the moment they could get down to work, and while Henry was worried that his lack of English could affect his chances of succeeding in training, Searle was quick to reassure him that he had already proved his capabilities in practice.

Given they were about to go into France, Henry's apparent difficulty with the English language was seemingly of little or no concern. And rightly so. It was better than the other way around, as was more often the case, where an Englishman might struggle with a lack of fluency in

French. Besides, Henry would have Alfred alongside him most of the time.

At the end of the course, de Wesselow described Party 27M as 'exceptionally promising', with all but one of the twelve going on to further training. And of those who progressed, at least seven would go into France.

***

The students were next off to the Scottish Highlands, where for a month they were assessed in a physical and rugged environment, staying at shooting lodges in the Arisaig and Morar areas on the western coast of Inverness-shire. Fortunately for them, it was now early spring and so the harsh winter weather had passed.

Training began with a hard slog over some unwelcome terrain, which included crawling on bellies and trekking up mountains. The students were taught map reading and compass work, and general fieldcraft, including how to live off the land. There were further sessions on elementary Morse code, some more weapons training using the Colt .45 handgun and the Sten sub-machine gun, more demolition training, which included laying dummy charges on selected targets, and sessions on close combat, with techniques such as silent killing.

Agents could expect to be parachuted into France and so the students were next sent to the Parachute Training School at RAF Ringway in Manchester for what was known to them as the 'dropping' course. Each agent was required to complete three jumps to qualify for their parachute wings. After first jumping from a tethered balloon in daylight from a height of 700ft, the second jump was from the balloon at night and the third from an aircraft, through a hole in the fuselage of a converted twin-engine Armstrong-Whitworth Whitley bomber.

Some of the remaining eleven members of the course had now fallen by the wayside, including two who were hospitalised from injuries suffered during the jumps. For those who had successfully completed their training they were rewarded with leave before reporting to their specialist training school according to the role they had been assigned.

It was while the Twins were enjoying some well-earned leave that Henry noticed a change in Alfred. It seemed as if his younger brother was not enjoying the time off at all. He had clearly hardened as a person and had stopped going to anything that might soften him in some way, such as the theatre or concerts. Even the sight of flowers or children playing in the park seemed too much. Alfred was no longer the family man that he had once been and seemed to deliberately insulate himself from all human emotion. He preferred to eat alone rather than socialise. Henry even likened him to a sulky schoolboy. But, although Alfred managed to pull himself around before it was time to start specialist training, the truth was that he was anxious to get back to France to have a crack at the Hun. It was as if nothing else mattered.

Those recruited by the SOE from outside the armed forces were given a commission, with rank and number, in one of the three regular services. This would hopefully give them some protection should they ever be captured – in which case, it was hoped they would be treated as commissioned officers rather than as civilian spies.

In the case of Alfred and Henry, they were both recommended for a commission in the British Army with the rank of second lieutenant, the note at the bottom of their recommendation form, simply titled 'ISRB Candidate', stated, 'This gentleman is required for very active work overseas', and requested they be commissioned with effect from 13 April 1942, the date they were expected to go into the field.

Accompanying their recommendation forms were two letters of reference; one from Buckmaster's deputy, Major Nicholas Bodington, and the other from Captain Selwyn Jepson, F Section's new recruiting officer. There were medical certificates (both brothers were assessed as Grade I), an additional note stating their birth certificates were not available (the brothers did not have them) and a request for the normal age restriction for a commission to be waived. The form also said that no entry was to be made in the *London Gazette*, as would normally be the case when service commissions were announced, as this was suppressed at the request of the SOE. All those recruited by the SOE were not to be paid from army funds. They were instead paid by the SOE, the amount being equivalent to their army rank and typically paid quarterly in advance into their bank accounts at home, rather than them having to receive money once in the field.

As expected, the request was approved and so, on 13 April 1942, Alfred and Henry Newton were commissioned with the rank of second lieutenant, both on the General List, with Alfred having the service number of 231950 while Henry was given 234267. It was now just a matter of waiting to see what would happen next.

5

SAINTE-ASSISE

As he approached the entrance to Orchard Court, 33-year-old Peter Churchill was feeling glad at the thought of going back into France. He had been another of those special types the SOE was always on the lookout for. Born in Amsterdam, he had read modern languages at Caius College Cambridge, and was fluent in French, Spanish, Italian and German.

Although he had initially been commissioned into the Intelligence Corps, Churchill had now been with F Section for just over a year. For his first mission he had been landed by submarine near Antibes, a part of the Mediterranean coastline he knew well from his holidays before the war, and had worked with circuit organisers in the south-east of France before making his way home via Spain. He had then returned for a second mission, during which he delivered two young wireless operators to the Riviera by submarine and canoe before making the return journey to London with one of the founder members of the French

Resistance. Now Churchill was about to be briefed for his third mission into France.

Inside Orchard Court, Churchill was met by Nicholas Bodington and after making the normal pleasantries, Bodington got straight to the point. There was something big on, and it had come from the very top. The Chiefs of Staff were at last taking notice of F Section's activities and achievements and had something of an intimate and specialised nature that needed attending to. More than that, the prime minister had been briefed and agreed that Peter Churchill was just the man to carry out the job.

The briefing went on. The Battle of the Atlantic was not going well. Losses amongst Allied convoys were high, and it was clear the German U-boats were acting on long-range radio transmissions coming from somewhere in France. These messages could be received by the radio operator on board a U-boat without it even having to surface. If the transmitter could be put out of action, even for just a week or so, the U-boats would be forced to surface to receive instructions, and that would give the Royal Navy a chance to hunt and destroy the wolf packs. British Intelligence believed the only transmitter powerful enough to do this was the very low frequency (VLF) transmitter at Sainte-Assise, near Melun, some 30 miles to the south of Paris. Aerial bombing of the transmitter was not accurate enough for such a precise attack, and because of its location would risk killing hundreds, if not thousands, of civilians. And so, it was to the SOE that the prime minister had turned to put the transmitter out of action.

Having had the aim of the mission explained to him, Churchill was taken into the next office where a scale model of Sainte-Assise had been laid out. It was accurate in all its detail. Churchill could see the transmitter station was about a mile long and in the centre of the complex was the aerial running between two main masts, with four sets of cables holding up each. It was pointed out that only one set of cables needed to be taken out to have the desired effect. If the outside cables could be cut then the mast would fall inwards, all helped by the added weight of the aerial, which would hopefully then be twisted and broken in the fall, putting the station out of action for several weeks, if not months.

If the idea of taking out one of the Nazis' most strategic assets right under their noses in the suburbs of Paris was not audacious enough, the task was made even harder by the fact that each set of cables consisted of three separate steel hawsers attached to the ground by iron rings on top of concrete blocks, some 9ft high and positioned 100 yards or so apart. However, only the top two cables would need to be broken, one of which was close to the perimeter of the complex and the next being towards the main mast. But that still meant scaling two of the concrete blocks and unless Churchill planned to take an extendable ladder with him, some other way would have to be found. Not only that, but the amount of equipment and explosives required to cut the cables was too much for one man to carry. And so, this was not a one-man job, which is where Alfred and Henry Newton came in.

Churchill was told about the Twins – described to him as a couple of tough eggs and circus acrobats by profession – and the reason why they were determined to get their own back on the Nazis. Scaling a high concrete block would be a piece of cake for them and, although they had yet to complete their training, they were an obvious choice. They had lived in the southern suburbs of Paris before the war and so knew the area reasonably well. Furthermore, the raid would be planned to coincide with a diversionary attack by RAF fighter-bombers coming in at low-level at the precise moment required.

Given that Churchill had already carried out two missions in the past four months, he was told that he had forty-eight hours to go away and think it over. There was no need for him to make his mind up now, but with the mission having been approved at the highest level, and with his name having been put forward to lead it, Churchill had in his own mind already accepted the task. Nonetheless, with the briefing over, he jumped in a taxi to Paddington to catch the train home to Malvern to think things over and for some well-earned leave.

When thinking deeper into what he had been told, Churchill was left with many unanswered questions. Presumably they would be dropped by parachute somewhere within easy reach of the transmitter station, but how many guards there would be and how they would synchronise the cutting of the cables had yet to be determined. There was another problem, too. A German army headquarters was situated in the nearby forest of Fontainebleau, just a stone's throw from Sainte-Assise, and so there would be no shortage of enemy troops around.

There was also the problem of the River Seine, which flowed on three sides of the transmitter station. Bridges were always guarded and so the three would need a safe house on the Sainte-Assise side of the river to avoid having to make a crossing. And there was the matter of how they would deal with the cutting of the cables, assuming they could get into the right position in the first place. This would be the most crucial part of the operation. Setting the time pencils too early would not give them enough time to get away, while setting them too late could risk the explosives being discovered and removed before they went off. And what were the chances of surviving such a mission? All these thoughts were still circulating in Churchill's mind when he got off the train, but once he was home there were more important things in his life to enjoy.

***

Meanwhile, the Twins' leave was brought to a sudden end. When the telephone call came, it was the voice of Buckmaster's assistant, Vera Atkins, on the line.

The indispensable Vera was the heart of F Section. She was officially Buckmaster's intelligence officer, but in her orderly mind she stored an encyclopaedic knowledge of information and regulations concerning the day-to-day life of an SOE agent in the field; the work, the travel, food rationing, curfews, documentation and so on. Vera was a perpetual source of information and it was she who dealt closely with the agents during the final days before they went into the field. She worked tirelessly for the rest of the war, and even beyond, and one can only wonder how much less efficient F Section would have been without her. On this occasion, though, Vera's message was short and rather abrupt. The Twins were to report to Orchard Court where their SOE journey had begun a few months before.

Again, the Twins were met on arrival by Park. Peter Churchill was already there. He had not needed the allotted forty-eight hours to decide to accept the mission. He had telephoned with the news the previous day and had now returned to Orchard Court to discuss the raid with Bodington and one of the briefing officers, Major Jacques de Guélis. And, of course, to meet the Twins.

By the time the Twins met Churchill they had also been given an overview of the mission and, like Churchill, had been given the opportunity to decide whether to take it on or not. Henry had been the first to speak up. It was just the kind of job he and Alfred were looking for, he said, mainly because it would give them a chance to hit the German U-boat effort. After all, it had been a German U-boat that had been the reason for the brothers ending up with the SOE in the first place.

The three were given the use of a separate room to discuss their initial thoughts as to how the task might be carried out. For the past day or so, Churchill had thought of little else. His plan was for them to be dropped from two aircraft – he in one and the Twins in the other – on the eastern side of the Seine and a few miles from Sainte-Assise. This would increase their chances of still being able to carry out the raid should anything go wrong with either party on the way to the area. They would then all meet up at a designated rendezvous point at the Bois de Saint-Leu, near Cesson, just a mile or so from the perimeter of the transmitter station. Should either party not arrive at the rendezvous by 9 p.m. the remaining party was to carry on and attach the explosives to the outer cable so that, at least, the top of the mast would be broken off.

According to what they had been told, the complex was not heavily guarded and so Churchill expected it would take them around an hour to get inside and set the explosives. And with a one-hour time pencil, the balloon should go up just before 11 p.m. to coincide with the air raid by the RAF.

Churchill had seemingly thought of everything. The Twins were impressed. The only thing they insisted on was to be armed with Stens. They were not looking to blaze away and risk spoiling the show, but if anything were to go wrong then they would simply take out as many Germans as they could.

It was now a matter of planning the raid in fine detail. However, the more they looked at what they were being asked to do the more they realised just how big the challenge was going to be. Getting into France would present little problem, but then there was the matter of getting close enough to the transmitter aerial to place the explosives in the right place to put it out of action, or at least cause significant damage.

That afternoon, the three made their way to St Pancras Station. Arrangements had been made for them to be given explosives and demolition training at one of the SOE's specialist training schools, and just a couple of hours later they arrived at Brickendonbury Manor in Hertfordshire.

Set in beautiful countryside just a short drive from the town of Hertford, the Brickendonbury Estate is now a unit of the Tun Abdul Razak Research Centre, but during the Second World War it was STS 17 (or Station 17) and was one of the most secret locations in the country. With its flower gardens, often featured in pre-war horticultural magazines, the impressively grand Jacobean mansion had been requisitioned by the government at the outbreak of war and was used by the SOE for the training of saboteurs.

Churchill and the Twins were met on arrival by the commandant, Major Cecil Clarke. He was a caravan enthusiast from Bedford but was now being employed as a leading expert in demolition and industrial sabotage. 'Nobby' Clarke, as he was known, was a rising star within the SOE and his teaching methods were unlike any other. His rather boisterous sense of humour and use of live explosives all helped enhance his lectures, particularly when he was trying to impress visiting dignitaries.

Despite the manor's grandeur, the three were accommodated on camp beds on a bare floor. Churchill had been to the school before, prior to his first mission, but for the Twins it was all a new experience. For three days they learned how to become experts in mayhem and sudden death. They were taught precisely where to apply a few pounds of explosive, or even a few ounces, to achieve maximum effect.

These were exciting times. In its early days, the SOE had depended mostly on the military explosives available at the time. Since then, though, new forms of explosive had been developed, such as the plastic explosive, PE for short, created by incorporating RDX (an organic compound and a more energetic explosive than trinitrotoluene, otherwise known as TNT) in a suitable softening agent to produce a putty-like material, pale yellow in colour, which could be cut and moulded into appropriate shapes. PE had changed the way saboteurs operated. It was more powerful, yet safer, than most other existing explosive materials and it would not detonate if struck by a bullet or when subject to shocks and dents during transit. It could be moulded into shape like dough and even coloured to help its disguise. All that was then needed was a detonator embedded in the mass of the explosive.

The Twins soon learned how to handle PE as if it were butter and quickly realised there was a great art to sabotage.

The emphasis was always to harm the Germans as much as possible and the French as little as possible, and the use of PE was far more accurate and less destructive than aerial bombing. They were taught how to make their own explosive from relatively easily obtainable ingredients, such as weed killer and agricultural fertiliser, and they learned how to take any manufactured article and convert it into a piece of equipment to maim and kill. They were even able to try things out for themselves by calculating how much explosive was needed to blow up a bridge or a building.

For the Sainte-Assise mission, the amount of PE required to cut the cables was worked out and then prepared in advance. This avoided them having to fumble around in the dark once inside the complex. All they would have to do was apply the PE in the right place.

Churchill was delighted with how the Twins were shaping up. They had shown just how good they were with Stens and, during the unarmed combat sessions with their instructor, Churchill never ceased to be amazed at how neither brother would ever hold back. Each was prepared to deliver heavy blows against the other as if he was a German guard. In the end, these sessions had to be stopped for fear that one, or both, would be hurt so much that the mission would have to be called off. Churchill later wrote that, in all his time with the SOE, he had never met anyone quite like the Twins. These two, he felt, were absolute killers and they seriously meant business.

During their time at Brickendonbury, Churchill and the Twins were able to study in detail the aerial reconnaissance photographs of the transmitter at Sainte-Assise and its surroundings, seemingly taken from every angle imaginable. From these images, they could work out where the German troop positions were most likely to be and in what strength, and from which direction they could best approach the transmitter.

With more information becoming available to them each day, the three were able to refine their plan. The Twins were to be dropped in a field around 3 miles to the east of the Seine during the early hours of the day of the attack. Churchill, meanwhile, would be dropped a couple of hours earlier as his drop zone was further to the east and a little more to the south, and so he had more ground to cover to reach the rendezvous. They agreed to meet up in an area of woodland less than a mile to the east of the transmitter station, where they would lay up during the day before setting off to carry out the raid later that night.

To help them with their preparation, concrete blocks were laid out in relation to a piece of woodland in the grounds of the estate so that they could rehearse the raid. Their first rehearsal was during daylight. Everything they required fitted into a rucksack, and to mount the block Henry stood with his back against its side while Alfred took a run-up and then placed one foot in his brother's cupped hands. Alfred was on top in a flash. And with Alfred laying on his stomach and reaching down below, Henry then ran at the block and leapt as high as he could to grab his brother's outstretched hands. Using all his strength, Alfred then hauled Henry up. In what seemed like no time at all, the Twins were ready to set the explosives. The individual packs of PE, each weighing around 1lb, had already been shaped to fit around the hawsers, with each pack having a pair of buckles and straps to attach them firmly. A fuse ran between each pack and to one end of the packs was attached a time pencil.

They later decided to refine the idea. After first helping Churchill to scale his block, the Twins would then quickly go to theirs, only this time Alfred would go up alone and set the explosives while Henry stayed on the ground to provide cover. They also agreed to wear army battle dress over civilian clothing, just in case they were caught on the ground having jumped from their aircraft.

Their concern about a suitable safe house for afterwards had also been resolved. A trusted farmer had agreed to take them in at his farm near Cesson, where the three intended to lay up for a couple of weeks until everything had quietened down, after which arrangements would be made to fly them all back to England.

That night they again went through the procedure, only this time under the cover of darkness and using a reduced amount of PE with ten-minute pencils. Unsurprisingly, they found that setting the explosives in the dark proved to be more difficult than before as everything had to be done by feel. Even so, it took them just forty-six minutes to complete the job. The explosions went off a minute apart and closer inspection afterwards showed that everything had gone to plan with all the fuse wires blown and each pack of PE having been properly attached.

The following day was spent on a long cross-country navigation exercise to brush up on their map reading and compass skills, and then later that night they carried out another rehearsal of their mission. Again, everything went to plan. The day after that was spent at the radio transmission station at Hillmorton near Rugby, where the layout of its large, very low-frequency transmitter, used to telegraph messages to the Commonwealth as part of the Imperial

Wireless Chain, was much the same as what they would encounter at Sainte-Assise.

***

It was now 24 May, and their training was complete. It was time to go and do the job for real. They were told they would be leaving in four nights' time, when the moon was half full, to carry out the raid during the late evening of 29 May.

The three were driven to the holding camp at Tempsford Hall in Bedfordshire, just to the north of Sandy, another enchanting eighteenth-century country house with walled gardens and huge lawns, close to the isolated airfield from where they would depart. The final few days were spent working on cover stories and forged documents for the Twins. It was then a matter of waiting.

The Twins sat quietly contemplating what might lie ahead, while reflecting on all that had gone on before. They both knew this could be the end of the road. They even discussed what they would do should they be discovered while placing the charges. In such an event, they agreed, they would go up with the explosion rather than give the Germans the chance to remove the charges.

Time passed all too quickly. Then, during the afternoon of 28 May, Nicholas Bodington and Jacques de Guélis arrived at the hall to go through the mission with Churchill and the Twins for one last time. By all accounts, the weather was forecast to be good throughout the night.

After they finished talking, Churchill handed over a letter that he had written to his parents should anything go wrong. He felt sad for the Twins. They had no such letter to write. They just sat together in the sun. There was no one who needed to be informed in the event of their deaths.

Sat in the shade of an old oak tree, they all enjoyed afternoon tea together. It was such a wonderfully peaceful English setting and the perfect way to spend their final hours before leaving for France. It was then time to go across to the storeroom to draw their equipment, which had already been laid out for them in three neat piles with their khaki parachute overalls for the drop. On top of the pile was a loaded Colt automatic and holster with three spare clips of ammunition and alongside each pile was a Sten gun.

There were two empty rucksacks on a table. Next to each rucksack were packets of PE and tins containing the detonators and time pencils required for the operation. On a smaller table there were three pill boxes containing an assortment of pills, some to keep them awake and others to knock people out, including the optional L-pill (L for lethal) which, if they were captured, could be kept hidden in the mouth and then bitten. Alfred and Henry never had any intention of taking the L-pill. They would rather go down fighting.

The three were then issued with their expertly forged French papers, and with their equipment sorted they all went across to the bar to spend their final moments relaxing as best they could and to wait for the transport to take them to the airfield. Finally, as the sun started to go down, it was time for supper: eggs, bacon, chips, toast and butter.

Churchill was due to leave first. His flight to the drop zone would take around two hours and so his planned take-off time was 11 p.m. This meant leaving the hall just over an hour before that to allow time for the short drive to the final dispatch point and to get kitted out prior to boarding the aircraft.

Exactly on time, a car approached the hall. Churchill bid the Twins farewell. He would next see them in France. As the car pulled up, they could see it had been blacked out with curtains in the back so that no one beyond this point would be able to see who was inside.

Bodington also got in the car as he was to accompany Churchill to the airfield. As the car pulled away, other well-wishers had gathered to wave off the occupants. For those who worked at the hall, it was an all too familiar scene. They did not know who the men were in the car, or where they were going, but they could not help but wonder if they would ever return.

De Guélis was to go with the Twins to the airfield in two hours, and it was again a matter of waiting, only this time at least they knew the mission was finally under way.

***

Two RAF Special Duties squadrons, operating a variety of aircraft, were based at Tempsford and used by the SOE for the dropping of agents and supplies. As his car pulled up at the airfield, Churchill could make out the silhouette of a converted four-engine Handley Page Halifax bomber waiting nearby.

The final departure point was a barn at Gibraltar Farm in the remote north-east corner of the airfield. An airman helped Churchill into his overalls, after which his parachute pack was fitted to his back. The rest of his equipment, including spare ammunition clips and rations, were packed into pockets wherever there was any available space. His

Sten gun was attached to quick-release grips across his chest and finally the rucksack of explosives for the raid was attached to his front. Churchill could barely walk.

Then, just minutes before he was due to board the aircraft, a car could be seen approaching in the distance. Churchill thought little of it. Someone from F Section often came to wish the agent good luck, but the first he suspected something might be wrong was when he could make out in the dim light it was de Guélis getting out of the car. He should have still been with the Twins.

As de Guélis got closer, Churchill could see he had a clouded look on his face. And it was then that the Frenchman delivered the bombshell. The mission was off.

Churchill was stunned into silence, as had been the Twins only a matter of minutes earlier when they had been given the news. The mission was off and that was that. 'Go on leave', they were told. The Twins were livid. Sainte-Assise was their mission. They were even prepared to die for it. How could someone possibly cancel it at such a late stage? And why?

It was later explained to Churchill and the Twins that the Germans had got wind of a possible raid after an earlier explosion at the transmitter complex. Unbeknown to anyone in F Section, some French patriots, seemingly acting completely on their own, had also decided to try and blow up the transmitter. Using PE inserted in the handles of their bicycles, they had gone off on what looked like an innocent fishing trip along the Seine. The group had then entered the complex and placed the bicycles against one of the main masts.

However, although the charges had gone off as planned, only slight damage had been caused to the mast and so the transmitter aerial remained in working order. And with more German troops now spread across the area, Churchill and the Twins would not have stood a chance.

Nonetheless, the Twins were still determined to go and try, but their request was denied. They were too important to lose on what could now be a suicidal mission.

Whether this incident happened exactly as it had been described to the Twins is not known, but it was the reason given for the cancellation of the raid. If it was true, then it was certainly not the first time, or the last time for that matter, that French patriots and the SOE worked towards the same goal in isolation. For now, though, the Twins would have to be patient and wait for another opportunity to return to France. And, as was usually the case, they dealt with the disappointment by going for a drink.

6

GOING BACK IN

With the Sainte-Assise mission gone, the Twins were given some leave before completing the rest of their training. In some ways, it was a shame that the mission had been cancelled as it would have been the quickest way to start getting back at the enemy. On the other hand, though, their final phase of training would better prepare them for their time in the field.

The Twins were next sent to Beaulieu, designated STS 31 and used by the SOE as its Finishing School. It was another country house in another beautiful location, only this time in Hampshire and set in a quiet and inaccessible part of the New Forest. Unlike the earlier elements of their training, the focus at Beaulieu was neither physical nor disruptive. Instead, this final phase was about mental agility and preparation for going into the field. It was all about clandestine operations, communication, concealment and security. And above all, it was to make sure that agents learned how to be French; to look like them, to behave like them and to eat like them, all in the hope that once in France they would not draw unnecessary attention to themselves.

In many ways, this final hurdle was more rigorous than what had gone before. SOE agents were taught how to look quite ordinary while carrying out quite extraordinary things. And again, no stone was left unturned. The clothes they wore had to be French, as was everything in their pockets, such as a used train ticket or a cinema stub. Every item carried had to be current and relevant. Everything had to be right.

For the Twins, this final phase of training was not a problem. They had, after all, spent most of their lives living in France. As far as their mission was concerned, they were told that nothing was expected of them in their first couple of weeks in the field. Rather than rush into things, they should use this time wisely to find out what had changed since they had left France some nine months before. They must blend in amongst the local population and not raise suspicion before making their move. They were also told they could expect to spend around six months in the field, after which they would be recalled to London to report on what they had achieved and to take some leave. But, if they ever felt they were in danger, or their mission had in anyway been compromised, then they were to get out of France as quickly as they could.

The Twins were now given their covering identities with relevant stories for their time in France, although these would change as often as necessary while in the field. Henry became Henri Marcel Dusseret, taken from his wife's maiden name. Born in Marseille, his father had been killed at Verdun during the First World War and he had briefly served in the French Army before the Nazi occupation – his fake military discharge papers confirming that all was in order. There was a similar cover story for Alfred, who became Henry's younger brother, Alfred Georges Dusseret. Since the death of their mother, he had become a self-sufficient bachelor and was now a photographer by profession.

The Twins spent hours perfecting their cover stories and had readily prepared answers should they ever be stopped and asked. They even had a response if ever asked their thoughts about the occupying Germans. There was to be nothing controversial or complicated about their reply. As far as the French were concerned, the Germans had won the war. There really was little else to say.

It was while they were sat in the beautiful grounds at Beaulieu that the Twins first heard they were to be sent into France to work as sabotage instructors within SOE's developing underground network. Some key targets had been identified and there were scores of French patriots who needed organising into efficient fighting groups. However, they had to wait until their final briefing to find out anything more.

★★★

Having returned to London, the Twins did not have to wait long for the call to come. They were woken one morning by the sound of the telephone, which Alfred answered. It was Vera – they were again summoned to Orchard Court and a car would be with them within the hour.

Their briefing was conducted by Nicholas Bodington. He told the Twins that the weather and moon conditions were just right for a drop that night, but otherwise the rest of the briefing was short and came across as rather muddled. Bodington clearly seemed to be in a hurry and kept being interrupted. He started a sentence only for the telephone to ring, after which he would disappear for several minutes before returning to carry on. It was all rather disjointed and the briefing had hardly been a convincing or motivating one.

Bodington then disappeared again, only this time he did not return and so it was left to another staff officer, Major Robert Bourne-Patterson, to pick up the pieces and tell the Twins as much as he knew about their mission and to answer any questions they had.

Bourne-Patterson did a far more convincing job. Essentially, the Twins were to be met on the ground by a man known as Gauthier who, apparently, had thousands of men waiting to be trained. Gauthier would take the Twins to his home, a château on a 300-acre estate in the Haute-Vienne in central France, and their mission was to act as his lieutenants and to train his men in sabotage. But they were warned, Gauthier might prove a little difficult to get on with. Although undoubtedly brave, he was known to be domineering and, at times, rather reckless. Furthermore, it was only recently that Gauthier had complained about the two previous agents sent into France to work for him, transmitting the message, '*Petits Suisses trop nous. Envoyez des durs* [Swiss cheeses are too soft. Send tougher ones].'

The Twins were told they were not going into France alone. A British wireless operator, code-named 'Célestin', was going too, and they would get a chance to meet him shortly.

***

Parked outside in Portman Square was a black saloon and sitting in the front was F Section's operations officer, Major Gerry Morel, an insurance broker by background and another who was fluent in English and French. Morel had been captured by the Germans at Dunkirk but had been released due to his ill health. Although he never made a full recovery, Morel recovered enough to return to England via Spain, after which he was recruited by the SOE. He had been the first agent to be inserted into France by a Westland Lysander and had now returned to England to become part of Buckmaster's staff. It was his job to escort agents to the holding point and go through the final preparations before they went into France.

In the back of the car was the tall, young and handsome figure of Célestin. He hardly looked old enough to be out of school. He was, in fact, 23-year-old Brian Stonehouse, a former art student. Born in Torquay and raised in northern France, he had joined the British Army following the outbreak of war but, being fluent in French, it was soon realised his talents were being wasted as an artilleryman and so Stonehouse had been snapped up by the SOE. He had been on the course ahead of the Twins at Wanborough and had trained as a wireless operator at Thame Park. Now he was going into France under the name of Michel Chapuis, a French artist.

Wireless operators, or 'pianists' as they were affectionately known, like Célestin were always much in demand as no long-term strategy in France was feasible without good communications between London and the agents in the field. Their specialist equipment was a short-wave Morse transceiver (a combined transmitter and receiver) weighing around 30lb. Its frequency range was quite wide, but because it was a small set it could not generate much power and so its signal was weak. This meant a long aerial was required, some 70ft or so in length, which had to be spread out and concealed as best as possible. Carrying such equipment around, and then operating it, particularly as the Germans had direction-finding equipment and vehicles seeking out the wireless operators, was about as risky as it got when it came to work for the SOE.

The Twins got into the car and Morel introduced them to Célestin – and then they were on their way. As they were heading northwards out of London, the coded messages for that night were already being transmitted by the BBC to the various reception committees waiting across France. One of the messages was, '*Les durs des durs arrivent*' – 'the toughest of the tough are arriving' – to indicate the imminent arrival of the Twins.

By late afternoon, the Twins were back at Tempsford where they had waited to leave for the Sainte-Assise mission only a matter of weeks before. Now they had to wait again since in June darkness falls very late.

The day was almost over by the time they arrived at the airfield to find a Whitley stood waiting. Guarded by four RAF sentries, its outline presented a rather eerie sight. Morel began the dispatch procedure. He checked everything about them – reviewing their documents for the last time, checking what they were wearing and asking them questions about what they would do in the case of this or that.

It was finally time for the Twins and Célestin to get into their jumping gear. A specially designed smock was worn as an outer garment to prevent any equipment getting caught on the exit hatch when jumping out of the aircraft.

They wore jump boots and a helmet, the idea being to discard the smock and helmet once on the ground. Under the smock, each man wore webbing with a pistol holder and various pouches added for personal rations and equipment. They were also carrying thousands of French francs as money could be used for any number of reasons and might just make the difference between life and death.

With their parachute pack fastened, they were introduced to the aircraft's crew. The navigator showed them a map, carefully pointing out the intended drop point near Tours, just a few miles to the north of the château and where there was a notable bend in the River Loire.

The jumping order was to be Henry first, then Alfred and finally Célestin with his radio transmitter contained in an art box inside a bulky container across his shoulder. They were also reminded that they needed to jump tight and not hang around. Any delay in getting out of the aircraft would mean them coming down on the ground several hundred yards apart.

Carrying their parachutes and suitcases of clothes and loaded with more equipment than they felt was physically possible, the three agents slowly followed the crew out to the aircraft. They could barely walk.

It was cramped inside the aircraft. The crew were to also drop propaganda leaflets over occupied France to mask the real reason for the sortie. The Twins and Célestin took up their positions on the fuselage floor near the cockpit. They were given sleeping bags to help keep warm and to make them feel more comfortable, and they were all given a flask of coffee and some sandwiches.

Now there was no turning back. Nervousness and apprehension were intertwined with a feeling of excitement;

this, after all, was what they had been trained to do. But there was no way of knowing how the next few hours would turn out, let alone what was in store for them all in the weeks and months ahead. Would they ever set foot on British soil again and, if so, when?

The first engine kicked into life and then the second, and in no time at all they were off down the runway and climbing into the night. At such a late hour, very few of the local villagers would have seen the aircraft climb away, but they probably heard it. They had become used to the sound of a lone bomber climbing into the air late at night.

On board the Whitley, the Twins and Célestin settled down for what was going to be a long transit. It was nearly 400 miles to their drop point and cruising at around 200mph meant that it would be at least two hours before they were in the area, maybe longer should there be any detours to avoid enemy defences. And that was assuming they did not run into any prowling night fighters on the way. The third of Bomber Command's so-called 'Thousand Bomber Raids' had taken place against Bremen in northern Germany just a few nights before and had been followed up by further raids against the same city every other night since, and so it was hoped the Luftwaffe's night fighters were elsewhere.

But as they approached the French coast the Whitley's guns suddenly raged into action. They had been jumped by a lone German night fighter that happened to be in the area at the time. Fortunately, the action was over as quickly as it had started. However, one of the crew indicated they were having to turn back. The aircraft's intercommunications system was no longer working, which made it impossible for the crew to co-ordinate the drop, and so the captain had reluctantly decided to return home.

It was nearly daylight by the time they landed back at Tempsford. Morel was there to meet them at the barn. The disappointment was obvious on everyone's faces but, as Morel pointed out, it was not the first time that an aircraft had to turn back; it had taken one agent four attempts before he was finally dropped into France.

After a few hours of sleep, everyone felt refreshed and in a better mood and ready to give it another go that night. Lunch was good, and the afternoon spent relaxing.

Then it was time to go and try again. This time it was a converted Vickers Wellington parked outside the barn. However, just as they were preparing to board the aircraft, the Twins found out their code names had now been changed to Auguste and Artus, for Alfred and Henry respectively, although they had no idea why. Perhaps their mission had been compromised.

Later that evening of 30 June, the lone Wellington climbed away into the darkness. This time the aircraft was less crowded and with extra space on board the three agents were able to settle down on a bunk. Apart from being lit up like a Christmas tree by enemy searchlights as they crossed the French coast, they droned on into the night, but with every hour that passed the tension on board increased. Only Alfred could stomach the sandwiches provided.

The dispatcher brought them hot coffee and rum before removing the circular wooden trapdoor covering the hole through which the three would jump. He beckoned Henry forward. In the dim lighting of the fuselage the sight of the heavily laden Henry Newton edging his way forward was a fearsome one. He connected his static line to an anchor point on the floor next to the exit hole and checked it for the last time. All he needed to do was jump through the hole and his parachute would be opened automatically by the thin wire, which would break under his own weight.

Alfred and Célestin took up their positions behind him. With the three about to jump through the same exit hole, they all needed to be ready to get out as quickly as possible; every second of delay amounted to nearly 100 yards of separation on the ground.

Sitting astride the exit hole and looking down, Henry could see the ground rushing past. The patchwork of fields and woods and the occasional village illuminated only by the moonlight gave the impression of a murky countryside below. The change in engine sound as the pilot reduced power meant they were now getting closer to the drop. Drops were made with the aircraft flying as slowly as possible just above its stalling speed, which was typically around 130mph, and from a height of around 600ft; high enough for the parachute to fully deploy but low enough to reduce the amount of time spent under the chute that, with no wind, could be as little as fifteen seconds.

They were now on the final run into the drop zone. The crew's eyes stared hard into the distance for the first sight of torch lights confirming that the reception committee were in place and the drop zone was secure. It was a risky business. To be seen from the air, the lights on the ground had to be bright, making them not only visible to the aircraft's crew but also to anyone else in the area.

However, no lights could be seen. Circling above the Loire, the Wellington loitered for forty dangerous minutes. Time after time, Henry watched the same bend in the river, the same woods and the same church go by. The aircraft then started to climb for one last chance to see if the crew could spot something on the ground, otherwise they would have to return home.

Finally, and quite by chance, four people on bicycles were spotted below, silhouetted against the reflection of moonlight on the road. They were cycling as fast as they could and every now and then were flashing torches into the sky.

On board the aircraft the decision was made to go ahead with the drop, even though it was now even more risky than usual. The aircraft had been circling far too long and had probably alerted every Vichy official, gendarme and Nazi sympathiser in the area. For a while the crew lost sight of the cyclists, but lights were then spotted again. This time they were laid out in the prescribed pattern marking the drop zone and the correct code letter flashed to show it was in friendly hands.

The Wellington went outbound again before turning in a wide arc to commence its run into the drop zone. The dispatcher shouted at Henry to get ready and raised his right hand above his head, the red light glowing dimly on the fuselage roof above. Heartbeats increased. Henry's legs were dangling through the exit hole in readiness to jump, the aircraft's slipstream pushing against them. Alfred and Célestin were ready to follow him out as quickly as they could. The dim red light then turned to green as the dispatcher gave the order to jump. There was no time for Henry to think. It was time to go.

★★★

Only those who have jumped in such conditions can know what it feels like during those first few moments after leaving the aircraft; the sensation of falling, the rush of wind against the face and the sudden jolt confirming the opening of the parachute. Then came the feeling of descending to earth in the cool night air, followed seconds later by a sudden crunch.

Henry came down amongst some trees. Alfred, meanwhile, found himself in a gulley after hitting some rocks. But there was no time to dwell. After gathering in his parachute he quickly removed his smock and helmet. He could hear rustling in the undergrowth. Drawing his Colt and flattening himself against a tree, Alfred slipped the safety catch. A squat, sturdy silhouette of a man emerged from some bushes. It was one of the reception committee. Alfred immediately instructed the man to look for Célestin who, he believed, had come down further along the gulley.

Célestin was soon found, quicker than might have been expected given how dark it was, and then Henry – he was found in a clearing nearby, rubbing his backside and cursing his bad luck having come down in the trees. They had all been lucky. Not all drops ended up with everyone together in such quick time.

Their guide quickly led them to the far side of the field, where the rest of the reception committee were nervously waiting. One of two women, who the Twins later referred to as 'the Goddess', was in charge. She told them there was no time to hang around. They were only a couple of miles from a lookout post and so the local gendarmes could be there at any minute. The whole area, she said, would be in a state of alarm because the aircraft had been circling for so long over the same spot.

There was clearly tension in the air. And there was no sign of Gauthier. However, now was not the time to find out why he was not there to meet them or why they had not been at the drop zone on time. They had to move on as quickly as they could.

The Goddess led them through the darkness to a barn. There was no light and no water, but at least they were now far enough away from where they had been dropped to stop and rest and for the Goddess to explain what had happened and brief them on what was going to happen next. It soon became apparent that the three had not been expected that night. They had been due the previous night and so the reception committee had waited at the drop zone until it was nearly daylight, but with no sign of any aircraft they had all returned to their homes in Loches.

As the Twins well knew, the normal procedure for a reception committee was for them to be on standby for three nights before and three nights after a full moon. But this group had clearly not been made aware of that. And so no one had been listening to the BBC transmissions that evening and therefore they had no idea that the drop had been rescheduled for that night. Fortunately, they had been woken by the sound of the aircraft circling above and the four had made their way as quickly as possible to the field. As for the drop zone, the Twins felt it had not been particularly well thought out. For a start, the gulley where two of the three had come down could have proved fatal and it was too close to the known lookout post. They could have all been captured or killed.

The Goddess had little sympathy for the Twins, her simple answer being that people were killed every day. And as she went on to explain, they had not jumped over the planned drop zone. With the aircraft circling overhead, the reception committee had simply picked the first suitable field so that the drop could be made as quickly as possible to avoid alerting even more people in the area.

The Twins had not landed in the bed of roses they had been led to believe, where all they needed was waiting for them. It was not a good start, but it simply highlighted the importance of good communication as well as the huge pressure on those on the ground in France who were willing to risk their lives to receive British agents and supplies.

Nonetheless, the Goddess seemed keen to get rid of the three new arrivals as quickly as she could, and it was now the Twins found out they were not going to Gauthier's château as they had been expecting. Instead, they were to go to Lyon to meet up with Gauthier's deputy, Joseph, who would look after them, while Célestin was to go to Limoges to meet up with Gauthier there. They would have to make their own way to the railway station at Loches, some 5 miles away, as it was unsafe for the reception committee to go with them in case they bumped into a patrol. And they would have to buy their own tickets once they were at the station.

The briefing went on, but the picture did not get any rosier. Once in Lyon, the Twins would have to wait inside a café opposite the railway station called Café des Étrangers. They would need to be there for the next three days at 11 a.m., midday and at 2 p.m., and they should make sure they had two papers on the table, one on Alfred's left and the other on his right, so that they could be identified. And once Joseph had made contact, they were to hand over a message for Gauthier, which read, '*Mettre les meubles en naphtaline parce que les mites vertes etalent velues*', translated as,

'Put the furniture in naphthalene because the green hairy moths spread'.

At best, the idea sounded amateurish – at worst, it was suicidal. Sitting in the same café for hours on end, day after day, would make them stand out like sore thumbs. Not only that, but they were told to leave behind their suitcases and money, supposedly for security reasons, which was yet another change to what they had been briefed in London.

The plan was sounding worse by the minute, but the Twins were left with no alternative. They handed over their large envelopes containing the money, convinced they would never see any of it again, and by the time they had all finished discussing and arguing about the plan it was nearly daylight. The Goddess and her friends disappeared, leaving the Twins and Célestin to set off down the road to the railway station.

Walking along a country road wearing suits and hats more suitable for the city seemed a daft idea and meant they certainly stood out to passers-by. If any of the locals saw them they would surely associate them with the noisy aircraft heard the night before. And if a patrol come along, then what?

There were several different police forces and groups in the unoccupied zone, one of the worse being General Joseph Darnand's collaborationist militia, the Service d'ordre legionnaire, or SOL. Too radical even for most supporters of the Vichy regime, these were Frenchmen who were wholeheartedly devoted to the bad cause. They lived and worked in their towns and villages and used their local knowledge to great effect. Many were described as thugs, sadists even, who enjoyed threatening their own country folk and who would stop at nothing to turn anyone in.

Fortunately, though, apart from one gendarme asking Henry for his papers in Loches, their long journey to Lyon passed uneventfully. With trains being few and far between, they were always overcrowded. With passengers crammed standing in the corridors, many of whom were themselves up to no good, no one even gave them a second look.

7

A HORNET'S NEST

Situated in east-central France, some 300 miles to the south of Paris and 200 miles to the north of Marseille, Lyon (also spelt Lyons) lies at the confluence of two large rivers, the Rhône and the Saône. As the third largest city and second biggest urban area in the country, Lyon is now a major economic centre for banking. Its metropolitan area boasts a population in excess of 2 million and every year visitors flock to the city in their thousands to enjoy its cuisine and historical landmarks.

Lyon was always of strategic importance during the Second World War. The main north–south rail line connecting Paris and Marseille passed through the city at the Gare de Lyon-Perrache, the Rhône and Saône were busy waterways and its road network connected with other major towns, while the safety of the Swiss border was conveniently nearby.

By early June 1940, the Germans had reached the outskirts of Lyon as half of its population, around 500,000 people, fled south, leaving a handful of disparate units to defend the city. Then, when France fell, the Germans entered Lyon virtually unopposed.

However, the initial occupation of Lyon lasted just a couple of weeks. The German withdrawal on 7 July was greeted with relief more than anything else and although the establishment of the Vichy regime and the demarcation line had temporarily silenced anti-German voices, there was left an uneasy peace.

For many French men and women who felt they could neither live nor collaborate with the Germans, Lyon became a place to gravitate to. As the biggest 'free' city in the unoccupied zone, resistance took root there, although a lack of political leadership initially stifled its growth as an organised movement. During the early years of the war, the French Resistance was fragmented, militarily weak and politically divided, but Lyon soon became the hub of resistance activities in the unoccupied zone, particularly from the summer of 1941 following Germany's invasion of the Soviet Union, which saw a rise in action by French communists. The sheer size of the city, with its network of narrow streets and an abundance of interconnecting passageways, derelict buildings and low standard blocks where people lived, all made Lyon an ideal refuge for anyone seeking anonymity, including SOE agents.

For the Vichy authorities, Lyon had become a hornet's nest. By the time the Twins arrived there in early July 1942 there were two resistance circuits established in and around the city, called SPRUCE and HECKLER. However, this increase in activity meant the city was heavily policed, with frequent swoops on buildings and searches on the streets. By and large, though, the Lyonnais were behind the French Resistance. Indeed, just days after the Twins arrived a mass demonstration was held in front of the Statue de la République in Place Carnot. Despite brutal handling by the Vichy authorities, the demonstrators were able to show that a large proportion of the city's citizens were fundamentally on the side of resistance.

One of the biggest problems faced by agents going into France at this time was the relationship between the French Resistance as an organisation and the SOE, which was at a quite delicate stage and not helped by the friction in London between F Section, R/F Section (a part of the SOE set up by the British and working in liaison with the Free French) and the de Gaulle organisation. There was jealousy and intrigue, and to some there was a mutual distrust to the point that at times it seems hard to believe they were fighting the same war.

Maurice Buckmaster later wrote that whatever liaison did exist between Baker Street and de Gaulle's organisation was conducted unofficially by individual officers whose tact and charm was the only weapon against jealousy and intransigence.

There was still confusion in the minds of some at the very top about the exact role they wanted the SOE to play. Views ranged from asking more of the organisation than it could possibly encompass to doubting the value of having the SOE at all. And as far as de Gaulle's leadership was concerned, Britain and America did not consider him to be France's official representative of a French government in exile. There was uncertainty about just how much support he had in France at the time, or his proposed policies once the country was liberated.

The distrust worked both ways, of course, and so British agents going into France were given the strictest instructions to steer clear of all political embroilment. They were expected to help French patriots, whatever their political beliefs, provided they could be trusted to help defeat the Germans.

However, there was a further problem. There were some in the unoccupied zone who still took a sour view of the British, although most recognised the vastness of the task faced by Britain at this stage of the war. There were still those who felt abandoned and were not able to see the broader view, and the unrest in the south was not helped by the Vichy Government continuing to meddle in people's private affairs.

And so, it was against this complex backdrop of unrest, sourness, mistrust and confusion that the Twins first arrived in Lyon. For the next three days, they did as they had been briefed, taking it in turns waiting in Café des Étrangers opposite the Gare de Lyon-Perrache at the specified times for their contact to turn up. But no one came.

Unsurprisingly, the Twins felt vulnerable and they were convinced that everyone inside the café suspected who they were. They were stuck as to what they should do next. They could not risk checking into a hotel as they had no idea which were considered safe and they had no food coupons, nor did they know which restaurants were working illegally on the black market. For their first three days in Lyon, the Twins lived on the sweets and chocolate they had been carrying when they were dropped into France.

Each night they took the train to Avignon so that they could get some sleep and keep warm before returning to Lyon the following morning to follow the same routine as they had done the day before. On the fourth day, it was Alfred's turn to wait at the café while Henry took the train to Limoges to see if he could find Gauthier or Célestin. It was a wasted journey. He really had no idea where to start looking, but he felt he had to try something. Alfred, meanwhile, had no joy either. Again, no one had turned up at the café.

The Twins' mission was seriously in danger of ending before it had even got started. Discussing what they should do next, they agreed to give it another few days in Lyon to see if anything turned up. But they could not risk going back to the café. The waiters kept noticing them, talking amongst themselves. It must have been obvious to anyone watching them what was going on. Instead, they would hang around in the quieter suburb of Vénissieux, in the south of the city.

At Brasserie du Rond Point they discussed their next move. If nothing turned up in the next few days, Henry would make his way across the demarcation line to Paris, where he would get in touch with friends from before the war and discuss with them the idea of setting up a new circuit from scratch. Alfred, meanwhile, intended to make his way to England via the Pyrenees and Spain to brief London on what had happened so far and to find out what they should do next.

It was a sound plan and the best they could have been expected to come up with under the circumstances. But on the sixth morning, and quite by chance, they spotted someone they recognised from England. They had been through training together. His appearance had slightly changed, but it was undoubtedly him. They knew him as Anatole Jukes, his cover name during training, but he was in fact 26-year-old Alan Jickell, a former lance bombardier in the artillery now working for the SOE with the code name 'Gustave'. He had recently arrived by *felucca* to work for an embryonic, but well-run circuit operating on the Riviera and centred around Cannes.

The Twins were faced with a most difficult decision. To make an unplanned contact with another agent in the field went against all they had been taught during training, but faced with little alternative, they felt they should seize the opportunity while they had the chance.

Gustave had sensed he was being followed and noticed a man standing close by. It was Henry. As they both stood looking into a shop window, Henry quietly uttered some words that only Gustave could hear. They then openly greeted each other with much handshaking and humour, as two French men would do having not seen each other for a long time, to convince any onlookers that it had been a chance meeting of old friends.

Joining up with Alfred, they continued their jovial discussion at a nearby café, while discreetly discussing what had happened so far and what the Twins should do next. The outcome was they would travel with Gustave to Cannes, from where they could notify London that they were safe and await instructions as to what they should do next. Gustave also handed over some of his food coupons so at least they could eat.

It was a long train journey to the Côte d'Azur. Having arrived in Cannes, Gustave set about arranging a meeting for the Twins with his own circuit organiser, known as Olive Urchin. This was the highly successful Francis Basin, who had set up his own network, OLIVE, on the Riviera, which eventually stretched along the Mediterranean coast to Marseille and as far north as Grenoble.

It came as something of a shock to Olive when he returned to his flat to find Alfred and Henry fast asleep on his bed. Word had not yet reached him they were coming. Nonetheless, he made the Twins feel welcome from the start. He even arranged a safe house for them to stay for a few days while he made enquiries as to what they should do next.

It was all quite different to what had gone on before. Grateful at last to have found someone who seemed to care, the Twins immediately started work in Cannes, training some of Olive's men in the use of explosives. They were also introduced to the circuit's wireless operator, a tall and lanky 26-year-old known as Julien. He was, in fact, Isidore Newman, a former primary school teacher from Yorkshire who had been dropped by submarine off the Riviera coast three months earlier.

Meanwhile, back in London, nothing initially seemed out of the ordinary. News filtered through that the Twins had landed safely in France, and it was known they had yet to contact Gauthier, but there was nothing unusual in that. It could often take several days, weeks even, to make initial contact in the field. Even their promotion to the acting rank of lieutenant had been promulgated with effect from 1 July, the day they had gone into the field, and everything seemed to be going as it should. However, when news reached Baker Street that the Twins had managed to contact another circuit in Cannes, it came as something of a surprise.

★★★

It was now 14 July. The Twins had been in France for two weeks and it was time for them to return to Lyon, where

Olive had arranged for them to finally meet up with Gauthier at a flat belonging to a female agent known only as Marie.

Exactly at the specified time, they arrived back in Lyon at Place Ollier on the eastern bank of the River Rhône. A flowerpot could be seen in the window of Flat 3 indicating that Marie was in and it was safe to knock.

Marie answered the door. At first glance she looked more like a schoolmistress than a woman working for the SOE. She was in her mid-thirties, medium height and wore little or no make-up, while her naturally wavy reddish-brown hair was pulled back in a bun at the nape of her neck. When she spoke to invite them inside, her American accent was unexpected, but most welcoming.

Unbeknown to the Twins at the time, Marie was the legendary Virginia Hall, the first female agent sent by F Section into France. A talented linguist, she had been educated in America and Europe, but a shooting accident before the war had resulted in her being fitted with a prosthetic leg, which she called Cuthbert, although this never held her back. She had been living in France at the outbreak of war and worked briefly with the ambulance service in the south of the country but, horrified at the signing of the armistice, she made her way to Britain, via Spain, having crossed the Pyrenees during the cold winter months.

As a citizen of the United States, at that point not involved in the war, she knew her nationality would allow her relative freedom to move around in France and so volunteered for the SOE. She returned to France in the late summer of 1941 as a correspondent of the *New York Post* and began writing articles from her hotel room in Lyon, although these were just a cover for the real reason she was in France.

However, when America entered the war the situation changed. While she was living legally in unoccupied France, it was an entity within a country occupied by a nation that was now at war with the United States. She no longer enjoyed immunity but instead risked the same as all Resistance members and SOE agents – arrest, imprisonment, disease, starvation, torture and ultimately death. Now using the name Marie Monin, amongst others, she had become the focal point for F Section agents operating in the unoccupied zone.

Marie had not been at Place Ollier long, having only recently left the hotel to avoid her increasing number of visitors arousing suspicion. The Twins could see that her flat was well furnished. There were just a couple of rooms; one that combined as the kitchen and sitting area, and the other was her bedroom, while she shared the bathroom down the hall with the other residents.

Marie listened intently to the Twins as they protested about all that had happened so far, particularly because they had yet to meet Gauthier. But, as always, she was unmoved. She simply explained that all agents spent most of their time in the field waiting – whether it be waiting for couriers, messages or weapons drops. In fact, Marie emphasised, they waited for just about everything.

Marie was interrupted by a knock at the door. She answered it and was followed back into the room by a large man. But it was not Gauthier, it was Joseph.

It was a start, but Joseph offered no words of apology nor seemingly had any sympathy for the Twins. He was, however, able to update them on Célestin, who had eventually managed to join up with Gauthier and was now transmitting messages to London. However, when asked where the elusive Gauthier was and why he was never seen, Joseph simply replied that Gauthier was a very busy man and only came to Lyon on a Thursday. As it was only Tuesday, they would have to wait another two days to meet him. And when the Twins asked about finding a safe house in Lyon where they could stay, Joseph again answered abruptly, suggesting that next time they were dropped into France they should bring a nanny along to look after them.

Joseph's arrogance was annoying. It was not what the Twins had expected and nothing like what they had been briefed in London. Henry finally snapped. Facing up to Joseph, he told him exactly what he thought of the comic-opera organisation and made it perfectly clear they should meet up with Gauthier on Thursday and no later. And they wanted to see Célestin just as soon as it could be arranged. Alfred, meanwhile, found it difficult not to laugh.

Joseph was left stunned. He could only listen in disbelief at Henry's outburst – but it worked. Joseph's attitude suddenly changed. He even became apologetic, explaining that things had been arranged for their arrival but had since changed. The château where they had been due to go was now under observation and was no longer considered a safe place to stay.

With everyone having calmed down, Joseph offered the use of a flat in Monplaisir, a working-class district in the eastern suburb of Lyon, where the Twins could stay for the next few days while things were sorted out. They were told not to arrive there before 7 p.m. to allow enough time for arrangements to be made. And with that, Joseph left.

Later that afternoon, the Twins took the train to Monplaisir and at exactly 7 p.m. they knocked on the door at the address given to them by Joseph. They were welcomed by a muscly ginger-haired man who introduced himself as Pierre Mutin.

The flat was dusty, but at least it was somewhere for the Twins to stay. However, it soon became apparent that their host was not necessarily trustworthy. During their conversation it became apparent that Mutin had been approached that same afternoon by a man he knew as Jean Isaac, who the Twins soon worked out to be Joseph. Mutin clearly knew more about the Twins than he should have done.

Joseph had told him that he was working for British Intelligence in Lyon and had been asked to shelter a couple of parachutists who had been dropped into France to work for his organisation. Joseph had also said that he would be well remunerated for putting the two men up, which the Twins worked out was probably the only reason why he was prepared to help. Worse still, Mutin had already told his wife that two parachutists would be staying at the flat and, when further questioned about who else he had told, Mutin confessed to having told one of his friends who was coming to supper that evening because he was curious to see what British parachutists looked like!

Henry was the first to react. Pulling his Colt from his waistband, he thrust it in the Frenchman's face, making it clear that should he breathe another word of their whereabouts to anyone else then he would happily blow his brains out. Mutin sunk to his knees, fearful for his life, as it suddenly dawned on him that Joseph's offer of a handsome remuneration carried with it a considerable risk. Faced with little or no alternative, the Twins decided to risk staying at the flat for just a couple of nights until their meeting with Gauthier could take place.

On Thursday they went to Café Terrais, where the meeting would take place. For more than an hour they waited inside, nervously watching the entrance door, without Gauthier ever showing up. Eventually, one of the waiters delivered a message with instructions from Joseph. The message was simple. The Twins were to return to the flat and wait until their meeting with Gauthier could be rearranged.

The Twins were again left feeling unimpressed and it meant at least one more anxious night at Mutin's flat. Fortunately, though, the meeting was arranged for the following day, this time at the Café de Monument. Again, the Twins arrived on time, and things were looking up. They had not been waiting long when Joseph walked in the door. With him was a round-shouldered man of medium height with dark hair and a ragged moustache, who seemingly took little care in his appearance. It was Gauthier.

8

FRUSTRATING TIMES

Seventeen days after they had been dropped into France, the Twins finally got to meet Gauthier, but his welcome was about as cold as it could get, with no word of apology for all that had gone on before. Although the Twins explained to him that London had sent them to be his instructors and lieutenants, it seemed to make no difference. All Gauthier seemed to go on about was how poor their predecessors had been. It seemed that he did not have a good word to say about anyone. It was not more officers that were needed, he kept repeating, but more money and weapons.

The man known as Gauthier was Philippe de Vomécourt, the youngest of three brothers, barons of Lorrainer origin and landed gentry of Limousin. Their ancestors had paid with their blood to preserve France. Their great-grandfather had been tortured and killed during the Franco-Prussian War of 1870, and their father had been killed during the First World War. Now, in the

Second World War, none of the brothers accepted that the French had lost the war and so they were actively keeping up the fight against their Nazi occupiers. It was their turn to fight for the freedom of France.

Philippe de Vomécourt had become known as Gauthier. With his job as a railway inspector came an *Ausweis*, an identification pass entitling him to travel freely around France. He also knew much about the rail network, now also being used to aid the German war effort, and this made it easier to cause disruption on the railway. Recruited to work for the SOE by his elder brother, Pierre, the two brothers set up the first circuits in France, called AUTOGIRO and VENTRILOQUIST. Helped by friends and often using their own money to fund activities, the brothers set up safe houses and places to store arms and ammunition, as well as finding suitable locations where supplies could be dropped from the air.

Dealing with Gauthier would have been a challenge for even the most experienced of agents, but the fact was London could not do without him. He was one of the SOE's key players in France and knew as much about resistance activities going on at the time as anyone. He was, however, someone who chose to work with as few people as possible. He had his handful of trusted associates and that was it. In the smaller communes, these were usually just one or two trusted individuals, but even in a large city like Lyon the number was kept down to a single figure at any one time. It was safer that way. No one, not even in London, was going to make him change his ways.

The relationship between those in London and the Resistance members in France was never going to be an easy one. There were often misunderstandings or broken lines of communications, usually the result of a wireless operator being captured or the betrayal of a circuit organiser, while elementary mistakes brought disaster to many brave men and women. It was already proving to be a difficult year for the French Resistance, suffering greater losses during 1942 than ever before. However, given that the Resistance had been born of the French people themselves and was still in its early years, the wonder is that there were not so many mistakes, but so few.

Little of this was known by the Twins at that time, but it does go part of the way to understanding why there was tension in the air. The more they told Gauthier about his organisation's incompetence and lapses in security, the more the Frenchman hit back. Organising the arrival of new agents and ensuring their safety once on the ground, he said, was not easy.

Inwardly, the Twins resented Gauthier's endless moans and groans, particularly when about those in London who, to him, seemed to do nothing but sit around drinking cups of tea. But, as the Twins quickly pointed out, they were not back in London drinking tea. They were sat next to him in a café in Lyon and were prepared to put their lives at risk for the liberation of France.

Realising that in this case he was not dealing with tea drinkers, Gauthier came up with an idea as to how they might be able to help him. There was a transmitter that needed to be taken across the demarcation line into the occupied part of France and he asked if one of them would deliver it for him, while the other could deliver a package of explosives somewhere else.

It put the Twins in a difficult situation, and it was not one they had expected to find themselves in when they had volunteered for the SOE. They had not come to France to run errands for a Frenchman and so they refused, explaining to Gauthier that it was a task that one of his own people could do. Instead, they wanted to talk about forming sabotage teams and destroying targets, which is what they had come to France to do. They also asked Gauthier to organise a couple of safe houses for them to stay in and some letter boxes where messages could be left.

However, this merely annoyed Gauthier even more. He was now up on his feet. The scene in the café was starting to become dangerous. People could not fail to hear what was going on.

For the Twins, it was now even more obvious than before. They could not work with a man like Gauthier. Alfred even asked for their money to be returned, only to be told that it had all gone. And when asked if Gauthier could arrange for them to meet up with Célestin, that request was denied too.

As far as the Twins were concerned, the meeting was over. They must inform London of what had happened. As they got up to leave, Gauthier suddenly became more reasonable, inviting them to sit back down so that they could talk things through. He may have suddenly realised that the Twins were no fools or perhaps he worried that one word from them would bring an end to the money and supplies coming from London. Whatever the reason, it brought an immediate change in mood.

Gauthier had another proposal for the Twins. Alfred, he suggested, could go to Marseille to meet up with some of his people there. There were 2,000 men waiting to be armed and hungry for the opportunity to go into action. He could see their set-up and learn about how they were operating. Henry, meanwhile, could go to an old airfield near Vierzon, which had seemingly been inactive since the fall of France, and assess its suitability as a place for the dropping of supplies.

This latest proposal seemed more like it and so the Twins agreed. The following morning, they went their separate ways, but when they met up again two weeks later neither had much to tell. The airfield at Vierzon had been taken over by Vichy forces and so there was no way it was going to be suitable for the dropping of supplies. Besides, Henry had arrived to find the whole area infested with Vichy officials and police of all kinds. It turned out that Admiral François Darlan, the former head of the French Navy and now the second highest-ranking Vichy official, was at the airfield reviewing the troops.

Alfred had a similar story to tell of his time in Marseille. He had been sent to meet one of Gauthier's men, code-named L'Allemand. This was Adrien Hess, who was running intelligence and sabotage groups along the Riviera. Again, there was no safe house where Alfred could stay. He spent his time moving from hotel to hotel and, at one stage, was even put up in a brothel in a side street off the Canebière. L'Allemand was also meant to have provided Alfred with an identity card, but nothing had been arranged and so it had been difficult for him to move around and find somewhere to stay.

As for the 2,000 men supposedly waiting to be armed, that had not turned out to be the case. Most were either on weekend leave or away on holiday, or unobtainable for some other reason. There were, however, plenty of dock-ers and younger lads around the Vieux Port who seemed willing to join a resistance organisation, but most wanted

to be armed immediately while others seemed more interested in the 5,000 francs (around £25) per month they had
been promised for their work.

Alfred had also been asked to investigate a possible target,
several goods wagons on a railway siding, but having got
there he found them to be empty and dilapidated. Besides,
there were so many wagons that it would take an artillery
battery to blow them all up. While there had been lots of
talking and good intent in Marseille, it turned out there
had been little in the way of action.

But Alfred's first impressions of resistance activity in
Marseille had been misleading. The truth was, there was
much going on there. Despite there being a strong Gestapo
presence in the city, many brave French men and women
were risking their lives to help Allied soldiers and airmen
escape to Britain, as well as countless Jews and refugees.
Besides, the French would have been equally suspicious of
Alfred so information may not have been forthcoming.

Alfred was not aware of the bigger picture emerging
in France. Only recently, a man called Jean Moulin had
parachuted into the Alpilles, a small mountain range in
Provence. He was acting on the authority of Charles de
Gaulle to unify the various resistance groups in France.

Collectively called the Maquis, these groups were
a constant nuisance for the Germans but there always
remained divisions between them, brought about because
of different loyalties and the politics of France. While
some groups were mainly political in their thinking and
offered only some interest in resistance operations, others
were primarily focused on resistance operations and had
only some political interest. There were also groups that
existed purely to oppose the German occupation and had

no political interest whatsoever. A power struggle had already started to emerge in France, leading to a growing mistrust between resistance groups as some leaders tried to establish a local power base that could be exploited post-liberation.

Moulin had gone to France to try and convince the different factions that they should unify under one leader, Charles de Gaulle. Moulin's mission lasted more than a year, but it was he more than anyone else who succeeded in welding the rival fragments of the French Resistance into something resembling a coherent and disciplined body.

As far as the Twins were concerned, they were not at all interested in the politics or strategies of these groups. They had simply gone to France to do a job and their services were available to anyone sharing the same hatred of the Nazis. It did not matter to them who they were teaching to fire a Sten gun, derail a train or slit a German sentry's throat. However, they were now convinced that Gauthier and Joseph were bluffing as far as their own organisation was concerned. The numbers they spoke about simply were not there. They were also certain that Gauthier wanted to get rid of them once and for all.

It had become apparent that Gauthier and Joseph had started a campaign of rumours, one of which was clearly aimed at keeping the Twins and Célestin apart. The Twins were told that the young wireless operator had been running around with women and was found drunk and talking carelessly in a bar. And so, if they wanted any messages passing on to London in future then they should be given to Joseph rather than contacting Célestin. Luckily, this was one rumour the Twins were able to dismiss straight away. They knew perfectly well that Célestin did not drink.

The Twins were also told not to contact Marie because she was only a courier and had a bad reputation in London. Neither were they to contact Gustave because he had become dangerous and unreliable, and possibly even a double agent.

In the meantime, it seems that both Gustave and Joseph had also been spreading bad rumours about the Twins. They only found this out one Sunday afternoon while travelling back to Lyon after a weekend in Marseille. They had spotted Gustave on the train, but it was too dangerous to talk in the crowded compartment. However, when the train stopped at Saint-Étienne, Alfred seized the moment during the general rush for the platform toilets. He asked Gustave if everything was alright. It was then that Gustave warned Alfred that it was they who needed to be worried. Gustave, and others, had been told to avoid the Twins, as they were now on the run and the Vichy Police were known to be hot on their heels.

Their brief conversation was both enlightening and disturbing. Alfred found out that Gauthier had spread another rumour about them and Marie, the general nature of it being that the real reason Marie got on so well with the Twins was because she was the mistress of one of them.

This latest rumour made Alfred particularly mad and he was still pondering over his conversation with Gustave when the train pulled into Lyon. He decided to make some discreet observations to see if he could determine what was going on. That evening, he followed Joseph from his place of work to a small café off Rue de la République. Observing him through the window, he could see Joseph talking to others, after which notes of paper were handed out, clearly carrying messages elsewhere. Alfred could only assume these were more messages scattering muck about the Twins.

Having left the café, Joseph stopped off at a nearby boarding house where one of his young couriers, a man called Gontran, was staying. But as he was not in, Joseph set off towards the district of Perrache.

Rather than follow Joseph any further, Alfred decided to try and find out why he had gone to see Gontran. He knew the young Frenchman had been entrusted with a suitcase full of weapons and explosives, which he was soon to deliver to a group of prospective saboteurs, and he thought it would be a good excuse to pop in to make sure that everything was all right prior to him setting off.

When Alfred knocked at the door, he was greeted by the landlady, who explained that Gontran had gone away for the weekend. Alfred came up with an excuse for his visit, saying Gontran had borrowed a book from him and had promised to return it by the end of the weekend. It worked – the landlady let him in, suggesting he went up to the room to see if he could find the book for himself. His room was on the fourth floor and should be open as Gontran never locked it.

As he entered the room Alfred's heart nearly stopped. Scattered all over the bed were weapons, explosives and detonators. The entire contents of the suitcase had been left lying around the room. Alfred could not believe how stupid the young Frenchman had been. He had gone away for the weekend and presumably used the case for his personal belongings. Either that, or Alfred was about to be caught in a trap.

Alfred decided to confront Joseph about this latest lapse of security. He set off for the square in front of the Gare de

Lyon-Perrache, one of Joseph's known meeting points, and minutes later saw him with Gauthier. They were both sat on the same bench they always used and in full view of cafés nearby. Alfred always thought it was one of the worse places to meet, but it was getting late and he did not want to tackle Gauthier at such a late hour, so he decided to leave it for now.

★★★

The Twins were tough, but they were not stupid. They were getting tired of trying to instil secure practices and procedures only to see others seemingly ignoring them. If only the 'tea drinkers' back in London could see how the organisation was being run. They sensed worrying times ahead, but the Twins had gone to France to do a job. They were looking for revenge on the Nazis and they were not going to give up now, just because of a Frenchman they did not get on with.

This ongoing clash between the Twins and Gauthier was a great shame. Each side had so much to offer the other, but the truth was the situation was never going to improve. Yes, they had got off to a bad start but their continuing reluctance to get on with each other can only be down to personalities and egos.

Joseph was no less courageous than the Twins. His real name was Jean Maxime Aron. He was a Jewish engineer and employee of the French car manufacturer Citroën. For people like Joseph, the consequences of getting caught were obvious. Even his new private secretary was drawn into resistance activities.

She was 26-year-old Denise Bloch, the daughter of French Jews. She also had a fixed hatred of the Nazis and had recently moved to Lyon from Paris after the Jewish situation in the capital had become perilous. The Twins were always wary of Denise's Jewish origin. They felt it might attract unwanted attention and so they tended to avoid being seen with her. However, Denise was another who showed great courage as a courier during the months ahead. Code-named Ambroise, she helped revitalise one of Gauthier's subordinate networks but was later captured and finally executed in a concentration camp just weeks before the end of the war. Denise had been another to have kept the flame of the French spirit burning throughout the dark years of occupation but was sadly to make the ultimate sacrifice.

***

Despite their ongoing differences with Gauthier, the Twins were moved to a safe house in Lyon and told that whenever they were needed a courier would come to the house with instructions from Joseph. In the meantime, the Twins spent much of their time talking to Marie. They trusted her more than anyone else and it was she who suggested there was a need to organise resistance activities around the town of Le Puy-en-Velay, some 60 miles to the south-west of Lyon, where she had many trusted friends. She would have a word with Gauthier.

This sounded far more like the kind of work the Twins had expected to be involved with and soon after came instructions from Gauthier. They were to go to Le Puy to meet up with a factory owner called Jean Joulian and his wife, Marie-Louise. Both were long-standing and trusted friends of Marie and with their help the Twins were to get a new Resistance circuit up and running in the area.

Le Puy is set in the rolling hills near the River Loire in the Haute-Loire department in south-central France. The Twins arrived there to find many willing volunteers and, as they wanted to make an early impression, they asked Gauthier to arrange for a supply drop to take place. This would not only show those who were prepared to join the Resistance just how good the organisation was and how things were done, but also provide them with some valuable experience when it came to the handling of future air drops.

A drop was soon arranged. It was planned to take place at night in a remote field on top of a hill overlooking Le Puy. It was the first time the Twins had gathered such a large group together, all wanting to do their bit for France. They came from all professions and backgrounds, young and old. It was dark and late at night, yet here they all were patiently lying in a thicket on a hillside above their homes, shops and offices, waiting for a lone aircraft that may or may not turn up. And if it did not turn up, they would all be back at work the next day as if nothing untoward was going on before returning to the hillside again the following night. These were good, honourable people, there was no doubt about that. The Twins felt reassured that at last they were achieving something.

The drone of an aircraft could be heard in the distance, faint at first but becoming louder by the second. As Alfred flashed the signal to indicate to the crew that the drop zone was in friendly hands, Henry organised the reception committee into their positions.

The aircraft made just one pass, dropping its load before turning away. It was all that was needed. Not all air drops were accurate, but this one was. The containers were gathered quickly and then loaded onto a lorry hidden in the trees. Within seconds the lorry had gone, and within a matter of minutes so had the reception committee. There was hardly a trace of any activity at all. It had been a good night.

Things were finally looking up. The Twins were much happier now they were working away from the influence of Gauthier. They had often discussed cutting loose from him to work on their own, but they knew they could not do so without the support of London. They decided to arrange for a message to be sent informing the powers that be in London of what they planned to do, confident that approval would quickly follow.

Although everything had been done to keep the Twins and Célestin apart, a chance meeting came about when they bumped into him while strolling along the Cours Belsunce in Marseille. During their brief conversation, Célestin told them he was looking for somewhere to stay. He had been feeling uneasy at his digs for a while and wanted to get away, but so far Joseph had been unable to find him a safe address that he could move to.

The Twins could sympathise with the young Englishman. The tension, loneliness and fear all combined to play hell with the nerves; even for the toughest of agents. They offered to put Célestin up at their own safe house until some other arrangement could be made, but in return they asked him to send their latest message to London just as soon as he could get the chance. Although Célestin was happy to do so, he told them it would not happen for a few days. His set was broken, and it would be a while before it was fixed.

It had also become apparent during their conversation that none of the Twins' messages had been passed on to Célestin for transmission, which explained why they had yet to receive any replies or updates from London. However, while this latest news could hardly have been a surprise, the biggest bombshell was still to come.

When the Twins next met up with Gauthier, they handed him their report for onward transmission to London, giving details of what they had achieved with their group at Le Puy and making clear their intentions for the future. The Frenchman took the report and, with a smile on his face, handed them a sealed envelope containing a message written in pencil. The message simply read, '*Cher amies, même en qualite d'officiers vous devez obeir immediatement et sans questions aux ordres que vous donne Gauthier*' ['Dear friends, even as officers you must obey immediately and without questions the orders given to you by Gauthier']. The message was signed by Pierrot, a code name used by Major Nicolas Bodington.

The Twins were livid. Although everyone knew they did not get on with Gauthier there had never been any question of them disobeying an order. Furthermore, if Bodington had anything to say to them then he should have said it in person so that at least he could hear their side of the story as well. What right did he have to take the accusations of a Frenchman over two officers of his own organisation without establishing all the facts?

There is no doubt that Gauthier could have handled the matter more discreetly than he did, but for the Twins it was finally the straw that broke the camel's back. If it had not been clear before, then their minds were certainly made up now. They could not, and would not, continue to work with the Frenchman.

Bodington's message had delivered a huge blow, leaving the Twins feeling disappointed and humiliated. They knew all too well that Gauthier would be quick to spread word about the message and it had taken the gloss off all the good work they had recently carried out at Le Puy. It would also damage their reputation amongst the French.

While they were understandably feeling down, like a heavyweight boxer kneeling on the canvas, the Twins were certainly not out. They were not going to give up – not now. From now on, they decided, they would do their own thing.

9

GREENHEART

Having fallen out with Gauthier once and for all, the Twins knew they needed to get a message to London as soon as they could. They needed to explain what was going on from their point of view and, as they could not wait for Célestin to repair his wireless set, they did what they always did in such situations – they went to see Marie. She knew every agent in the south of France and so they hoped she could arrange for their message to be sent.

Marie was fully aware of what had been going on. In fact, she knew more than the Twins about what had happened. Bodington had arrived on the Mediterranean coast at the end of July to meet up with several key individuals and to assess for himself the state of F Section's activities in the unoccupied zone. During his visit, he had travelled to Lyon to see various people and to try and undo the chaos that was seemingly reigning there.

The root of the problem stemmed back to the turn of the year after London had sent a couple of agents to

Lyon to work as co-ordinators alongside Marie and an organiser known as Alain (real name Émile Georges Duboudin). But much of the ongoing chaos was caused by Alain himself after he had struggled to form sabotage teams in and around the city for his own circuit, SPRUCE, and then fell out with those sent by London to help him. One of these was the strong, energetic and voluble Robert Boiteux, code-named Nicolas, a half-Jewish London-born Frenchman in his mid-thirties. He had been on the course ahead of the Twins at Wanborough and had arrived in Lyon just before them. But the hunt for Nicolas had been on from the first minute he landed in France after he narrowly escaped arrest when the agent he jumped with, Robert Sheppard, code-named Patrice, had landed on the roof of a building being used by the German military police.

While the luckless Patrice's mission was over before it got started, Alain was also sent a wireless operator, Edward Zeff, a half-Jewish man of great nerve and resource who went by the code name Georges 53. Alain did not get on with either Nicolas or Georges, and even the imperturbable and resourceful Marie had been unable to resolve their quarrels. In the end, London had to step in and so it was left to Bodington to try and resolve the issue, the outcome being that Alain was ordered back to England as soon as could be arranged, leaving Nicolas to go it alone having won the backing and support of the key players in Lyon.

As for other contributing factors to the chaos in Lyon at the time, it seems the Twins were not the only ones to have suffered problems with Gauthier. The Frenchman had also managed to fall out with 20-year-old Tony Brooks, the youngest SOE agent to be sent into the field. Code-named Alphonse, he had been dropped into the Garonne to explore the possibility of using French railway workers to disrupt the rail network connecting the key cities of Marseille, Lyon and Toulouse.

Like the Twins, Alphonse had been given Gauthier as his contact in France, but it seems the Frenchman considered him far too young for clandestine operations in the field and soon sent him off to Toulouse. But Gauthier had clearly underestimated the young Alphonse. So successful had he been since arriving in France that he had now set up his own circuit of local saboteurs called PIMENTO.

It was during his visit to Lyon that Bodington had met up with Gauthier, which led to the message for the Twins. From what Marie was now telling the Twins, it appears that throughout the meeting the Frenchman had been his usual difficult and demanding self, wanting this and wanting that. It was then that Bodington had hurriedly scribbled the message, simply to satisfy Gauthier on at least one point and without even thinking about the consequences.

The Twins explained to Marie that the situation between them and Gauthier had now become impossible. In her usual and relaxed way, Marie told them she fully understood and agreed to make sure their message was sent to London just as soon as she could.

As always, Marie kept her word and a reply was received from London the following day. The message was short but sweet – 'The Twins will work on their own'. When they later bumped into Gauthier at a meeting point near a newspaper kiosk on the Quai de Rhône, it gave Henry the greatest of pleasure to deliver him the news. And without giving Gauthier the time to reply, Alfred went into a tongue lashing that left the Frenchman in a daze.

***

The Twins had now been in France for two months. They had learned much during that time, although in their view this was more about how not to run a circuit than anything else. With their tie to Gauthier officially cut, they soon settled into their new way of life in the Haute-Loire. Alfred became an insurance broker and Henry a rural architect, both occupations that gave them a legitimate reason to move around the countryside. While Alfred could go from village to village inspecting policies and organising contracts, Henry could visit farms to supposedly discuss matters such as establishing loans for repairs and maintenance under the new Vichy administration. Once he was at a farm, he could then wander around the fields and roads making notes of their suitability for all sorts of ill practices. And now they had the backing of Baker Street, the Twins quickly set about organising their own circuit. Given the name GREENHEART, it soon started to grow.

From the outset, there had always been French men and women who were prepared to do something to oppose the Nazis. However, in the unoccupied zone at that stage of the war it was never easy recruiting for the Resistance, unlike in the north of the country where the mere presence of Germans encouraged people to resist. The recent demonstration in Place Carnot had shown the strength of local support, but the Twins needed more than demonstrators. They needed people for whom there were no reservations and who had no conscience about whether what they were doing was right, proper or legal. Not only did the Twins need to find men and women with the right spirit, they needed the right personal qualities as well. They needed courage, self-discipline and a willingness to remain silent. They needed to sustain a normal and unassuming manner in everyday life, rather than be impulsive or reckless, and they must live with the fear of one day being captured or betrayed.

It would always be almost impossible for any circuit organiser to be certain of the motives of those who came forward and so the Twins adopted their own method of recruiting. Instead of promising large amounts of money to greedy individuals, they worked on winning over the locals by playing on their patriotic feelings. It worked – nobody wanted or expected to be paid in return for what they did, which meant the Twins were able to use what money they had wisely, such as to cover individual expenses or to buy small gifts and drinks for people in return for what they were doing.

Most importantly, though, the Twins surrounded themselves with people they could trust, almost all of whom they had been put in touch with by Marie. In Lyon, there was Eugénie Catin, an energetic and enthusiastic 28-year-old housewife known as Fernande. She was one of their most trusted aides and worked as their courier. She dreamt of nothing but dead Nazis.

Another courier was Marie-Fortunée Besson, who went by the code name Bohémienne. A slim and pretty woman with glossy black hair, she is best described as the essence of femininity with the heart of a warrior and an instinct for trouble. She lived with her husband, Alphonse, on the corner of Rue Claude Veyron and Rue du Docteur

Crestin, in a flat belonging to the Desautel factory where he was the *chef de personnel* and factory foreman. A dark, curly-haired man of slim stature, always scruffily dressed and invariably with a cigarette drooping from his lower lip, he was a man of immense strength and went by the code name Thermogéne.

In Le Puy there was Hubert, the manager of the insurance company who had 'employed' Alfred as one of his brokers, and the rather stocky and jovial Marius, whose real name was Eugène Labourier, a haulage contractor in his mid-thirties who had taken on Henry as a rural inspector.

There were also those who had influence within the region, including the Mayor of Langogne, gendarmes from Saint-Paulien and firemen from Le Puy, while others had access to useful assets such as vehicles and official documentation. The list goes on.

It was Marius who the Twins appointed to be their right-hand man. Should anything happen to them, he knew enough about the organisation and how London worked to hold the group together until another agent could be sent from England. Marius and his courier girlfriend, Andrée Michel, the invaluable Maggy to her friends, had joined the Resistance more than a year earlier and had been members of the NEWSAGENT network before transferring to GREENHEART. It was Marius who had been behind the recruitment of a group of gendarmes while attending a luncheon party with Henry, as well as the recruitment of an officer of the Le Puy fire brigade who the Vichy authorities had appointed to head a group of collaborators tasked with tracking down and arresting British agents and their reception committees. The authorities thought he worked for them, but he was really helping the Resistance. It was a smart bit of recruitment.

At last, things were looking up. The Twins were also pleased to hear that Célestin had found a château outside Lyon from where he could transmit and receive messages and had forged a good working relationship with a newly arrived courier known as Christianne. This was 44-year-old Blanche Charlet, a small, dark-haired and attractive Belgian who was another of SOE's early female agents to be sent into the field. Her job was to carry messages between Gauthier, Joseph and Célestin, although she, like Célestin and the Twins, had quickly become dissatisfied with Gauthier's attitude and his disorganised group, and was now actively looking to move elsewhere.

***

Although there had now been more than a dozen SOE circuits formed across France, only a handful could be considered fully established. Others had either become disjointed in their activity or had come to a sudden end after circuit organisers had been arrested or killed. And so GREENHEART was a much-needed and most welcome addition to SOE's operations and in what seemed like no time at all was ready to receive its first dedicated air drop of supplies.

On the night the drop was planned everyone turned out. The mayor, his secretary and many other notable dignitaries had all joined the reception committee to do their bit. Not only were they expecting to receive supplies, but Marie had also arranged for an agent to be dropped in. Even Joseph got involved, claiming the agent parachuting in that night was a friend of his, and so he had sent one of his own men along to join the reception committee.

The man Joseph had sent along was Rodolphe, real name Henri Sevenet and an old family friend of the de Vomécourts. Rodolphe had recently been dropped into France to try and persuade Gauthier to go to London for a rest and further training. It seems the Twins had not been the only ones getting tired of Gauthier and his ways but, Gauthier being Gauthier, he had refused to go. As far as he was concerned, there was nothing he could learn from the SOE's training staff in England as they were clearly less experienced than him. And so, having failed to persuade Gauthier to go to England, Rodolphe was left to get on with his secondary task, which was to prepare a small circuit called DETECTIVE with the specific aim of attacking the Tours–Poitiers railway line.

Everything was in place for the drop, but no aircraft turned up. It was the same the following night. Again, they all waited until the sun was almost up, but still no aircraft came. It was a huge disappointment. This should have been GREENHEART's first drop. The Twins had so wanted the night to be a success, particularly as they had rallied so many people together. It was important to get off to a good start. Otherwise, how could they expect the locals to believe what they were being told?

Not only were the Twins left feeling somewhat embarrassed by the fact that no aircraft had turned up, they were also annoyed – even though they knew all too well that a no-show was always likely to happen. But they felt they needed to be seen doing something and so they sent a message to London making it clear how they felt, although their moans will have fallen on deaf ears.

The past couple of nights had been a great disappointment for everyone involved, but friendships and trust were maintained. It was considered a mere setback, that was all. Just because a supply drop had been requested it did not mean that one would happen. Similar groups across occupied Europe were competing for the same limited resources and so this early feeling of frustration was a timely reminder to everyone, particularly those who were new to it all, that patience would be the key to success.

However, the Twins could still not shake off Joseph's interference in what was going on in the Haute-Loire. They found out he had recently been to Le Puy claiming to have become the chief of all Resistance activities and telling people that the Twins were about to be sent back to England to be reprimanded for their inefficiency, meaning he was to take over the group's work in the Haute-Loire.

Joseph had also been full of promises. Black market prices were already extortionate, but for items such as bicycles and fuel he was prepared to pay double the price negotiated in Le Puy. He had also produced some documents, written in English, referring to targets that would need to be destroyed as and when the Allies landed in France, one of the targets being a railway tunnel in the area.

Within a couple of days of a reconnaissance of the tunnel being carried out, German troops had been spotted inspecting it. From what the Twins later found out, it appears that after carrying out their reconnaissance of the area, with a view of blowing up the tunnel, Joseph's group had then gone to a local bistro where they were heard bragging about their work.

It was yet another example of a lapse in security and more interference from Joseph in what the Twins felt should have been their line of work. They were the trained saboteurs. Besides, they would have tackled the problem in a different way. Instead of trying to blow up the tunnel, which would require an enormous amount of explosives, they knew that a small amount of PE applied to a train in the right place would have derailed it once inside the tunnel, and so they could have achieved the same result in a much more efficient way.

While such setbacks and interference might have dissuaded some from carrying on, the Twins simply knuckled down more. GREENHEART was a small group in comparison to others, but at least it was manageable and secure, unlike some circuits that had become too big too quickly, making them unwieldy and easy to infiltrate.

In a matter of just a few weeks, the Twins had knitted GREENHEART into a well-organised circuit. They had always been mindful of security, but even more so now the circuit was firmly established. They insisted that no written records should ever be kept of the group's activities, for fear they might one day fall into the wrong hands. Everyone was given a code name, and everything was committed to memory. And now they had no one to answer to, they could freely go about training their group. They gave sessions on how to organise air drops and receive supplies, as well as how to use weapons and make the best use of explosives. Every day was spent cycling around the countryside teaching something to someone. Their members were thoroughly schooled in all the tricks of the trade. They had also formed combat groups, individual teams of eight, who kept their eyes and ears open at their places of work or around their homes, and then got together during the dark hours to discuss what they knew.

Although things were going well, the Twins burned with a passionate desire to get things going. However, they knew it would be a while before they could gather enough weapons and explosives to conduct small-scale operations. They also knew the day would come when the Allies landed in Europe. It could be next year or the year after, but the day would undoubtedly come. And when the call from London came, they needed to be ready to rise against the occupiers and disrupt their movements as much as possible, to help pave the way for the liberation of France.

In the meantime, the Twins looked for other ideas to carry out some low-key sabotage and their first opportunity came at the Rochet-Schneider factory in Lyon. The factory had produced automobiles before the war but was now turning out 6-ton lorries for the Vichy Government, although the word was that the vehicles were being loaded onto transporters and taken straight to Germany to aid the Nazi war effort. And so, they decided to sabotage the entire output.

There are many ways to sabotage a lorry, such as using explosives, but the Twins knew they could achieve the same result without putting the French factory workers at risk. Each vehicle was to be greased with a mix containing paraffin and a high proportion of pumice and steel powder, while the engine was treated with a concoction that would gum up and corrode every component. After a short period of time the lorries would seize so badly that they would be of no further use.

It was a simple, yet extremely effective way of sabotaging many lorries and shows how the resisters were using their initiative to achieve an aim while minimising the risk of reprisals against their own people. The Gestapo soon worked out the lorries had been sabotaged and, realising the damage had been caused somewhere between the production line in Lyon and the delivery point in Germany, an investigation was carried out. However, although their sleuths visited the factory in Lyon, nothing was ever found to suggest the act had been carried out there and so the conclusion was that the sabotage must have taken place somewhere else.

It was a good start, but the Twins were already facing a major problem and it was not something they wished to share amongst their group. They had no direct link with London. With no wireless operator of their own, all their messages had to be passed to Marie, who then passed them on to someone else for transmission. All they could do for now was to carry on producing their reports, which included all aspects of their work, such as identifying suitable drop zones, reporting on any German units seen, providing descriptions of radio detector vans, which were increasing in number, and passing on details of known Vichy vehicles and activities in their area. But nothing was ever heard back. The Twins were never convinced their reports were getting through.

Financially, too, GREENHEART was in difficulty, although Marie helped whenever she could. Thermogéne and Fernande had already dipped into their own savings to help the cause, the idea being they would be repaid as soon as more money was received. But it was an arrangement kept quiet from the rest of the group to avoid causing any uneasiness or concern. Henry even went to Paris to sell some of the family's land and other belongings as a way of raising some funds. This meant crossing the demarcation line, something generally to be avoided, but he somehow made it safely to Paris and back, and with the money raised the Twins were able to reimburse Thermogéne and Fernande.

Without a dedicated wireless operator and financial support, it was not going to be easy to carry on. In truth, the Twins were only just keeping GREENHEART alive, but then things suddenly took a turn for the worst. And as was so often the case when circuits were infiltrated or agents betrayed, things happened quickly and without warning, and triggered a chain of events that had a devastating impact elsewhere.

Firstly, on the morning of 24 October, Célestin and Christianne were arrested near Lyon. Six days later, Christianne's fiancé, Dominique Mendelsohn, was also arrested, and two days after that L'Allemand was arrested in Marseille. Then, just a day after that, Joseph was arrested in Lyon.

When piecing the events together afterwards, it seems that Célestin and Christianne were both arrested in Château Hurlevent at Feysin in the southern suburbs of Lyon after his transmission had been picked up by German detector vans. It was only the second time he had transmitted from there, but his luck had finally run out. Christianne had been with him at the time because she was carrying papers and an urgent message from Gauthier that needed sending to London. It appears she had spotted what looked like caravans when she arrived at the château, but satisfied there was nothing to worry about, she had gone to find Célestin, who she knew would be transmitting from the attic. Soon after that the lamp in the attic had gone out. The power must have been cut. Sensing danger, Célestin immediately stopped transmitting and they both hurried down the stairs to an exit at the rear of the château, Christianne hiding the papers behind the lift shaft as they went. But the rear exit was covered. They were both arrested, and the château searched. The papers and wireless set were found.

Célestin and Christianne were taken to Petit Dépôt Saint-Jean in Lyon, where they were separated and then questioned. It was Joseph's secretary, Ambroise, who first raised the alarm. She had been in Lyon that day and saw Célestin being led into the police station by two men, followed by Christianne. Realising they were also in danger, Denise, Joseph and Rodolphe all fled to Marseille.

The circumstances behind Mendelsohn's arrest are unclear, as are those relating to L'Allemand, but the following day Ambroise decided to return to Lyon to deliver crucial information about landing grounds that she had earlier received from L'Allemand. Not wishing to let Ambroise travel alone, Joseph and Rodolphe dutifully went with her, but it was a mistake that cost Joseph dear. He was arrested outside the railway station in Lyon after getting off the train. The Gestapo had clearly expected Ambroise to be with him, but she had left the station by another exit, as had Rodolphe, who also had a lucky escape.

It was Fernande who told the Twins about the arrests – but that was not all. There had been further arrests after a trap had been set at Joseph's office on Rue de la Gare, and everyone who had subsequently called there was captured. The rumour was that explosives had been found and a diary kept by Joseph confiscated, and at least five or six people had been caught. Gauthier, however, was not one of them.

Although none of those arrested so far were members of GREENHEART, its members were still at risk. Arrests amongst one group would often lead to the downfall of another. People knew people, who knew other people, and so it did not take long for word to spread.

The situation was bad enough as it was, but the matter became even worse when Fernande got word that Joseph had betrayed the Twins. Now the Vichy Police were asking about two men they knew only as Auguste and Artus.

There was no way of knowing for certain whether this latest rumour was true, but if Joseph had betrayed the Twins there was clearly no time to waste. They immediately sent Fernande off to warn the rest of their group and to drop all activities until further notice.

While news of these arrests was extremely worrying, it could not have come as a complete surprise to the Twins. Célestin was known to make longer transmissions than he should, and as for Joseph's arrest – they had seen it coming. They had always felt that men such as Joseph, and Gauthier for that matter, hated the Germans so much that they had started to consider them unintelligent and easily outwitted. If this was true, then it was a costly mistake.

***

For a while the Twins kept their heads down. But they did not stay low for long. Once they found out the police only had a very loose description of them – average height, dark-haired and dressed in grey – they knew it was not much for them to go on. It was a description that fitted half the male population of France.

With everything having calmed down, for the time being at least, the Twins set about their work once again. Marie even came to them for help. She was co-ordinating a plan to get Célestin and three other British prisoners out of the Vichy-controlled prison at Castres. Captured SOE agents and Resistance members were being held there in appalling conditions and were being retained as hostages ready to be shot should any attacks be carried out against German or Vichy officials in the unoccupied zone.

With rumours starting to spread about the Germans soon moving into occupy what had been the unoccupied south, there were concerns about what would happen to the prisoners should the prison fall into German hands. There would then be little chance of getting anyone out. And so, Marie had a plan to free the four prisoners during the early hours of 12 November.

The three other prisoners who Marie was planning to break out of Castres were Xavier, Justin and Alexandre – or, to use their real names, Richard Heslop, Denis Rake and Edward Wilkinson – who had all been arrested by the Vichy Police during a night stop at Limoges prior to them attempting to cross the demarcation line into the occupied zone. For the break-out, Marie had already secured the use of a vehicle that could be used as a German staff car and an SS uniform for the driver.

Her plan was for the staff car to pull up at the prison. Two fake gendarmes and two men posing as Gestapo officers would get out of the car and produce the required paperwork for the transfer of the four British prisoners elsewhere. The two posing as Gestapo would then bundle the prisoners into the car, followed by the gendarmes, and drive off at speed. Should the prison guards become suspicious or try to stop them, the four would stay and shoot it out while the prisoners made their escape.

All Marie needed for her plan to go ahead was a couple of gendarme uniforms and two willing volunteers to fill them. She knew the Twins had good contacts and so she could rely on them to get the uniforms and men together just as soon as they could.

The Twins would do anything to help Marie. However, given the urgency, it was not going to be an easy task as it meant finding two suitable volunteers to go into the prison to pose as gendarmes. They decided to take on the role themselves. It was just the sort of job they looked forward to.

While Henry stayed in Lyon, Alfred went off to Le Puy to meet with Marius. The following day, he returned with two gendarme uniforms and forged paperwork authorising the transfer of the prisoners. However, when the Twins tried the uniforms on, they still looked more like backstreet thugs than gendarmes. It had also become apparent that the technicalities of the paperwork required for such a transfer of prisoners to take place was far more complicated than they had initially thought. They would not fool anyone.

Instead, the Twins decided to take on the role of the Gestapo civilians and leave it to others of their group, who were real gendarmes, to do the rest. But as they thought more about the idea, they realised it would be difficult to ask real gendarmes to carry out the job. Their true identities would most likely be blown and what would happen then? It would leave them and their families at risk. No, it was not that simple.

★★★

The Twins were still pondering over their plan when everything suddenly changed. The Allies had landed in French North Africa three days earlier and, in response, the

Axis powers carried out *Fall Anton*, the military occupation of Vichy France by German and Italian forces. It was 11 November 1942.

In that one moment, the French people were reunited in the common misery of occupation. Gone was the feeling that some were living in comparative freedom and gone was the illusion of Pétain being the saviour. It marked the end of the Vichy regime as a nominally independent state, although it continued its existence as a puppet government in occupied France. It was the end of the *Zone Libre*, the unoccupied zone, and that meant change. And it was not going to be for the better.

10

REVENGE

The war was not going particularly well for the Allies, and for most of 1942 it had been a difficult year. German U-boats continued to inflict terrible losses on Allied shipping in the Atlantic, while in the Mediterranean, British convoys attempting to reach the beleaguered island of Malta had been hammered relentlessly from the air. In the east, the Germans had advanced deeper into Russia, in North Africa Rommel had torn through Libya into Egypt, while in the Far East, Singapore had fallen, and the Japanese were in Burma with India in their sights.

However, 1942 ended on a note of hope. While serious thoughts of the Allies mounting landings in Europe were still some way away, the SOE was now in a far healthier position than it had been at the start of the year as more circuits were being established across France. But, as an occupied country, France was starting to pay the price for Allied successes elsewhere, suffering more from air raids by British and American bombers and enduring harsher privations as the Germans sucked the country dry of food and manpower. Thousands were dying from malnutrition and disease, and as the war droned on a ubiquitous lethargy fell upon the French people. There was no longer any distinction between those in the north and south of the country. They shared a common fate. Vichy was irredeemably under German domination and, by continuing to exist, it gave apparent sanction to German atrocities.

As news of German and Italian forces arriving in the south of France reached London, word filtered back to the circuits and resistance groups. There was to be no initial opposition or response. While the Twins were disappointed to hear such news, they could understand. There was a bigger picture to consider and things were happening at pace. The Germans had now taken control of the whole of France, and so it was vital that officials back in London were kept up to date with the latest information. SOE agents about to be inserted into the south of the country needed to know what changes had been introduced in towns and cities such as Lyon if they were to survive. What might be considered relatively minor details could make the difference between being caught or not. Changes to cinema opening hours and what day of the week meat might be available were as important as knowing whether any changes to the rail network had taken place or making sure that agents were carrying the right papers and documentation. New agents had to be briefed.

The resistance circuits would have to wait for further direction. But many, like Fernande, were less understanding. With the Germans arriving in great numbers, she was determined to do something and went to the Twins to ask for half a dozen grenades. But Alfred had to say no, to which her retort was that she would throw bricks instead. Hubert, too, asked when they were to go into action. His group was standing by, waiting for the word. The barracks in Le Puy were being prepared for the arrival of German troops, which were expected within the next few days, and so now was a good time to strike. Again, Alfred had to be the deliverer of bad news.

Alfred admired their patriotism, but the truth was there was not a circuit in France that could have done anything to oppose the Axis occupation of the south. It was hard having to tell them all they were not about to go into action. They had been planning for this day, intending to cause as much disruption as possible, and while they might not have been able to do much, they could at least derail trains carrying troops and supplies. But all that would now have to wait. It was all very frustrating.

The Twins now faced a different kind of challenge. Having recruited their group and primed their thirst for blood, constantly telling them that their time would come, now that the Boche had finally arrived they were to do nothing. Somehow, they had to keep them all motivated or risk losing their willingness and support. It would not be easy.

They did eventually agree to let the groups carry out activities which were best described as a nuisance rather than anything big. At least it would keep them all onside. And there was, as far as they knew, still the plan to get the prisoners out of Castres. Henry had even found two gendarmes who were willing to desert their posts so that the prison raid could go ahead.

Leaving Henry and the two gendarmes waiting on the corner of Rue Garibaldi, Alfred went to Marie's flat. But as he walked into the ground-floor entrance hall to the flats, he instinctively sensed something was not quite right. Deciding to take the stairs rather than the lift, he made his way up to Marie's flat.

Standing outside her door, Alfred noticed that the coded sign that was normally visible to indicate it was safe to knock was not there. Its absence spelt danger and although there had been no other sign of any suspicious activity, nor any sign of a raid, he decided not to hang around. He went straight to the lodge where the concierge and her husband lived. They were old and trusted friends. They told him Marie had been forced to go into hiding. It was Alfred's worst fear. They had lost their link with London.

When later piecing together the events of the previous few days, things had clearly moved fast. First, the American Consul had informed Marie that the forthcoming Allied landings in North Africa – due to take place any day – would almost certainly see the Germans occupy the south of France. And with the Germans about to arrive in Lyon, Marie was advised to leave. The Gestapo already knew of a woman known to them as the 'Limping Lady' and she was on their most wanted list.

Marie had gone to meet up with her strongest ally in the city, known as Pépin, real name Doctor Jean Rousset, at his surgery in Place Antonin Poncet. After destroying papers and documents in his cellar, they discussed what should happen next. Marie did not want to leave Lyon until she had secured the release of the prisoners being held at Castres and tied up other loose ends, but Pépin disagreed, arguing that she would be of no use to anyone should she be arrested. And so, Marie had left Lyon and was now on her way to safety across the Pyrenees. Pépin, however, was not so lucky. He was arrested two days after the Germans moved into Lyon.

Knowing that Marie had gone, Alfred re-joined the others to tell them the news. There was no way the prison raid could go ahead and so the gendarmes were told to return to their unit as quickly as they could before they were missed. The Twins, meanwhile, were left to walk the streets of Lyon discussing what they should do next.

They stood for a while looking down on the railway line connecting the neighbourhood of Les Brottaux with the Gare de Lyon-Perrache. The sight of the train passing beneath them carrying German troops said it all. It was too much for Henry. Picking up a large stone he hurled it at one of the carriages, more in frustration than anything else. They did not hang around to find out what happened next.

As for the prisoners who the Twins were intending to help escape from Castres – they were already free. Unbeknown to the Twins at that time, the four had been amongst a group of prisoners released by sympathetic French prison officials just before the Germans arrived in the south.

***

A mist and drizzle had descended over Lyon, which summed up the mood in the city. The once busy streets were now almost empty. Bars and restaurants, usually packed with revellers until the early hours, were now frequented by small groups of people looking for comfort and reassurance as idle waiters stood by. Where there had once been an acceptance of the Nazi occupation in the north and the rules of the Vichy authorities in the south, there was now fear and apprehension.

The following day, the Twins could only stand and watch as more Germans moved into Lyon. They commandeered houses and offices and occupied the best hotels in the city. The Hôtel Terminus, which occupied a grand position opposite the Gare de Lyon-Perrache, became the headquarters of the *Sicherheitsdienst* (SD), the intelligence branch of the SS, and the Gestapo. Eighty SS officers, under the command of Rolf Müller, were amongst the first to arrive, fifty of whom remained in the city while the others were dispatched to outlying areas.

There were now five Resistance networks operating in and around Lyon, of which GREENHEART was one, but during the early days of occupying the south, the Gestapo had only limited information about circuit members and their activities. There was no shortage of people keen to help the new occupiers, but it took the Gestapo time to build up a cadre of long-term and trustworthy collaborators and informers, and so initially relatively few arrests were made.

That, of course, would change, but the fact the Germans had moved into the south simply played into the Twins' hands. They had, after all, joined the SOE and gone to France to seek revenge on the Nazis and not so much on the Vichy regime, although they had no time for them as well. And now there were plenty of Nazis about.

Later that afternoon, the Twins were strolling around the north-east part of the city when they spotted a couple of German radio detector vans parked nonchalantly on the road running down from the Canal de Jonage. Sensing an opportunity to provide their occupiers with an early reminder that life in Lyon was going to be anything but straightforward, the Twins decided it was time to act. They knew a place nearby where they could get their hands on some explosives and, having made a couple of charges with clamps, they waited until it was dark before making their move.

It was 10.30 p.m. by the time they arrived back at the spot where they had earlier seen the vans parked. Fortunately, they were still there. Stopping for only a matter of seconds to quickly attach the charges underneath the two vehicles, the Twins then moved on. The charges had been set to go off long after the Twins had fled the scene, and later that night the residents were woken by the sound of two explosions as the charges ripped the vans apart.

It was a small, yet defiant act and had taken place within hours of the first Germans arriving in the city. But the Lyonnais were soon finding out for themselves what those in the north had been suffering for the past two years. There had been rumours and tales of Nazi brutality before, but now they were reality. And that was not all – informers and collaborators were already busy denouncing their countrymen to the Germans. A good living could be made by selling a neighbour or someone who had previously been considered a friend, while those resisting the occupation – people like the Twins – had to tread more carefully than ever before. Informers and collaborators were lurking in every café and on every street corner.

What had previously been the unoccupied zone was now split between the Germans and Italians, with almost the entire area to the east of the Rhône being handed to the Italians. The Lyonnais did their best to carry on as before and went about their daily business as best as they could. However, while on the surface it might have appeared that little had changed since the Germans had moved into the city, the fact was the Gestapo were everywhere. Dressed in civilian suits, they skulked in darkened doorways or hovered around public places, their eyes and ears keenly attentive to any slip of the tongue from some unsuspecting Frenchman or woman.

★★★

With Marie gone and the Germans having moved into Lyon, things felt very different to how they had been before. It would take a while for everything to settle down in the city and so the Twins decided the best thing to do for now was to go to Le Puy.

Leaving Lyon behind, they first took the train to Saint-Étienne, where they decided to break their journey to go out into the hills to the west of the town to look for any suitable areas for the dropping of supplies. As was usually the case, they were armed and carrying a couple of hand grenades and a small amount of plastic explosive.

While resting on a ridge overlooking the main road, they could hear a car approaching in the distance. A small black Citroën appeared and came to a stop just a few hundred yards away. Four men in civilian clothing got out of the car and then disappeared into the woods on the far side of the road.

With pistols cocked, the Twins took cover to see what happened next. A few minutes later, the four men reappeared and got back into the car. At first, they guessed the Citroën's occupants had stopped for a comfort break. But then, having travelled only another 100 yards or so up the road the car stopped once more. And, again, the four men got out.

The car was now closer than it had been before. The Twins could clearly see the men deliberating over something, presumably a map. From the way they were dressed it was obvious that three of them were German, probably Gestapo, while the fourth was perhaps French. And, as before, the four men crossed the road and went into the woods.

Seeing the car had again been left unattended, the Twins had just one thing in mind and it was too good an opportunity to miss. They stuck some plastic explosive into their empty flask with a primer bound by a length of fuse and a ten-minute time pencil. Then, as quietly and stealthily as they could, they made their way towards the car, expecting its occupants to reappear at any moment.

Just as soon as Alfred had pressed the time pencil and screwed the cup on the flask, Henry stowed it under the near-side front seat of the car, and within seconds they were making their way back up the ridge. Once back under cover, they waited for the explosion to go off, hoping the occupants would reappear and set off again in the car before it did. Blowing up the car would be good but killing its occupants was even better.

Although they had set a ten-minute time pencil, it was a cold day and so it could easily take longer for the car to blow up. The minutes passed – five, then six. The men now appeared out of the woods and for a while they stood around chatting amongst themselves. Seven minutes had now passed, then eight and then nine. Finally, the four men got back in the car and it moved off.

Ten minutes had now passed. It could not be long before the car blew up, but then another minute went by, and another. Then it happened. Just as the car was about to disappear in the distance, the peace and quiet of the countryside was suddenly shattered by the sound of the explosion, followed immediately by the sight of the Citroën lifting off the ground. In one seemingly choreographed movement, the car swerved across the road and crashed into the trees.

There was no sign of any movement from the car, or any sound coming from it. The Twins could not have timed it better. In that one moment, everything they had trained for came to fruition. They could never fully avenge their family, but at least this went some way towards it. At last, they had got some revenge. And it felt sweet.

As the noise of the explosion died down, a motorcycle could be heard approaching in the distance. It was a German dispatch rider and when he saw the twisted wreck of the car smouldering in the trees, he stopped. He could see there was no sign of life. Not wishing to hang around alone at such a remote location, he quickly got back on his motorcycle and sped away.

It was a long walk on to Le Puy, but the Twins had a renewed spring in their step, and as they walked in silence through the night, they were both feeling rather pleased inside.

By the time they arrived in the town it was daylight. They went their separate ways as both men had people to see. However, after meeting up and chatting to various people, Alfred became concerned. He had found out that a member of their group who was storing arms and explosives in the cellar of his large house had been openly heard expressing his hatred of the Germans to several people, one of whom was a known collaborator with a German wife.

No matter how patriotic the man might have wished to sound, it was careless talk. Fearing the house might soon be raided and the arms seized, Alfred and another member of the group, a young man only just out of his teens, spent the night clearing the cellar and loading everything on to a lorry.

Alfred knew of another suitable hiding place, but it was on the other side of town and so they needed to pick the time carefully to transport their goods if they were to minimise the risk of being caught. They had no choice but to drive through the centre of town – there was no other way – but hopefully their lorry would look just like any other lorry on the road that was simply going about its daily business. Deciding it was best to make their move when the roads were at their busiest, they waited until the following morning to set off.

With the young man driving, Alfred sat on top of the tarpaulin concealing their load. As they approached the town centre, they could see that everything ahead of them was at a standstill. It was a spot check by the police. The street was too narrow for them to turn around and there was soon a queue of vehicles and horse-drawn wagons behind. With nowhere to go, they both needed to remain calm.

Alfred could see a member of the *Feldgendarmerie*, the German military police, making his way down the queue towards them, stopping to talk to each driver. Hopefully, the lorry would not be searched. But then Alfred watched in horror as carts and vehicles up ahead were being searched, and he knew it was most likely their lorry would be searched too. There was no way of hiding what they were carrying, and they had no excuse for doing so.

When he eventually reached their vehicle, the German cautiously looked up at Alfred and asked the driver what they were carrying. Thinking on his feet, Alfred spoke first before the young driver even had a chance to reply, jokingly saying they were carrying enough arms and explosives to blow half the town to hell and back. Grinning back, the German pointed out it was not the time for humour and suggested they quickly moved on before he turned them both in. It was one of those anxious moments in life when everything could have, and probably should have, gone wrong. They had been extremely lucky.

With the arms and explosives offloaded at the new hiding place, Alfred returned to Le Puy to join up with Henry, where they brought each other up to date with what they had each been up to during the past couple of days and discussed what they should do next.

★★★

They were missing Marie, there was no doubt about that. She had been the focal point in Lyon and their only way of keeping in touch with the other circuits in the region. And she had been their contact with London. The Twins knew that if GREENHEART was to survive they must somehow resume contact with London. They needed money and they needed weapons and decided it was best to get word to Fernande and for her to go off to Marseille to see if she could contact a wireless operator there.

Fernande soon returned. She had managed to contact a wireless operator in Marseille, but he was unable to recode any coded message sent by the Twins. This meant that any messages they wanted transmitting to London would have to be written in clear writing. This was not something the Twins were prepared to do – not only would it be too risky for Fernande to carry any messages that had been written in clear, but it would also give away all kinds of information to anyone who happened to see them.

Marius drove the Twins back to Lyon. They would have to see what they could do from there. Firstly, though, they needed to find somewhere in the city where it was safe to stay. Word was that a close friend of Marie, a woman called Germaine, had now carried on where Marie had left off.

When the Twins found Germaine Guérin at her flat on Rue Garibaldi, they were again somewhat surprised. She was another whose appearance at first deceived. An elegant and expensively dressed brunette in her late thirties, she wore an ample coat of rouge and lipstick and her flat was furnished with lavish and beautiful things. As the part-owner of a successful brothel in Lyon, she was not the type who needed to get caught up in this sort of business, but she seemed to know all the right people, whether they were in the high parts of society or from the darkest dives of Lyon. Above all, though, Germaine was fiercely patriotic and like Marie shared the same sense of excitement when flirting with danger.

Germaine had heard much about the Twins already and so she was pleased to be able to help. Amongst her many properties she had a flat on the mezzanine floor of a building on Rue Boileau that was not in use. They could stay there.

It was just what the Twins needed. The building had two separate exits and from the kitchen in the flat they could easily get out into the back yard. And should it ever become necessary, they would be able to exit the building, scale the wall and be out and away into a different street in a matter of seconds.

The first to call at Rue Boileau was Thermogéne, who brought the Twins up to date about some new members for GREENHEART. Through one of their group, an engine driver, they had managed to recruit a handful of railway workers into the circuit. This was good news. It was always useful to have railwaymen involved, whether they were engine drivers, ticket inspectors or station masters.

Thermogéne had also come to ask for half a dozen limpet mines. The railwaymen, he said, were getting fed up at the sight of more and more fuel tankers being moved around the country for the benefit of the Germans, and they wanted to do something about it.

Henry was hesitant. He had yet to meet these new circuit members and trusted no one. Besides, limpet mines were difficult to get hold of and these railwaymen probably had no idea how to handle them. They could easily muck the whole thing up. Alfred, however, was more understanding. The last thing he wanted was to dampen Thermogéne's enthusiasm. Furthermore, he could understand the railwaymen's frustrations and annoyance at having to transport precious fuel around to boost the German war effort, while the French were being rationed and had to make do with bicycles or get around on foot.

In the end, Alfred won the argument, much to the delight of Thermogéne. There was more news as well.

An elderly relative of one of their group had discovered a hoard of weapons and ammunition on his land. He had found it all lying in thick bracken. It had probably been dumped there some time ago and it now looked as if it had all been abandoned.

Such a find was rare, and the arms could not be left for someone else to discover, particularly the Germans. The problem was, though, the cache was 250 miles away near Theillay, which meant crossing the River Cher, a main tributary of the Loire. It would not be easy, particularly as the area was known to be crawling with Germans and there would be plenty of checkpoints and searches when it came time to cross the river.

Despite the obvious risks, the Twins felt it was an opportunity not to be missed, although another suitable hiding place needed to be found. However, to transport the arms and explosives over such a long distance by road would be too risky. A lorry would almost certainly be stopped and searched at some point, and so they decided their best chance was to carry whatever they could recover between them.

By lunchtime the following day, the Twins were in Châteauroux. The journey had been easy enough. The trains were crowded as usual, with only a few checks along the way, and their papers and cover stories had been perfectly adequate for such a trip. However, they knew the rest of their journey would not be quite so easy. The normal route when travelling north-eastwards from Châteauroux towards Theillay passed through the town of Vierzon. However, Vierzon was known to be a German stronghold and trying to cross the Cher there was too much of an unnecessary risk. Their best chance was to the west of the town, but there were only three known cross-ing points within 15 miles of Vierzon – near the villages of Thénioux, Châtres and Mennetou – and their bridges would almost certainly have checkpoints.

Instead, the Twins decided they would cross the river at a more remote point, somewhere between Thénioux and Vierzon, in an area of farming and forestry where the course of the river ran furthest from the nearest road. Leaving Châteauroux on foot, they stopped only to hide a bag containing fresh clothes and shaving equipment. It was a precaution they always took. They knew they needed to make their way home at some point, but it could easily be a couple of days or more before they returned and looking dirty, wet and scruffy would only draw unnecessary attention.

The hours of daylight were short at that time of year and it was dark by the time they reached the river. It was never going to be easy finding somewhere to cross at night. Luckily, they came across a small fisherman's punt con-cealed on the riverbank. Neither were used to handling such a craft, but they somehow managed to reach the far bank. Then, having successfully made their way along the northern bank, albeit with some difficulty in the dark, they managed to cross the Canal de Berry using an unguarded rickety old levy-bridge.

It was dawn by the time they reached the field where the arms had been dumped. After a little searching they found what they were looking for. Rummaging through the stack, they discovered a dozen carbines, which had quite obviously been there for some time as they had already started to rust. They were too cumbersome to carry over such a long distance so they decided to leave them behind for a local resistance group to pick up. Besides, they had found more appealing items – two bags containing grenades and other explosives. These were always useful and much easier to carry.

Deciding it was too risky to make their way back by day, the Twins took cover in the woods to the south of Theillay. Rather than just sitting around waiting for it to get dark, they decided to look around to see if they could find any targets of opportunity. They soon discovered that they were laying up alongside the main railway line that runs northwards towards Orléans and on to Paris. It was one of the main communication links between the north and south of France.

The Twins were both thinking the same thing – here they were alongside a main rail route with two bags containing grenades and explosives. It was another of those opportunities that was too good to miss. All they had to do was to wait for a German troop train to come along.

However, they knew that trying to derail a train with what they were carrying was out of the question. Nonetheless, they might just be able to do something. They needed to be careful. The Germans knew how keen resistance groups were to target the railways and patrols were always on the lookout, particularly along the main routes, although the reality was that with thousands of miles of railway track in France it was all but impossible to guard against every threat.

From their hidden vantage point looking down on the track the Twins watched train after train go by. But none, so far, had been what they were looking for. Patiently, they waited for the right train to come along and every time one was heard approaching, they were ready with a grenade in each hand, only to then decide that something better would surely come along.

Another train was heard in the distance. This one was coming from the north but whether it was carrying German troops would remain to be seen. As the train got closer, the Twins could see it was carrying anti-aircraft guns and their crews. They looked at each other in excitement. Then, as the train passed level with their position, they both stood up and lobbed the grenades into the trucks before the crews even had a chance to react. The look of terror on the faces of the Germans, who suddenly realised what was happening, was priceless and within seconds the muffled sound of four explosions could be heard above the noise of the train as it passed by, followed by the yells and screams confirming the grenades had found their mark.

The train was more than 100 yards away by the time it came to a halt, by which time the Twins had disappeared into the distance, sheltered by the dense woodland. Still carrying the bags containing the rest of the explosives, they made sure they were a few miles away before deciding to stop and take a rest.

Although they were safe enough for now, they still had to be extremely careful. There was still a couple of hours of daylight to get through before they felt it would be safe to use the roads. Finding somewhere under cover, they waited for darkness to fall. It had been another good day.

As dusk fell, they moved on towards the river, but having reached the edge of a field they suddenly had to stop and lay nervously in silence. They had come across a German patrol taking a rest. Only a hedge separated them from being seen. Eventually, after a tense half an hour or so, the patrol moved on, leaving the Twins to hop over the hedge, cross the road and press on across the fields towards the river.

It was now dark, making navigation extremely difficult. The road they had just crossed was probably the one running north-westwards to Thénioux, but they knew they had yet to reach the river, which in this area ran south-eastwards towards Vierzon, and they could hear trains in the distance. The problem was, they had not expected to come across another railway line at that time. They had certainly not come across one on their way out.

The word 'lost' would, perhaps, be unfair and reflect poorly on their cross-country navigation skills, but they were certainly unsure of where they were. Nonetheless, Henry was carrying explosives and here was another railway line. And so, as far as he was concerned, it was another opportunity to put the explosives to good work.

Alfred tried to persuade his brother otherwise, but Henry was determined to try and cut the rail line. Even better, he could see that the track crossed a sunken road; a perfect place to cause the most damage. Besides, using the explosives now meant they did not have to risk carrying them any further. They still had to cross the river and then catch a train south. And even if they did manage to get the explosives all the way back to Lyon or Le Puy without being caught, they needed to find somewhere to hide them before later carrying out a similar job. They might just as well do it now.

This time it was Henry who got his way. They quickly prepared a charge and climbed on to the track to look for a suitable place. Having found what they were looking for, a fishplate connecting the adjacent rails, they secured the charge and covered it with earth.

On this occasion, they did not get the chance to witness the result of their work. There was no sound of a train coming and they needed to cross the river as soon as they could. They assumed there was still some way to go to where they had previously crossed, but even if they could find the same place in the dark, they knew there would be little or no chance of ever finding the fisherman's punt they had left hidden on the northern bank.

There was no time to waste and so they gave up on the idea of trying to find the punt. Faced with little alternative, they scrambled around in the dark looking for a suitable place to cross the river. And having found somewhere that looked reasonable enough, in they went, wading out into the darkness until the water became so deep that they had to swim. The water was bitterly cold and the current quite strong, but they reached the other side without any difficulty and headed off towards Châteauroux.

In the cold night air, there was no chance of their clothes drying out, but at least they were back on the southern side of the river, which meant there was less likelihood of coming across an enemy patrol. By staying on the road, they were able to make better time and soon worked out where they were, and it was something of a relief when they found their bags of dry clothes.

Having shaved and smartened up, they made their way through Châteauroux to the railway station to continue their journey south. There was just one check of their identity papers, after which they boarded the train and were soon on their way.

The Twins had already split up, as they usually did when using the train, although they still tried to make sure they were travelling in the same carriage so that they could keep a distant eye on each other. Besides, Henry was going to Lyon while Alfred had business in Le Puy.

However, on this occasion the train was overcrowded and so they were sat in separate carriages, which turned out to be just as well. As the train chugged slowly towards Limoges, Henry had an uneasy feeling he was being observed by the man sitting opposite him. Henry tried to bury his head in a newspaper, but the man insisted on making conversation, asking him what he was doing there and saying how pleased he was to see him again. Henry did his best to look puzzled. He was travelling under one of his many false identities, on this occasion he was carrying the papers of a certain Jean Boileau, a carpenter from Lyon, and so he tried to explain to the man that he had made a mistake. But the man insisted there was no mistake; he would recognise one of the Boorn Brothers anywhere.

It was one of the most uncomfortable moments in Henry's life, but he remained calm. Keeping his voice at a low enough level to avoid creating a scene, he kept insisting that he was Jean Boileau and not one of the Boorn Brothers as the man had claimed. In the end, Henry's calmness and perseverance won the day, the man eventually accepting that his appearance was strikingly similar. But things could have turned out so differently had Alfred have been sitting anywhere near Henry at the time. Then it would have been all but impossible to have convinced the man otherwise.

It was only after the man had later left the train that Henry could breathe a sigh of relief. The man had been right, of course, and Henry had instantly recognised him. He had been a theatrical agent before the war and had handled many of their engagements!

Alfred, meanwhile, arrived in Le Puy to meet up with Marius but his journey back to Lyon was delayed and took several hours, rather ironically the result of some railway saboteurs – probably their own men. Alfred had experienced for himself what it was like to be on the receiving end of disruption on the railway, but any thoughts of being annoyed at having to miss his meeting with Henry quickly disappeared. He could not help but have a smile on his face.

Henry (left) and Alfred as the Boorn Brothers in 1938. Highly successful cabaret artists, they topped the bill at music halls across Europe and South America before the war.

Henry with his father, Ernest, a former racing jockey known by the family as 'Patter' Newton.

A poignant picture of Alfred's three sons on the motorcycle commandeered by the Newton family. Gigi is seen riding the bike while Jimmy is behind him and little Coco is sat in the sidecar with one of the family's dogs.

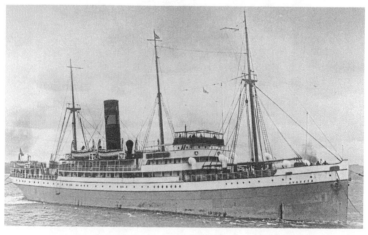

Built in 1923 for the Yeoward Line, the steam passenger-cargo ship SS *Avoceta* was requisitioned during the Second World War to carry passengers and supplies between Liverpool and Gibraltar. It was her sinking in the North Atlantic by a German U-boat on 25 September 1941 and the tragic loss of seven members of their family that left Alfred and Henry Newton with a burning desire for revenge. (John Clarkson via Philip James)

Kapitänleutnant Rolf Mützelburg, commander of *U-203*. He would later state he had misidentified the *Avoceta* to be a 12,000-ton petrol tanker; a different shape altogether and nearly four times the size of the steam passenger ship that he had, in fact, sent to the bottom. (UBA)

Henry (kneeling on left) and Alfred (standing far left) with other British escapees from France at the Miranda de Ebro concentration camp in Spain in late 1941.

It was on this H-Class destroyer, HMS *Hesperus*, that the Newton brothers sailed from Gibraltar bound for Liverpool in January 1942, by which time they had already been told of the loss of their family. (Via Ray Woodmore)

The Twins arrived at Wanborough Manor, Surrey, on 11 February 1942 to begin preliminary training with Party 27M. (Courtesy of the Puttenham & Wanborough History Society, via Patrick Yarnold)

Parachute training took place at Ringway, Manchester. SOE agents were required to complete three jumps to qualify for their wings: one from a tethered balloon at 700ft and a second jump from the balloon at night. The third jump was from an aircraft, through a hole in the fuselage floor of a converted Whitley bomber. (Via the Dallow family)

Lieutenant Henry Newton.
(TNA HS 9/1097/1)

Lieutenant Alfred Newton.
(TNA HS 9/1096/8)

Peter Churchill, an intelligence officer, joined SOE's F Section in 1941. The Twins were to carry out a daring raid with him in May 1942 against a radio transmitter at Sainte-Assise that was being used to transmit vital messages to German U-boats in the Atlantic. The mission was cancelled after it had become compromised, just as they were about to board their aircraft. (TNA HS 9/315)

The Brickendonbury Estate in Hertfordshire was requisitioned by the government during the Second World War and used by the SOE. Designated Station 17, it was one of the most secret locations in the country and it was here the Twins came in 1942 to be trained as saboteurs. (With permission of Tun Abdul Razak Research Centre, Brickendonbury, Hertford, SG13 8NL, UK)

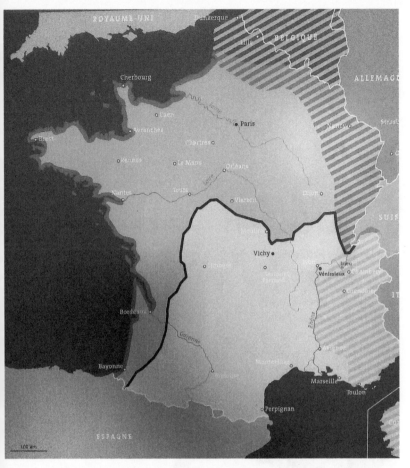

Following its armistice with Germany, France was left with an unoccupied zone in the south of the country and inland from the Atlantic coast, administered by the French from the town of Vichy, while the Germans occupied and governed the northern zone from Paris. The demarcation line separated the two zones.

A fashion artist before the war, young Brian Stonehouse became a wireless operator with the SOE. Code-named Célestin, he parachuted into France with the Twins on the night of 30 June 1942. (TNA, HS 9/1419/8)

Philippe de Vomécourt, known as Gauthier, was one of three French brothers working with the SOE. The Twins had been sent to France to work for him, but they soon fell out and went their separate ways to form their own circuit. (The National Archives)

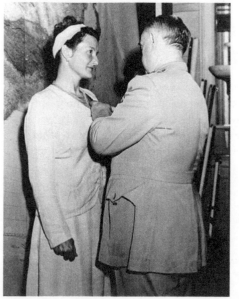

Virginia Hall, code-named Marie, an American with a prosthetic leg who was later to become known as 'Marie of Lyon', was the focal point for all SOE activity in east-central France. She was known to the Gestapo as 'the limping lady' and became the only civilian woman in the Second World War to be awarded the American Distinguished Service Cross.

The Place Ollier in Lyon, on the eastern bank of the River Rhône. Marie lived in Flat 3, and it was here the Twins first met her in July 1942.

Amongst the members of the Twins' GREENHEART circuit were railway workers who knew the rail network better than anyone else. They soon became experts in sabotage and took every opportunity to hamper the network in France.

The collaborationist Milice Française was set up by the Vichy French to assist the Germans in their campaign against the Resistance and the SOE. Made up of local French Nazi sympathisers, the Milice quickly became the most feared group around, perhaps more so than the Gestapo.

When the Germans moved into the previously unoccupied south of France in November 1942, cities such as Lyon became particularly dangerous places for agents to operate.

One of Alfred's fake identity cards, dated 31 December 1942, showing his name as Alfred Normand.

It was here in Lyon, on the corner of Rue Claude Veyron and Rue du Docteur Crestin, that the Twins were captured on 4 April 1943 during a Gestapo raid on a flat occupied by Alphonse Besson (code-named Thermogéne) and his wife, Marie-Fortunée (Bohémienne). The white building next to the flats is part of what was then the Desautel factory, where Besson was the foreman.

After the Germans moved into Lyon in November 1942 the Gestapo took over the Hôtel Terminus as its headquarters. It was here the Twins were first taken after their arrests and where they suffered numerous interrogations at the hands of the Gestapo. (Mercure Lyon Centre Château Perrache Hotel)

Klaus Barbie has since become known as the 'Butcher of Lyon', having personally tortured countless French prisoners and members of the SOE, including the Twins. (Klarsfeld)

Now a national memorial, the Montluc military prison in Lyon was used during the Second World War to hold perpetrators opposing the Nazi occupation and the Vichy regime, including SOE agents and members of the French Resistance. By the time the Twins arrived here in April 1943, the prison had already gained an awful reputation as a torture and killing place for the Gestapo. Nearly 1,000 were executed within its walls.

Conditions at Montluc were harsh. Some 15,000 were held here during the Second World War, with the small dark cells containing only a filthy camp bed and a bucket. As the prison reached bursting point, up to seven prisoners were held in each cell at a time. (With the kind permission of the Mémorial National Prison de Montluc, Lyon)

No. 84 Avenue Foch. This rather unassuming building is now private flats, but during the Second World War it was the SD's headquarters in Paris, and it was here that captured SOE agents, including the Twins in 1943, were taken for further interrogation.

In January 1944, the Twins arrived here at the Royallieu-Compiègne internment and deportation camp. Around 48,000 passed through the camp during the Nazi occupation of France before being deported elsewhere. Part of the camp has been preserved and can be found on the Avenue des Martyrs de la Liberté in Compiègne. (With the kind permission of the Mémorial de l'internement et de la déportation Camp de Royallieu, Compiègne)

Restored cattle trucks and a memorial stand at the railway station in Compiègne as a permanent reminder of the mass deportations that took place from here. It was in trucks like these that the Twins were deported to Germany, with as many as 150 prisoners packed into each truck.

It was just outside the town, on the edge of the forest of Compiègne, that prisoners were loaded onto the cattle trucks for deportation. On 27 January 1944, the Twins were amongst 1,584 prisoners deported from here to Buchenwald, a journey lasting three awful days. The single-rail track heading eastwards is still in place and runs left–right in front of the line of trees, with the memorial marking the last deportation to Buchenwald on 17 August 1944.

The gate building was their first sight of the concentration camp at Buchenwald. The clock above the main watchtower is frozen at 3.15 p.m. to mark the time the camp was liberated by the Americans on 11 April 1945. The site is now preserved as a permanent exhibition and museum. (With the kind permission of the Buchenwald and Mittelbau-Dora Memorials Foundation)

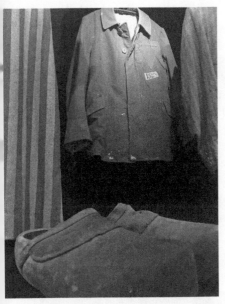

The green clothing and wooden clogs, as worn by the Twins at Buchenwald. The triangle shown on this example has no letter, denoting it was worn by a German prisoner, whereas the Twins wore a red triangle with the letter 'E' for *Engländer*. On the left is the more familiar blue-and-white striped clothing worn at concentration camps, but by the time the Twins arrived at Buchenwald in January 1944, supplies of this style had long been exhausted. (Rebecca Jacobs, with the kind permission of the Buchenwald and Mittelbau-Dora Memorials Foundation)

Looking east across the main square, the *Appellplatz*, towards the crematorium and its infamous chimney. The main gate building on the right stands opposite the main square, while the *Effektenkammer* can be seen in the distance on the left. (With the kind permission of the Buchenwald and Mittelbau-Dora Memorials Foundation)

Maurice Pertschuk had been with the Twins throughout their ordeal at Buchenwald, but the gallant 23-year-old went to his death on 29 March 1945, just days before the camp was liberated. (Buchenwald and Mittelbau-Dora Memorials Foundation)

It was in the basement of the crematorium that Maurice Pertschuk's short life came to an end, hanged from a hook. At least twenty other agents and members of the Resistance (probably many more) are known to have been executed in this way. (With the kind permission of the Buchenwald and Mittelbau-Dora Memorials Foundation)

The plaque inside the crematorium in memory of the Allied officers murdered at Buchenwald between September 1944 and March 1945. The list of names includes Lieutenant Maurice Pertschuk. Most of the others went to their deaths sometime between 9 and 11 September 1944. (With the kind permission of the Buchenwald and Mittelbau-Dora Memorials Foundation)

The Twins (Henry on left) with Maurice Southgate on their return from Buchenwald at the end of the war.

13th September 1945

Flt/O. ATKINS

Dear

I am very pleased indeed to forward
you the enclosed notifications that you have been
awarded the M.B.E. (Mil.) for your good work in
FRANCE.

We are all delighted, and send you both
heartiest congratulations. I have told Colonel
BUCKMASTER who is particularly pleased, and who I
believe will be writing to you.

I have tried to leave a message for you
at Paddington 8044, but I think they must all have
died there. There is never any reply.

With kind regards,

Lts. A. and H. NEWTON.
4 Spring Street,
Paddington, W.2.

A file copy of the letter from Vera Atkins to the Twins, dated 13 September 1945, informing them of their award of the MBE. (TNA HS 9/1097/1)

Alfred's medals (from left, MBE, 1939–45 Star, War Medal 1939–45) and the inspiration behind this book. (Rachel Jacobs)

11

A CLOSE-RUN THING

The Twins' flat on Rue Boileau had become affectionately known to their friends as 'Fort Boileau' or simply 'the Fort'. When Alfred finally arrived back in Lyon, he noticed that the sign in the window, which was inconspicuous to anyone else, was in place to confirm that Henry was in and it was safe to enter.

There was much to talk about. Germaine had managed to get in touch with a wireless operator working for another circuit and had heard about a large amount of cash left behind by Marie before she had fled Lyon. This meant the Twins would have some funds to keep GREENHEART going and there was hope they might be able to resume contact with London in the near future.

Henry also told Alfred that he had been given a list of registration numbers of cars requisitioned by the Gestapo and addresses of newly recruited collaborators. Thermogéne had already made up bundles of small leaflets with the names of the collaborators on, and these could easily be picked up or passed around so that the decent French people would know who to avoid. Morale had also picked up following the sound of RAF bombers over Lyon. They were on their way to bomb the Italian city of Turin. Seven times in the past three weeks aircraft had been heard overhead, which even had the German anti-aircraft batteries around Lyon opening up.

There was clearly much going on, but not everything was going their way. News had filtered through of several arrests being made in Lyon and word was out that the Gestapo had now received orders from the German High Command to deal ruthlessly with anyone caught carrying out acts of sabotage on the railway. That evening they went to visit Germaine. With Marie gone, Germaine's time was always in demand, but the Twins wanted to find out more about the money left behind by Marie and to talk about how they could secure the use of a wireless operator. There were other matters to discuss as well, now the Germans had settled in Lyon.

When the Twins arrived at Germaine's flat, they found she was not alone. She had someone else there with her who she thought they might be able to help, a priest known as 'the Bishop'.

Having introduced the Bishop to the Twins, Germaine left the room so the three could talk. The Twins eyed up the Bishop with suspicion. They trusted no one. They could see he was young, of medium height and slender in build, with a receding hairline and bright blue eyes, and he was wearing an ordinary beret rather than a traditional clerical hat. Speaking in perfect French, albeit with a slight accent, which he put down to having grown up in Alsace near the German border, he introduced himself as Abbé Ackuin.

The Bishop explained that he had first met Marie at Pépin's surgery the previous summer, after he had travelled to Lyon from the north of France where his team were involved in some vital work photographing sections of the Atlantic Wall. Now he was ready to hand over the spools of film and claim the money Marie had promised him for the work. But as she had gone, he had heard about Germaine and he had now turned to her for help. He even had with him a letter, written in English and signed by someone in London, claiming it had been given to him by a British agent in France in order to verify who he was and instructing that he should be paid accordingly for any work carried out.

The Twins each looked at the letter in turn. Believing it could be a trap, it was Henry who spoke first, claiming he did not understand the content of the letter because it was written in English. He then told the Bishop they were not involved in any subversive activity at all, nor were they connected in any way to anyone who was, and so they could be of no help to him.

The Bishop was unconvinced. He even tried talking to the Twins in English, but neither fell for that. Having reverted to French, the Bishop then offered to work for them or to at least hand over the films, provided they gave him some money. But if they were not prepared to do that, then he would be grateful if they could put him in touch with Nicolas or, failing that, any other British agent working in Lyon.

The Twins were now even more suspicious of the Bishop than they had been at the start. Something did not seem right. He had also suddenly become less confident and appeared more nervous. They were convinced he did not know for certain who they were, or what they were up to – the Bishop was clearly guessing, bluffing even.

When Germaine came back into the room she was accompanied by a handful of men, all known resisters. She could not have picked a worse time, given they had an unknown person in the flat. Amongst them was one of her many devoted boyfriends, a wealthy man called Dubois, who immediately recognised the Twins and set about greeting them in the normal French way, and a man known as Louis (real name Marcel Leccia), who was a police inspector supposedly working for the Vichy counter-espionage service but behind the scenes was a fervent resister and saboteur. He did not help the situation when he greeted Alfred and Henry as the famous Twins.

Minutes later, another group of resisters arrived. Having so many people in the same flat, and with someone who was a stranger to them all, was careless at best, if not dangerous. Alfred and Henry had said nothing to confirm they were the Twins, but the Bishop had clearly heard every word. If he was not who he said, then he would clearly be able to identify them all. Something had to be done.

Before they could do anything about it, the Bishop had already edged his way towards the door and was off, hurriedly making his way down the flight of stairs. The Twins bolted after him, but they were already a few seconds behind. By the time they reached the ground floor he had disappeared into the crowd and the darkness of the night. To try and find him would be all but impossible. They made their way back up to the flat, but by the time they got there it was empty. Sensing trouble, the others had all quickly made their escape.

The Bishop had disappeared, but to where was anyone's guess. And what would happen next? Germaine clearly needed to go into hiding somewhere else. As for the others, they had all been seen, although no true identities or addresses had been revealed. Everyone who had been at the flat that evening must now take extra care.

Lyon is a very large city, sometimes described as the Birmingham of France, and so it was possible to keep out of the way until things had quietened down. But it was another timely reminder that strangers could not be trusted. The Twins had already seen GREENHEART grow to nearly 200 members, but it was now time to take a breath. They could not allow it to get any bigger for fear of infiltration, and once a circuit had been infiltrated it would inevitably lead to its downfall, and ultimately to the capture and death of many good people.

For now, the incident at Germaine's flat had put on hold the idea of getting more money or securing the use of a wireless operator. It meant the Twins could not do all the things they wanted to do. Almost every day Thermogéne or Marius came to them with an idea, only to leave disappointed.

Their circuit members were keen, despite the risks, and the Twins did not want to have to reject every idea being put forward. Their stock of explosives was getting low, but they were keen to let their group do something and so they decided to approve the latest idea, which was to blow up half a dozen water pumps at a marshalling yard to cause further disruption to the railway. At first, the Twins could not see the importance of water pumps, but it was quickly explained to them that water was required to make steam and without steam the engines could not go anywhere.

The problem was, the marshalling yard was further north and it was never easy transporting a large quantity of explosives on the railway, but Thermogéne had an answer for that as well. At the Desautel factory where he worked, they made industrial fire extinguishers, some of which were quite large, and instead of filling them with foam they could be filled with explosives. These could then be moved around relatively easily as extinguishers were being transported around France on a regular basis. They would not be considered overly suspicious and a large extinguisher full of explosive would make quite an explosion.

***

While their men set about the task, Alfred went to see Germaine to try again to talk about money and securing the use of a wireless operator, and Henry took the opportunity to return to Cendrieux to catch up with old friends. Henry was pleased to meet up again with Flavie, the young French girl who had courageously acted as courier for the Nuisance Committee. The Nuisance Committee was no more, she explained, but individually they were all well. After the Twins had left, they had all joined other groups, although Flavie did say that just one word from the Twins would bring them all back together again.

That was not going to happen, not yet at least, but Henry was pleased to hear the old members of the Nuisance Committee were keeping up the fight, albeit with different groups. When he told Flavie about the loss of the Newton family she was deeply shocked, as was he when she told him that her father, André Perdioux, had been deported to

Germany. And with Perdioux gone, the rest of the family had been unable to keep up the rent on their home and the owner had the family moved out. It was such a shame. So much had happened to them all since those happy days just eighteen months ago.

Alfred, meanwhile, had met up with Germaine as planned, but she told him that word about the money left by Marie had quickly spread. Everyone wanted to get their hands on it. And as far as access to a wireless operator was concerned, again everyone wanted the same thing. But Germaine knew the Twins were doing good work and rather than leave Alfred feeling disappointed having seemingly got nowhere, she said she would arrange for someone to go to his flat the following day to try and help.

Sure enough, the following day, a visitor arrived at Fort Boileau. It was Joseph Marchand, a 51-year-old Lyonnais businessman who was a chief associate of Nicolas. Marchand explained that Nicolas was busy rebuilding SPRUCE after most of the circuit's weapons had been ditched in the river when the Germans entered Lyon and many of the group's half-hearted resisters had decided to quit. He went on to add that Nicolas now intended to work closer with the other agents in and around Lyon as the best way to pool resources and expertise.

Other than that, very little else was discussed with Marchand during that first meeting. It had been more about meeting up and preparing the way, ahead of a meeting between Nicolas and the Twins, which would hopefully take place sometime soon.

★★★

While the defiant talk continued and plans were being made to hit back at the occupiers, the reality was, the German occupation of the south had brought a temporary lull in subversive activities. Christmas 1942 came but the mood on the streets of Lyon was not as it had been in previous years. The cold was intense, there were too many Germans around and far too many rules and curfews for people to think about celebrating the time of year. High-end shops suffered as stock had been confiscated, the official reason given because the owner was a known terrorist, as luxury items such as handbags, perfumes and jewellery ended up as gifts for mistresses of the Gestapo.

Many good agents had arrived in Lyon during the year, but with limited resources they had only been able to achieve so much. Their efforts needed to be corralled and it was Nicolas more than anyone who was trying to do that, but so far without much success. London reacted by sending into France 35-year-old Captain John Hamilton, a ship owner and former Paris businessman, who was parachuted into the Rhône valley on 29 December to assess the situation in Lyon and report back.

Hamilton managed to get to Lyon and was staying at Marchand's flat when it was raided by the Gestapo. The Germans had not particularly been looking for him, but the poor and unfortunate Hamilton was taken away. He had been in France just two days and was later executed at the Gross Rosen concentration camp.

Hamilton's story was yet another sad tale of a mission being over before it had even got started. And so, for now, the various circuits in the south were left to carry on doing much their own thing, as they had been doing so far. But the New Year brought renewed Gestapo activity.

There were constant roadblocks and snap searches on the street. Even women and children were being stopped and searched, particularly the women, as the Germans well knew that many women were acting as couriers for the Resistance. Things had also taken a turn for the worse with the creation of a new French militia, the Milice Française, born from Joseph Darnand's SOL to combat the French Resistance and SOE.

The Milice quickly became the most feared group around, perhaps more so than the Gestapo, because its members were French who understood local dialects and had extensive knowledge of the towns and countryside. Because they were indistinguishable from local people, they were able to manipulate informants and permeate circuits with a confidence that was impossible to the Gestapo, and they had the power to spread their corrupting influence amongst the discontented and the timid. And by the time suspicions were aroused, it was often too late, with many falling into the trap. It was the Vichy regime's most extreme manifestation of fascism, with torture being the preferred method of extracting information from those captured and interrogated.

With so many arrests now being made, it was becoming too much of a risk for the Twins to stay at Fort Boileau. So many people knew it was their home, there were too many callers and it would not be long before the flat was put under surveillance, if it had not been already.

There was more bad news as well. A new Gestapo chief had arrived in Lyon and was now driving all German counter-sabotage activity. This was the notorious Klaus Barbie, later to become known as the 'Butcher of Lyon' for personally torturing countless French prisoners and members of the SOE.

At the time he arrived in Lyon, Barbie was still only 29 years old. He had earlier been assigned to Amsterdam after the Germans had occupied the Netherlands, but in 1942 was transferred to France where he was based in Dijon in the occupied zone. When the Germans crossed the demarcation line to occupy the south of France, it was to Barbie the Nazis turned to sort out the hornet's nest of Lyon. He established his headquarters at the Hôtel Terminus, where all sorts of atrocities were carried out, and quickly built up a trusted personal army, reportedly more than 100 strong and made up mostly of French men and women. They were a nasty mix of Nazis and political fanatics, as well as thugs. Barbie even had special kiosks set up across Lyon where people could go to denounce their fellow countrymen.

It was now early January 1943 and this new wave of German and Vichy counter-sabotage activity meant the Twins would have to find somewhere else to stay. But before they did, they had a more pressing matter to deal with. Fernande had arrived with some news. The Gestapo were on to the man they knew only as Nicolas, and word was that a trap was being laid that night at a restaurant on Rue Puits Gaillot, one of the places where Nicolas was known to eat.

As it was already early evening, there was no time to lose. Alfred decided to go straight to the restaurant rather than waste time trying to find Nicolas anywhere else. Within fifteen minutes he had taken up a position across the road from where he could safely observe the front of the restaurant without being seen himself. He was in good time. Nicolas would not have arrived yet.

It was not long before a black Citroën car pulled up across the road. Then a second car arrived and a couple of men wearing civilian clothing got out, presumably Gestapo. Alfred waited. And waited. He waited until Nicolas's normal time of arrival had passed and started to wonder if he had arrived too late. Perhaps Nicolas was already inside the restaurant having arrived earlier than he would normally have done.

Knowing he could not just stand there and watch, Alfred decided to take a chance. He needed to go into the restaurant and check the first floor where Nicolas always sat to see if anything was going on. With his hand delicately poised inside his pocket, Alfred slipped the safety catch on his pistol and crossed the road, brushing past a group standing outside the entrance to the restaurant. He quickly made his way up the stairs and through the dining room, but Nicolas was nowhere to be seen. Alfred again checked his watch. It was now getting late. Nicolas was not coming now. Someone must have already warned him off.

Leaving the restaurant by the rear door, Alfred made his way through the darkness back to the Fort Boileau, much to Henry's relief. Germaine was also there. She had brought food and newspapers for the Twins, but there was more worrying news. A shop owned by a friend had been raided and one of her couriers was missing.

All kind of things were now flashing through their minds. Was the trap for Nicolas and the courier's disappearance a coincidence, or had someone been caught and spilled the beans? There had been other arrests, too, one being a wireless operator working for Nicolas called Grégoire (real name Pierre Le Chêne), who was one of three brothers working for the SOE. It turned out that Grégoire had been caught at his wireless set and this had triggered more arrests and consequences elsewhere, one being his older brother,

Henri, having to wind up his own circuit, PLANE, in the railway centre of Clermont-Ferrand to make his escape over the Pyrenees while Henri's wife, Marie-Thérèse, had fled to a safe house elsewhere.

Sensing trouble, the Twins knew they had to get out of Lyon – and very soon. They were still discussing their options with Germaine that same evening when heavy footsteps were heard on the staircase outside. They all held their breaths. The footsteps were then heard going up the flight of stairs to the first floor and seemed to stop outside the flat above. A voice then started shouting. Henry looked through the letterbox of the front door. What he could see horrified him. The hallway was full of Germans and police. There was more shouting upstairs before someone realised that they had gone to the wrong flat and they were on the wrong floor. The heavy footsteps could then be heard making their way back down the stairs to the ground floor.

Everything seemed to happen in a flash. Alfred grabbed Germaine's hand, dragging her into the kitchen. Henry, meanwhile, already had the window open and was the first out, dropping quietly on to a sloping roof and then down into the back yard below. Alfred went to lift Germaine so that he could lower her out of the window to the waiting Henry, but she wriggled free, telling the Twins to get away. She was a French woman, she said, and this was her home. She was going nowhere. She would take care of the Germans while they made their escape. And as Germaine started to take off her dress there was loud knocking at the door.

The brave Germaine was staying behind to give the Twins a chance to get away. It was hard to leave her, but they knew they had to go. Besides, Germaine was a strong and determined woman and so to try and persuade her otherwise would just be wasting valuable time. There were walls and fences to climb and there was no time to hang around.

The last Alfred saw of the fearless Germaine was her calmly going to the door in just her underwear, the warm smile still on her face. And with that, the Twins were off into the night.

12

THE NET CLOSES

The escape from Fort Boileau had been a close-run thing. By the time Alfred got out of the window, Henry had already disappeared. Each brother knew there were times when they simply had to do their own thing, particularly when the Gestapo were knocking at the door.

Alfred headed straight for Thermogéne's flat on Rue du Docteur Crestin, but his nerves were on edge. He was convinced someone was following him and when a hand slapped him firmly on the shoulder, he was convinced his luck was up. It was only when he heard Henry's voice behind him that he breathed a sigh of relief.

It was late by the time the Twins arrived at the flat. Bohémienne made them all coffee as they discussed the night's events. The more they talked about what had happened, the more they were all convinced that someone must have been caught, and that same person must have been forced to talk. The only other explanation was there was an informant. Either way, it made no difference. They all knew what was in store for them should they be caught by the Gestapo and, whichever way they looked at the situation, they knew the net was closing on the Twins.

The following day they were still worried about what had happened at the Fort. They had left the flat in such a hurry that there had been no time to take with them a bunch of important papers that had been hidden there and what little money they had. Although the papers did not contain the names of any individuals, they did include valuable information. Their intelligence network had provided them with all sorts of details ranging from information about factory production to details about vehicles commandeered by the Gestapo, enemy troop dispositions and known informants, to details about prisons and who was being held where. There was also information about the rail network. If the papers were found their content could potentially lead the Gestapo to those who had provided the information in the first place, such as a factory worker, prison guard or railwayman.

The Twins discussed what they should do next. Word was already out on the street that the Germans had raided the flat and a prisoner taken. However, there was still a chance the flat had yet to be stripped bare. They knew it was incredibly risky to go back, but they needed to know for certain whether the papers had been found or not.

Disguised as gas engineers, the Twins made their way to the Fort. When they rang the doorbell there was no answer, which came as something of a surprise as they had half-expected someone to have been left inside just to see who called at the address. Either that, or a trap was being set. Satisfied for now that no one had been left behind, they decided they would later return under the cover of darkness and enter the flat.

Early the following evening, Fernande arrived at Rue du Docteur Crestin. She had seen a light on at the Fort Boileau. Someone was probably inside. While it was possible the Gestapo had now decided to put someone inside the flat for a couple of days to arrest any callers, the Twins thought it unlikely. The Germans knew all too well that word would already have spread amongst resisters that it was no longer safe to call at the flat. Even if there was someone inside, the Twins were confident that they could quickly overpower them, particularly if they caught them by surprise.

The Twins knew they must take a chance as they could not leave it any longer. As usual, Thermogéne and Fernande were quick to volunteer to go with them. With four they stood more of a chance than with two, particularly if it came to a shoot-out. They would go later that same evening, while it was dark, and if there was no obvious presence in terms of the French police or Germans at the Fort then they would storm the place, recover the papers and get out again as quickly as they could.

Having made their way back to the Fort, Alfred rang the doorbell and waited to see if someone answered, while the others had taken up position close by. But again no one answered. And as before, it meant that no one was there, or it was a trap. It made no difference either way, they had come to do a job.

Alfred inserted his key into the door, opened it and went inside. The others followed. They could see straight away that the flat was in a mess. Many items, such as the clock, ornaments and food, had gone. So, too, had the money.

Worst still was the sight of blood on the carpet. Other than that, though, there was no indication the flat had been thoroughly searched. There was no time to waste. Henry went straight to the hiding place in the kitchen to see if the papers were still there. They were. He grabbed them quickly and with that the four were gone, back into the darkness and away.

Back at Thermogéne's flat, there was much talk and excitement about what they had just done, although they were all still left pondering over how the Gestapo had found out about the Fort. Fernande had spoken to the neighbours earlier in the day and they had confirmed the raid was carried out by a mix of plain-clothed Gestapo, German soldiers and Vichy Police, and someone had been heard shouting for Auguste and Artus.

This latest piece of news merely confirmed what they had already feared. The Gestapo were after the Twins. However, those who knew about the Fort were all trusted friends and none of them had been arrested, which meant the information about the Twins living there could only have come from an informant. But who? They were convinced their own circuit had not been infiltrated nor had there been any arrests amongst its members. They then started going through the names of people they knew to be friends of Germaine, and who knew it was her home. But of the names they came up with, none had been back to the flat since she had left, and they probably did not know the flat had since become home to the Twins.

It was all very puzzling indeed. The Twins then went through the names of everyone they had ever met during their early meetings with Germaine at the flat, way back in November when they first needed somewhere to stay. And it was then that it suddenly came to them. It was almost certainly down to one person – the Bishop!

Not that the Twins knew it at the time, but the man they knew as the Bishop was a Nazi informer called Robert Alesch. When the Germans first occupied France he was working in parishes around Paris, and for a while he assisted a local resistance group. But when the Germans found out about his activities, and that he was a native of Luxembourg, which was then part of the Third Reich, he was summoned to the office of a senior Abwehr officer. As the Nazis considered him to be a German, Alesch was told he could help his country by acting as a double agent. It was either that or face deportation to a concentration camp. So, Alesch had become the double agent Abbé Ackuin, otherwise known as 'the Bishop', and he soon started exposing members of the French Resistance. While listening to the confessions of prisoners in Paris he learned of an escape plan and immediately reported it to his superiors. Then, having foiled the escape in Paris, the Bishop was sent on his next task in Lyon.

Marie had been wary of the Bishop from the first moment they had met. Her instincts told her there was something not quite right about him. She even shared her concerns with Pépin, but he thought her worries were unfounded. He had heard that the Bishop preached anti-Nazi sermons and he had personally seen him handing out pictures of de Gaulle. A German sympathiser, he said, would never do that. But Marie had always remained unconvinced. She even contacted London about him, but she was told the Bishop's bona fides checked out. Her concerns were heightened further when she learned of the arrests in Paris, just days before the Bishop had arrived in Lyon. But it seems that Marie was told by London to continue working with him and supply him with what he needed.

Having concluded it was the Bishop who was the problem, the Twins felt sure that Germaine must have been followed to the Fort that night, and once there it would have been easy to call in the raid. As for their own names, Auguste and Artus, being known to the Gestapo, that could hardly have been too much of a surprise.

***

Although it was all a concern, the Twins were not overly worried at this stage, even though they had been told throughout their training that if the Gestapo ever got on their backs then they should get out at the earliest opportunity. They could always return to France, but they were no use to anyone languishing in a prison or a concentration camp or, worse still, dead.

The Twins really should have got out at this point, while they still had the chance, and left the circuit in the temporary hands of others, but instead they decided to carry on. They did, however, agree to lie low for a few days.

As always, Thermogéne and Bohémienne stepped in, saying the Twins could stay with them for as long as they needed until they could find somewhere safe to go. While they were extremely grateful for the offer, the Twins were also mindful of the risks their hosts were taking. Not only would the Twins be staring death in the face if they were to be caught at their flat, but so would Thermogéne and Bohémienne for harbouring them. And that was something the Twins were not willing to accept, despite the protests of their hosts, who were clearly prepared to take the chance.

For now, though, Thermogéne and Bohémienne got their way. In truth, the Twins had little choice but to stay put. They had nowhere else in Lyon to go, although they felt sure the Germans did not know who they really were. Besides, they were enjoying themselves and were more determined than ever to carry on. It was what they had joined the SOE to do. They even wanted to step up a gear and hit the Germans harder than ever before.

It was fighting talk, but the reality was the Twins did not have the support they needed to be able to step up a gear. Yes, they had people, and good ones at that, but they needed more of everything else – more money, more weapons and more explosives. Most importantly, though, they still needed a direct link with London. And if they could not have that, their work would have to come to an end.

With the Twins deciding to stay with Thermogéne and Bohémienne for a while, Fernande went back and forth keeping circuit members up to date with what was going on. She was one of only a trusted few who knew where the Twins were staying.

Another who knew where they were staying was Gustave, who was the first to call on the Twins. He had gone to see them at the Fort and, noticing it was cordoned off, had feared the worst. It was only when Fernande tracked him down that he discovered the Twins were safe.

Gustave had brought some good news. He had heard that a message received from London included the news that Alfred and Henry were promoted in the field to the rank of captain. While news of their promotion was both satisfying and flattering, it hardly solved their problem. The Twins needed a wireless operator and they needed support. Perhaps those back in London thought they were doing such a good job that they could manage everything on their own. What was more promising, though, was when Gustave told them Nicolas had the money left by Marie and was now prepared to share some of it out. He would be in touch and hopefully things would get moving once again.

When Nicolas arrived at Rue du Docteur Crestin he sensed the morale of the Twins was low. It was the first time they had met, but he had heard much about them from Marie before she left Lyon and knew they needed help. Now that he had some money, he had come to see what he could do.

Nicolas gave the Twins 100,000 francs (approximately £500), half of which they owed to members of their group in Le Puy, and a further 10,000 francs to cover what they had lost at the Fort following the Gestapo raid. It was a considerable portion of the 1 million francs Nicolas had available to him, but he knew from what he had been told that the Twins were doing good work.

With the help of the money he had now given them, Nicolas suggested the Twins go to Mâcon where his contacts there were in urgent need of leaders. It was a tempting offer, but Mâcon was 50 miles to the north and working with others was, perhaps, a step too far. The Twins had taken great care to make sure their own circuit was close-knit and secure, and to now start working with others was a huge risk. Besides, GREENHEART was doing well and still had some great ideas, and the last thing they wanted was for someone else to steal those ideas and get all the credit for the work. And, as they said, if London could send them their own wireless operator, there was no reason to join forces at all – with anyone. Reluctantly, the Twins turned down Nicolas's proposal, although Nicolas did agree to have a message sent to London requesting a wireless operator be sent to the Twins.

A couple of days later, Alfred asked Gustave if their message had been sent to London. It had not, although this was not due to Nicolas going back on his word. There were already too many messages waiting to be sent and not enough wireless operators to send them. It was risky to send too many at once and so theirs was in the queue. They must be patient.

After a week of laying low, the Twins considered it safe enough to get going once more. They would first venture out on to the streets of Lyon under the cover of darkness to see if anyone approached or followed them.

When the time came to set foot outside the flat, they decided to walk separately and on opposite sides of the street, as it was most likely that anyone looking for them would be looking for two men rather than one. At first, everything seemed fine. They took it in turns to cross the street and pass each other, all choreographed of course, with discreet hand signals to notify each other that everything was alright. But after a while, Henry indicated he thought he was being followed. In response, Alfred took up a position on the opposite side of the road. He was far enough behind Henry to see if anyone was shadowing him, but not too far behind his brother to lose sight of him altogether.

There did seem to be someone following Henry. There was a man behind his brother, although in the darkness it was difficult for Alfred to work out who it might be. Deciding he needed to act before it might be too late, he quickly caught Henry up, crossed the road and ushered his brother into a bar and straight out onto a street the other side.

The pursuer was now hot on their heels and then came a shout ordering them to stop. It was the police. Henry was the first to move. He quickly spun round, faced the man, taking him completely by surprise, and caught him fully in the groin with a hard kick. The man screamed in pain and sunk to his knees, as the Twins made off into the night.

***

Safely back at the flat with Thermogéne, Bohémienne and Fernande, they all discussed what had happened earlier and chatted about what they should do next. It seemed there was another problem as well. An appeal for French men of working age to volunteer to work in factories in Germany in exchange for the return of French prisoners of war had not received the desired response, and so the Vichy Government had announced the *Service du Travail Obligatoire* (STO, the Compulsory Labour Service Law), which meant compulsory forced labour in Germany with French manpower being used to replace German workers sent to fight in the war.

Every French man between the age of 17 and 55 was liable and when men failed to report for transportation, the Milice and Gestapo drove through the streets of Lyon hunting down any man of working age. One major drag-net, which had lasted three days, took place after 600 men had failed to report for transportation and resulted in the

Gestapo sealing off the whole of the north-east suburb of Villeurbanne. Those without exemption were herded to the station and put into railway carriages destined for the concentration camp at Mauthausen.

They all agreed that it was no longer safe for the Twins to stay in Lyon. It was time for them to take to the countryside until things had quietened down. Fernande was sent off to contact Marius to arrange for him to come to Lyon and collect them by car. It was a plan they had put in place long before the Germans moved into Lyon. There were farmers throughout the Haute-Loire and Puy-de-Dôme who were prepared to put the Twins up should the need ever arise.

However, it was not just about Alfred and Henry. There were similar plans for the others, too. All had safe places to go or somewhere they could call in for something to eat or a change of clothes.

With the help of Hubert, it was arranged for the Twins to stay at a flat in Le Puy where the deaf old landlady asked no questions. So long as the rent was paid on time, she was happy. Marius picked the Twins up from Lyon as planned. They decided it best to travel the last part of the journey separately to avoid attracting unnecessary attention when they arrived in Le Puy, and so Henry was dropped off to the west of Saint-Étienne and Alfred near Langogne. They would meet up at Le Puy in three days.

Alfred was the first to arrive at the flat. It was his job to check it over. With it being on the first floor and with a window facing out on to the back of the building, he was happy there was a good escape route should it ever be required. Satisfied with the flat, he waited until it was dark before leaving to meet up with Henry at a prearranged meeting point on the edge of town. It was safer to meet that way rather than Henry going straight to the flat, just in case Alfred had been arrested there and a trap then set for him.

Henry turned up exactly on time, but he was in a terrible state. His clothes were torn and caked with blood and filth and he was stumbling along and mumbling to himself. Back at the flat he fell on to the bed, exhausted. Alfred could now see him more clearly. Henry had a large bruise on the side of his face, but there was no sign of a wound to account for the blood. Alfred also noticed the empty magazine in Henry's pocket and his Colt pistol had just one round left in the other.

Leaving Henry to sleep, Alfred gathered up his brother's clothes, bundled them into a bag and took them to Hubert for disposal elsewhere. Returning to the flat, he could see that Henry's condition seemed to be deteriorating. He poured a brandy and fetched a glass of water and a couple of aspirins. Waking Henry, he helped him sip the brandy and water and gave him the aspirins. Alfred could see that Henry's eyes were wide and staring vacantly into the distance. Henry broke into a fit of laughter and then came the tears. He then started mumbling about a German staff car and its arrogant Nazi occupants being blown sky high, before he drifted back to sleep.

The following morning Henry was much better. He washed and shaved as normal and dressed in some spare clean clothing. But it came as something of a surprise to Alfred when Henry said he wanted to go straight back to Lyon. Without weapons and explosives, he said, they could not achieve anything worthwhile. Their only chance was through the likes of Nicolas and Gustave, and that meant returning to Lyon.

Alfred knew from his older brother's tone that it was not something to be discussed. They were both now starting to wonder if they would ever get the support from London that was so desperately required. Leaving Le Puy behind, they caught the train to Saint-Étienne and from there they caught a bus to Lyon. But whatever had happened to Henry the previous night stayed with him. He never talked about it with Alfred. Alfred later put Henry's condition down to something akin to a nervous breakdown. It was all quite strange and most unlike Henry.

They were soon back at Rue du Docteur Crestin. Nothing had happened while they had been away. Neither Fernande nor Bohémienne had managed to contact Nicolas or Gustave and so there had been no word from London.

Alfred decided to go and find them himself, but rather than risk being spotted, he thought he would stand a better chance of going unobserved if he changed his appearance. This he did, courtesy of a trusted hairdresser who darkened and styled his hair, trimmed his newly grown moustache to pencil thinness and blackened it using mascara. As a finishing touch, Alfred put on a heavy pair of horn-rimmed spectacles and dressed in a tweed suit. To a casual observer he might easily be mistaken for a shop assistant.

A few days later, Alfred arranged to meet up with Germaine's boyfriend, Dubois, at a local bar. A trusted Vichy inspector had apparently found out where Germaine was being held and what she had disclosed during interrogation. Dubois had suggested that he and Alfred first meet up and then go together to meet the inspector to find out more.

It provided Alfred with an early opportunity to try out his new disguise. When he got to the bar, he spotted Dubois and as he walked up to him it was clear the Frenchman had not recognised him. The disguise had worked, but what happened next took Alfred completely by surprise. As Dubois ordered a drink, someone joined them from the crowd. It was the Bishop.

Before Alfred could say anything, Dubois blurted out how much Alfred's disguise had fooled him and, with that, the Bishop made his excuses and left, saying he was off to meet another British agent who had only just arrived in Lyon.

Alfred was not convinced. The Bishop was more likely to go straight to the nearest telephone and inform his masters that Alfred had changed his appearance or, worse still, to get someone to come to the bar to arrest him. But what bothered Alfred more was the fact that Dubois seemed convinced the Bishop was a trusted friend.

Alfred decided against arguing otherwise. Against such stupidity, what was the point? Besides, it was time for them to go and meet the inspector. As it turned out, though, there was not much for the inspector to tell other than Germaine had been transferred to a prison in Paris and the Gestapo had placed little importance on her arrest. They considered her to be just another pawn in the game and nothing higher than that.

There was clearly nothing more they could do for Germaine and Alfred had already had enough for one night. Not wishing to hang around the streets of Lyon any longer, he made his apologies and left.

As Alfred wandered back towards Rue du Docteur Crestin his mind was in a spin. He was full of rage. What on earth was going on? He wondered how Dubois could have been so stupid as to have been taken in by the Bishop's story. Another explanation was that Dubois had been turned by the Germans and was now working for them, but if that had been the case the Gestapo would surely have been at the bar waiting for him to arrive. Even so, he was annoyed. Not only were they taking on the Germans, but they were being hampered by infiltration and the betrayal of some misguided French. It finally dawned on him that they were never going to get any support from London. They were clearly not a high enough priority. Maybe those back in London thought they were doing a good enough job in Lyon as it was, simply by ruffling feathers and making a nuisance of themselves, all of which was true and all of which was diverting the Germans away from others who were clearly bigger fish in the pond.

***

For the first time since landing back in France seven months ago, Alfred started to question whether he and Henry should stay. Most would have already got out by now, either to Switzerland or across the Pyrenees.

Thoughts were still swirling through his mind when Alfred suddenly became aware of footsteps behind him. He wondered just how long someone might have been following him and was instantly cross with himself for being distracted by his wayward thoughts. Lyon was a dangerous place at night and he still had some way to go before he was back at the flat.

Alfred crossed the road and turned into a side street but still he could not shake off the sound of footsteps behind him. Convinced he was being followed, he quickened his pace and turned another corner, taking the opportunity to glance over his shoulder to see who was behind. He could see there was someone there, just as he had thought. The man was tall, possibly young, and there was someone else on the other side of the road, a man wearing a trench coat and a hat. Alfred moved swiftly on, giving his pursuers no indication that he knew he was being followed.

The street ahead was dark and empty. Seeing a doorway, Alfred stepped off the pavement and into the dark shadows. He could hear the footsteps approaching, getting closer and closer, but now they became more hesitant. Then the footsteps stopped, the pursuer perhaps thinking that Alfred had disappeared into a safe house somewhere along the street.

Slowly the footsteps started again. Now they were very close. Then there was the shape of a man. He stopped to look in the doorway but whoever he was could not see Alfred crouched in the dark shadows. And in that same instance Alfred pounced, one hand stretched across the man's mouth while the other arm went around his neck, tightening remorselessly. The man struggled frantically but he was no match for Alfred. A muffled gurgling sound was followed by silence as the man crumbled to his knees. And as he did so, Alfred finished him off by repeatedly bashing his head against the wall, until he was certain the man was dead.

Turning the body over, the man's face was barely recognisable, but it was clearly not the Bishop as Alfred had expected. Some Frenchman had just paid the price for taking the side of the Germans. Alfred briefly thought about trying to find any papers or identity on the man's body, but he knew there was no time to hang around, particularly as there was almost certainly a second man in pursuit.

Alfred was soon off again into the darkness of the night, but all the twisting and turning that had gone on before as he had meandered from street to street meant he was now in a part of the city he did not know. With no option but to turn around, he retraced his steps. It was something he would not normally do, but eventually he recognised where he was. By now, though, his nerves had almost gone. Alfred felt shot to pieces. He was not enjoying this one bit.

***

Back at the flat, Henry and Thermogéne sat with Alfred discussing the evening's events. Alfred, being Alfred, chose to dismiss the whole episode as being just one of those things. Fernande had also arrived with worrying news from elsewhere. There were shocking reports coming from Marseille, where part of the old town had been cordoned off as the Gestapo tried to get to grips with the resisters, and from Bordeaux as well, where it had been reported that hundreds of hostages had been executed following recent resistance activity. Meanwhile, closer to home, further bombs on consecutive days had gone off in an office near the Gare de Lyon-Perrache that was being used by the Vichyites for recruiting voluntary labour for Germany and a newspaper kiosk near Rue de la Gare. And just two nights before, a German soldier had been found dead in a park, while only that morning another was found floating down the Rhône. Now there was talk of a curfew being imposed in the city.

Lyon was a jungle of resistance activity, but the Twins knew the net was closing in on them and their luck was running out. It was now time to get out, once and for all. They decided to leave together the following night.

It was an anxious following day waiting at the flat, but early in the evening they made their move. They decided to leave when the streets were at their most crowded so that they could blend in amongst the crowd. However, they soon became convinced they were being followed.

They cut through the narrow streets to the busy Cours Gambetta and jumped on a tram car, before almost immediately jumping off again while it was still moving and running down a side street. As they entered a building, a shot sounded somewhere behind them. Quickly climbing the stairs, they climbed out of a window on the second floor and jumped onto a roof. Huddling together in the shadows, they heard voices at the window through which they had just passed. A couple of wild shots rang out behind them as the Twins worked their way along the roof and then down a drainpipe into a small yard. Seconds later, they were over the wall and out into a neighbouring street.

Again, the Twins had got away by the skin of their teeth. But there seemed to be no easy way out of the city and they reluctantly made their way back to the safety of Rue du Docteur Crestin to contemplate what they should do next. Their bid to escape Lyon had failed.

13

END OF THE LINE

Just how much the Gestapo wanted to arrest the Twins at this stage is not clear. The Germans clearly knew who they were and what they looked like, and with greater numbers there had seemingly been opportunities to bring them in. It is quite possible – probable even – that Alfred and Henry were being used like pawns in a game of chess. They were probably being tailed in the hope they would lead the Germans to someone else. It was a common tactic used by the Gestapo to get at bigger fish in the pond. And if that was the case, then it was probably Nicolas the Gestapo were after. After all, it had been Nicolas who the Bishop had been so keen to be put in contact with when the Twins had first met him at Germaine's flat back in November, and it was Nicolas who, many years later, was described by the SOE's official historian, M.R.D. Foot, to have been the most important agent to go to Lyon that year.

For now, though, the Twins were still free, albeit on the run. The days following their failed bid to escape

Lyon were spent cooped up in the flat on Rue du Docteur
Crestin, their nerves almost at breaking point. They could
not even move around Lyon safely anymore.

Over and over, they discussed their options. The railway
and bus stations were clearly under constant surveillance
and so their best hope of getting out of the city was in one
of Marius's lorries. But then what? They would be back in
the countryside without any contact with London, with
no way of organising supply drops of weapons and arms.

Without weapons and arms, they could not provide
their circuit members with what they needed to continue the fight against the Nazis. As far as their mission
was concerned, they were no longer achieving a thing.
It was, effectively, over. Reluctantly, the Twins came
to the same conclusion. They would have to return to
England. Even Henry agreed that to do anything else did
not make sense.

Their plan now was to leave GREENHEART in the
capable hands of their trusted friend Marius and return to
England so that they could take a break and find out from
London why they had not received the support they had
expected. They would also use their time away to arrange
for their own wireless operator to be allocated to their
group. Having done that, they would return to France,
hopefully in a matter of weeks, to continue their work
with the circuit, only next time there would be no need
to return to Lyon. With their own wireless operator, they
could carry out their work from the countryside.

With Fernande being their only link with the outside
world, she was back and forth keeping the Twins updated
on what was going on elsewhere. The latest bit of news
was that word had finally filtered through from Nicolas

that London was sending someone to Lyon to co-ordinate a new campaign against the Nazis.

The Twins were in no position to support any such campaign. They were, in fact, in no position to do anything. Besides, what none of them knew at the time was the man sent by London to co-ordinate the new campaign was Captain John Hamilton – and he was already in the hands of the Gestapo!

The Twins brought Fernande up to date with their own plan, after which she was sent back to Nicolas to inform him of their intention to return to England and to ask if he could organise a Lysander pick-up just as soon as could be arranged.

Leaving Henry at the flat to deal with any messages from Nicolas, Alfred decided to have one more go at getting out of Lyon and make his way to Le Puy so that he could brief Marius on their plan. Early one morning, just as soon as the city streets were starting to get busy, he cycled to a rendezvous point where one of Marius's lorries was waiting. The lorry was not going all the way to Le Puy, but it was going to Roanne and, provided it was not stopped at a checkpoint when leaving the city, at least it got Alfred out of Lyon, after which he could continue the rest of his journey by train.

The lorry was there on time and Alfred quickly jumped on board. It was a tense journey out of the city, but it passed with surprising ease. They were not stopped at any of the checkpoints and three hours later Alfred was in Roanne, where he hopped off the lorry and jumped on a train to Langogne, and then completed the last leg of his journey by bicycle.

From what Marius told him, the arrival of the Germans in Le Puy had seen things take a turn for the worse. Businesses were being raided and items removed, all presumably to help the German war effort. Alcohol and other such luxuries were being confiscated, presumably for the benefit of others, and young men were being rounded up for forced labour elsewhere. Many had already taken to the hills rather than face an uncertain future in the hands of the Nazis.

It was now a matter of being patient until the Twins returned from London. With greater support, they could all pick up the fight once more. In the meantime, Alfred knew GREENHEART was being left in very capable hands. However, it was still an emotional farewell when it was time to say goodbye to Marius and his wife. They had no idea when they would all be together again.

The thought of going back to Lyon made Alfred feel sick inside, but his return journey was as uneventful as his journey out of the city had been. It seemed a good route, but he also knew he had been lucky. Back at Rue du Docteur Crestin, he was brought up to date. Henry had heard from Nicolas, but he had been told that an increased presence of German detector vans in and around the city was making it all but impossible for transmissions to be made. And even when transmissions were made, messages had to be kept to a minimum. Nonetheless, Nicolas had assured the Twins that their message to get out was now top priority, although it was extremely unlikely that London would allocate them a Lysander. From what he knew, the number of Lysander drop-offs and pick-ups had been reduced following the infiltration of circuits and other breaches of security. Their best way out, Nicolas suggested, was to go over the Pyrenees.

The thought of going over the mountains again and then languishing in some camp in Spain, as they had done a little more than a year before, did not appeal to the Twins at all. There was more bad news as well. Word had filtered through that Patrice had been recaptured on the Spanish border after he had been one of those released from prison before the Germans arrived in the south, and word had also now spread of John Hamilton's capture in Lyon. Furthermore, a curfew had now been imposed, more young men were being rounded up for forced labour and hostages were being shot for crimes committed against the Nazi occupation. It all seemed so depressing. There was little to be optimistic about. For the Twins, it was the last straw.

★★★

Alfred soon arranged a meeting with Nicolas to check once again if a reply had been received from London and to discuss what they should do next. As the meeting was arranged at a nearby café, Henry went along too as cover, keeping a safe distance from his brother and watching out for anyone who might be tailing him. Both were armed with pistols and each had a hand grenade in their pocket just in case. They had a good idea what awaited them if they were caught and neither intended going down without a fight.

Choosing to chat outside the café rather than going in, Nicolas told Alfred their message had been sent but so far there had been no reply, although he was expecting one later that night. He would arrange for Gustave to call at their flat in the morning with any news received. Nicolas was also keen to hear Alfred's thoughts about the man they all knew as the Bishop, as he had heard that he had been making enquiries as to how he could get in touch with Nicolas by saying that he was a friend of the Twins. But Alfred's terse reply merely confirmed Nicolas's own suspicions. It seems the Bishop was using their names as a way of getting to others.

Before returning to Rue du Docteur Crestin, Alfred moved on to the Café des Hirondelles where Rodolphe had asked to see him. During their brief conversation, Rodolphe told Alfred that he had become aware the Twins had run into problems and was now offering to help get them both out of the country. At first Alfred was interested, but Rodolphe was unable to help with a Lysander pick-up, although he did offer one of his guides to help get them across the Pyrenees.

Alfred was grateful for the offer of help, but it was much the same old story. Even if the Twins did decide to go out over the Pyrenees, they would do it on their own rather than trust anyone else.

All the Twins could do for now was to go back to the flat and wait to hear from Gustave in the morning. Their eyes did light up, though, when later that evening Thermogéne told them that one of his factory workers had spotted a couple of suspicious delivery vans hanging around on the roadside leading up to the Canal du Jonage, and they had been there for the past couple of nights.

From what they were being told, it sounded like they could be German detector vans and, while it was easy to think no more about what Thermogéne had said, the Twins knew they would soon have to leave France. This was probably going to be their last opportunity to do something worthwhile. German detector vans were always a high priority when it came to finding targets to destroy and as they were down to their last two limpets, there could be no better way of putting them to good use. They would go and have a look, but not during the hours of curfew – that was too risky. They must wait until the following day.

Gustave arrived early the following morning. The curfew had only just been lifted, but he was keen to get to the Twins as soon as he could. He had news from London. The Twins had been instructed to return to England via Spain. There was to be no Lysander pick-up, which was disappointing, but at least London had acknowledged that it was time for the Twins to get out while they still had the chance. Gustave had been told to pull out as well.

As they talked more about their time in France, they all agreed they were tired. They had known each other since their first days at Wanborough, but now their nerves had all but gone and they were all desperately in need of a rest. There was nothing unusual in that. They had all done their bit for now and had lived to fight another day.

The Twins and Gustave agreed to make their way out of France together. It made perfect sense. However, before they all set off, Gustave would first try to contact a fisherman he knew on the Mediterranean coast who might be able to drop them off in northern Spain. It would at least save them the long and treacherous journey across the Pyrenees. Gustave left, telling the Twins to stay where they were until he got back in touch with them in the next couple of days.

With nothing to do until Gustave got back to them, the Twins decided to make best use of the time by taking out the two German detector vans, assuming they were still there. They could not do anything until much later and so the rest of the day was spent getting ready to clear out and removing any evidence that they had ever been at the flat. The thought of leaving something behind that might condemn the brave Thermogéne and Bohémienne to an early death did not bear thinking about.

As soon as it was dusk, the Twins cycled off towards the Canal du Jonage, Henry with a bag containing the two limpets slung over his shoulder and Alfred with a Sten gun in his. Avoiding the main roads, it took them an hour to make their way through the narrow streets to the point described by the factory worker, but when they arrived they were disappointed to find the vans were not there.

The Twins had no intention of giving up. Dismounting, they hid their bicycles and started to walk. They were certain that any detector van would use the high road to maximise the line of sight needed to detect wireless transmissions and so they continued along a lower parallel lane rather than risk proceeding along the road above.

It was now dark, making it easier for them to continue unseen, but it was equally hard for them to see a thing. After a while without success, they decided to return to their bicycles and continue further along the lane. More in hope than anything else, they cycled slowly along, their eyes straining above through the darkness to see if they could spot anything silhouetted against the night sky. Then, out of the gloom, they could make out the shapes of what looked like two vans.

Leaving their bikes on the side of the lane, the Twins stealthily made their way through the scrubland leading to where the vans were parked. They could now make out that the vans were parked back to back and could see the rear doors of one were slightly ajar, and as they got closer still, they could hear muffled voices coming from within. There was no doubt they were detector vans. Better still, there was no one guarding them. What arrogance, they thought. More than that, it was careless, and now the Germans were about to pay for such nonchalance.

With Alfred providing cover from a vantage point, his finger firmly poised on the trigger of his Sten, Henry quietly inched towards the vans. He could hear the German voices coming from inside and the telltale sound of Morse code. He then fixed the limpets to the vans.

Seconds later, the Twins were off again into the darkness. As they pedalled away from the scene as fast as they could, the sound of two explosions, barely seconds apart, shattered the silence of the night. The excitement of it all gave them renewed energy to pedal even faster, the grins on their faces as wide as they could possibly be. It was a great way to sign off.

The following day, the Twins were back to moping around the flat with nothing to do, other than to hope Gustave got back to them before the Gestapo arrived. Fernande, as always, kept their spirits up by visiting them, even though the Twins kept telling her not to take any more risks. On this occasion, though, Fernande had a letter with her from Germaine and it had just been given to her by the Bishop!

Fernande went on to explain that the Bishop had unexpectedly called on her saying he had a letter from Germaine, which she had given to him when he saw her in the prison in Paris where she was being held. He said he had been granted the privilege of visiting her because of his priestly vocation and knowing that the content of the letter involved the Twins, he had come to ask for their address so that he could go and discuss it with them. But, Fernande added, she had refused to tell the Bishop where they were staying, although she did tell him that she might be seeing them sometime in the next week. And with that, the Bishop had given her the letter and left, and now she had come straight to the flat to tell the Twins.

From the handwriting, it seemed that the letter had indeed come from Germaine. It was addressed to Mere Poule (Mother Hen), a code name used by Fernande, and its translation simply read, 'Send the two chickens out into the country' – the 'two chickens' being a prearranged nickname for the Twins.

At that point, the Twins really should have got out while they still had the opportunity to do so. They had always had their doubts about the Bishop, but the fact that he had supposedly been able to visit Germaine in prison and get the letter from her was itself highly suspicious to say the least. However, rather than leave, the Twins instead decided to wait for Gustave to return to the flat, which he did the following day with news that the fisherman could not take them to Spain. There was, however, a trusted guide who could take them across the Spanish border.

The three now finalised their plan. They decided to make their move the following day, with the Twins making their way to an agreed rendezvous point to the south of Lyon to meet up with Gustave. And all being well, within a couple of days they should all be enjoying a cup of tea in the British Consul in Barcelona.

★★★

It was now 4 April 1943, a Sunday. The last few weeks had been hell, but that evening the Twins sat down to a farewell supper with Thermogéne, Bohémienne and Fernande, their closest and most trusted friends, courtesy of a hamper of food put together by Fernande. It was a wonderful evening together. The Twins could not have spent their last hours in Lyon with anyone better. Everyone seemed so relaxed and the food washed down exceptionally well with a fine bottle of wine. They talked about their good times together and looked forward to the future when the Twins returned to carry on the fight.

As it got closer to 9 p.m., the time the curfew was enforced, Fernande got ready to leave. She had, as usual, been briefed with messages for Marius and the others.

But then the doorbell rang. It caught them all by surprise. They wondered who risked calling so late into the evening.

Telling the women to stay where they were, the men grabbed their Colts and Stens and moved quickly upstairs to look out of the window to see if they could make out who was calling, but the road below was empty. Thermogéne called down to see who it was. The unfamiliar voice of a young man replied, claiming to have an urgent message and asked to be let in.

Thermogéne said he would go downstairs to see what the man wanted. He might have urgent news from Gustave. Before he could get to the door, the Twins saw a military lorry swerve around the corner and come to a halt outside the flat, and before those inside the flat could take in what was happening outside, Germans were piling out of the lorry as a machine gun covered the door, while a second lorry pulled up to cover the far end of the road.

It all happened in a matter of seconds. The Twins dashed for their planned escape route that would take them out of the window at the back, but they could see German soldiers waiting below. The building was surrounded. The front door then crashed open as more than a dozen soldiers stormed the building, while a voice could be heard below shouting, 'Auguste and Artus!'

Thoughts of trying to shoot their way out flashed through their minds, but it was no good. The Twins, and the others for that matter, would be dead before they knew it. Instead, Alfred pulled the light cord plunging the bedroom into darkness and turned off the upstairs landing light. It might just buy them some time by adding to the confusion inside the flat. Even the Germans were unlikely to start shooting in the dark.

However, the darkness only gave them a temporary reprieve. There were far too many Germans inside the flat. Even the Twins could not get out of this mess, but they were determined not to go down without a fight. For a while they fought in the dark, two against fifteen, chin jabbing and using the legs of a broken chair as truncheons. It was a scene more like a western bar brawl, but at least neither side started firing aimlessly. It would have been carnage.

The fight seemed to last several minutes but gradually the Twins were overcome and soon they were pinned to the floor. Bleeding and having finally been restrained, they were then led down to the kitchen on the ground floor. Their war was over – and most probably, so were their lives.

As they were led outside the Germans started searching the flat. The Twins could see Thermogéne, Bohémienne and Fernande all stood facing the wall, their hands above their heads. It was a woeful sight. They feared for them all. Henry immediately protested the innocence of the others, saying they had merely let them have a room in good faith. His protests were a waste of time, although he hoped his words reconfirmed with the others their cover story when the time came.

But they all knew what was in store for anyone caught harbouring members of the Resistance or British agents. For all of them, it was finally the end of the line.

14

THE BUTCHER OF LYON

The Twins never found out who had betrayed them, or if in fact they had been betrayed at all. Other than their hosts and Fernande, there were, as far as they knew, only three others who had ever known they were staying at the flat on Rue du Docteur Crestin. These were Nicolas, Gustave and Patrice. As Alfred and Henry later stated, 'all these people are above suspicion', and it might well have been the case that the Twins had been under surveillance and followed back to the flat, and then the raid called. Either that, or Fernande had been followed to the flat after the Bishop had called on her with the letter from Germaine.

Whatever the circumstances behind their arrest, the Twins were certainly amongst those identified by the Bishop to be part of the SOE's wider network in Lyon. Many were rounded up in a series of raids, decimating SOE's operations in the city and leaving those back in London scratching their heads as to what they should do next.

The Twins had been so close to leaving France but, like many similar tales of woe, they had hung around just a little too long. As for their prospects now, they did not look good at all. Survival from here on would be against all the odds. The Germans could have instantly had them all shot. The Twins would be treated as spies and the three French, as members of the Resistance, had broken the terms of the armistice agreement.

However, for now, their lives were to be spared. And, as with most cases of those captured by the Gestapo, it was to be the start of a well-trodden track. Arrest was followed by torture and torture was followed by deportation, and deportation usually meant death at one of the many concentration camps.

The Twins were taken straight to the Hôtel Terminus, now the magnificent Mercure Lyon Centre Château Perrache Hotel. Its surroundings, leading to Place Carnot, have changed enormously over the years and this rather grand-looking early twentieth-century building carries no reminders of its dark days during the Nazi occupation, but in 1943 it was the Gestapo's headquarters in Lyon.

From the entrance on the Cours de Verdun Rambaud, the Twins were taken straight up to the third floor. After a short wait, Henry was the first to be dragged away before Alfred was hustled into a room where a rather hefty, unpleasant-looking man in his mid-forties and wearing the uniform of the SS was sat behind a desk.

The man was called Larsen, who the Twins later described as the 'typical fiction Gestapo man'. He spoke in perfect English to ask Alfred his name, his cold eyes staring through his pince-nez and without any emotion in his voice. Then, his character suddenly changed. Larsen started shouting at Alfred, accusing him of being a dirty spy and a terrorist.

Alfred had always wondered what such a moment might feel like. Now he knew. He was still hurting from the fighting at the flat, but he was not at all afraid. As he looked at the German in more detail, Alfred could not help but notice Larsen's small, dark moustache matching that of his Nazi leader.

Larsen spoke again, this time in the same toneless voice as when he had first spoken. He said he had been to London and knew the city well. He even claimed to know all about Alfred and his cover story, and so there was no point wasting each other's time. Alfred might just as well tell him everything as it was far better coming from him. If he was not prepared to do so then the Gestapo, Larsen emphasised, had ways of making people talk.

Alfred was certain Larsen was bluffing. While the Germans had clearly heard of the Twins, that was probably as much as the Gestapo knew. Besides, Alfred was tough and was prepared to go through whatever lay in store. The Gestapo would get nothing of use out of him.

Alfred simply said there was no cover story. He was Alfred Norman, born in Rochdale on 17 February 1914. He was an artist by profession and had lost his family in 1941 during the Blitz on London. He had joined the army at the declaration of war, but his responsibilities mounted to nothing more than folding and counting army blankets at a depot near Aldershot. Then, in 1942, he had been called to the War Office where he was told that because of his knowledge of the French language he was to be sent to France to recover downed aircrew and help them get to the Spanish border. But because he had not come across any aircraft that had been shot down in the unoccupied part of France, he had spent his time drinking and going to cinemas. And that was it. There was nothing else to say.

This rather simplistic story had been agreed with Henry before they had gone into France, and neither brother swayed from it during the difficult times ahead. They had been told during training to stick to their stories for as long as possible after arrest, but at least for the first twenty-four hours to allow time for news of their arrests to spread and for their contacts in France to disappear.

Under torture, it would never be that easy. Nonetheless, their story was plausible and easily remembered and it could be recited time and time again, although how much of it the Germans would ever believe remained to be seen. One thing that became apparent from the outset, though, was that any hopes the Twins might have had about being treated better because they were officers in the British Army were misguided and naive. They were, indeed, officers in the British Army, and so these facts could easily be checked. But, as far as the Germans were concerned, they were not to be treated like any other army officer. They were instead treated like all captured Allied agents and members of the French Resistance – and that did not bode well.

Larsen commented on Alfred's identity card, insisting it was easy to spot as a forgery along with the dozens of others he had seen during his time in France. Alfred did not reply. He knew it was a good forgery and was even tempted to gloat that it had been produced in Langogne with the help of the mayor and then thoroughly checked by town hall officials, but that would only have led to unnecessary questions and arrests there.

Then came the first beating – later described by Alfred as 'the beating of my life'. But, as it was now the early hours of the morning, Larsen decided to save the rest for another time, telling Alfred he was disappointed in his attitude and he would see him later that day.

It had been a similar experience for Henry, who had met Klaus Barbie for the first time. There was clearly worse to come, but for now the Twins were taken away in one of the Gestapo's black Citroëns to Fort Montluc, only a matter of a few minutes away.

Situated on Rue Jeanne Hachette, Montluc Prison now stands as a national memorial open to the public for guided tours. Fort Montluc was built during the 1830s as one of a series of fortifications surrounding the city, with the military prison being built in 1921. Following the signing of the armistice, in the Second World War it was used to hold military prisoners and perpetrators opposing the Nazi occupation and Vichy regime, mainly Gaullists and members of the French Resistance. When the Germans moved into Lyon in November 1942, the prison was requisitioned, after which it became an internment camp for prisoners prior to them being transferred elsewhere. During the Nazi occupation, some 15,000 prisoners are believed to have been held at Montluc, nearly 1,000 of whom were executed within its walls.

By the time the Twins arrived at Fort Montluc in April 1943, the prison had already gained a reputation as a torture and killing place for the Gestapo. The small, dark cells, each measuring around 6ft x 9ft, contained only a filthy single camp bed and a bucket. The stench was unbearable.

Later that morning they were back at the Hôtel Terminus, where they were again held on the third floor, waiting for their interrogations to begin. They were not allowed to talk and as they looked at each other they could see they were a shocking sight. This was what war had done to them. They were both handcuffed and Henry's eye was badly swollen from the fight at the flat, while Alfred's face was caked with dry blood with a trickle of red still running from a bad gash above his eye.

As they sat there in silence, Alfred noticed that Henry was trying to attract his attention. From Henry's discreet hand signals and his eye movements, Alfred worked out that Henry was going to try and make his escape through the window, even though it was closed, and they were on the third floor.

Henry's dramatic idea was to escape the building and get out of Lyon so that he could inform their group members in Le Puy where they were all being held. Then, one night after dark, he would take a group of volunteers to Fort Montluc and mount an assault to bring out those being held. It was an incredibly ambitious plan, madness even, but in desperate times people think and do desperate things.

Being the younger and more agile of the two, Alfred decided that he should be the one to take on the mad idea. Gesturing to Henry he was going to make the escape instead, Alfred started to work out in his own mind how he would go out through a window that was presently closed while wearing handcuffs – and there was the fact that he was on the third floor. He wondered what it would be like to jump from such a height and how it might compare to a parachute descent from an aircraft. That was always a high rate of descent, but at least jumping from a building meant he did not have to worry about the wind. There was, however, the likelihood that he would either break his legs or be shot.

Having quickly thought about it, Alfred reckoned he had around ten seconds or so to make his escape before the guards could react and take a shot at him, and that was assuming he survived the fall. He knew there was only the slimmest of chances of getting away with it, but he was prepared to give it a go. Besides, if he died while attempting to escape then the others would be able to put the blame for their arrests on him.

If he was going to give it a go, then he needed to go now. But, just as Alfred was about to make his move, Larsen appeared. It was too late. He had missed his chance. It was time to go for some more questions instead.

As he followed Larsen to what would surely be another beating, Alfred was still cursing himself for being too slow. But then he noticed an open window midway along the corridor, just a matter of a few yards away. And with that, Alfred was off. Putting himself in God's hands, he ran past Larsen and leapt through the window.

It was an incredibly brave attempt to escape, but wire netting had been strung across the courtyard below; the Germans having anticipated that someone might try such a thing. Dazed and shocked by the fall, Alfred freed himself from the netting and staggered to his feet. He could see the courtyard was enclosed and there was no easy way out. He found a door, which he opened, but after entering a corridor the next door he came across was locked. Alfred was now becoming weaker by the second. He could hear people shouting, but he could not go on any further. His legs finally gave way and after that there was only darkness.

When Alfred eventually came to, he realised he was in a strange bed. The handcuffs were still on and he first wondered if he had been dreaming. His whole body hurt, particularly his shoulder and ribs, which were badly bruised and causing him excruciating pain. He later found out that he had fractured his shoulder and hip. He also struggled to move his left hand and noticed that his fingers seemed to be locked in a rather uncomfortable position where they had broken. He also noticed his blood-soaked clothes, torn and in a terrible state. Slowly things started to come back. He remembered going out of the window, but thereafter seemed a blank, although there were vague memories of falling in the yard and then trying to run. And then the doors and the corridor, after which came the ambulance car and from that he worked out that he must be in a hospital bed. It had not been a dream.

Alfred had, in fact, been in hospital for three days. The hospital was in Charbonnières-les-Bains, in the north-west suburb of Lyon. A nurse tried to befriend him, asking him who he really was and who his friends were so that she could get word out to them that he was alive and well, but Alfred was not going to fall for such a Gestapo trick. Then came a visitor with news that he was soon to be transferred back to Fort Montluc.

***

Henry, meanwhile, had been subjected to severe beatings at the hands of Barbie's stooges. With Alfred in hospital, the Gestapo's efforts had focused on him. The interrogations had started the same morning that Alfred had made his death-defying leap for freedom and three days later they were still going on.

For some bizarre reason, Barbie had got it into his head that Henry was a Czech national and one of the assailants behind the assassination in Prague of the high-ranking Nazi official, Reinhard Heydrich. Afterwards described as the darkest figure within the Nazi elite because of his leading role in the Holocaust, Heydrich had been General of Police and chief of the Reich's Main Security Office, which included the Gestapo and the SD. His car had been ambushed by two SOE-trained agents, one Czech and the other Slovak. At the time Henry was being interrogated, ten months had passed since Heydrich's death.

Perhaps Barbie really thought Henry looked Czech or genuinely believed he was connected to Heydrich's assassins in some way. But, for whatever reason, Barbie saw Henry as someone he could get a confession from, either to get his own masters off his back or to consciously propel himself further into the Nazi limelight having tracked down a key assailant.

Barbie had underestimated the stubbornness and resilience of Henry Newton. During one beating, carried out by half a dozen of Barbie's thugs, the torrent of savage blows beat Henry to his knees in a state of semi-consciousness. It was only because Henry made it look like he was out cold that it stopped him from being beaten any more.

Even then, one of the thugs returned. Henry was in a daze, but he was aware of the man approaching, although he was helpless to prevent the boot coming down full force across his chest. The pain was excruciating. And with that, he finally passed out.

Barbie seemed determined to make Henry a scapegoat for Heydrich's death, which might be a reason why he was kept alive. Henry even remembered Barbie saying to him many times that he was no use to him dead.

In between the interrogations and beatings at the Hôtel Terminus, Henry was left shackled in his cell at Fort Montluc. His whole body ached. The cabbage soup and water were barely enough to keep him alive.

On the third day of questioning, it was Larsen's turn to have a go at breaking him. It made a welcome change. Barbie had been a ruthless thug, whereas Larsen adopted an altogether different style with a barrage of questions, repeated time after time, many of which seemed meaningless. What's your name? Where were you born? Where did you go to school? What was your teacher's name? When did you leave? Where were you when war broke out? The questions went on and on like a broken record.

But Larsen could not get anything out of Henry either and so Barbie took over again. It was back to the same ugly style. Still convinced that Henry was Czech, or perhaps Polish, two of Barbie's men started rattling at him in each language to see if they could get a reaction. And when that did not work, a rather odd and sinister-looking pair of handcuffs, with an electric flex dangling from them, appeared.

As his stooges forced the handcuffs on to Henry's wrists, Barbie told him he would be forced to speak in his native tongue, whatever it really was. Several of Barbie's victims later testified to him after he used modified handcuffs on them as well. Whether they were the same ones or whether Barbie had a macabre selection of such items is not clear. But whatever the case, Henry was subjected to the same brutal treatment. As the current seared through his body, he writhed in pain, his face contorted – but still he said nothing. And then came darkness once again.

Back at Fort Montluc, Henry collapsed in his cell, too weak even to reach his bowl of cabbage soup. For the next two days he was taken back and forth to the Hôtel Terminus. Barbie even tried a different tack. Still fixated on getting him to confess to the killing of Heydrich, Henry was plunged into a tub of icy cold water. Grabbed by his hair, his head was repeatedly dunked under and each time he was held under for longer. It was another of Barbie's preferred techniques. Henry's lungs were bursting, but still he remained silent.

The following day, he was taken up to a room on the fourth floor and his lower half stripped. Sat on a table, his legs dangling, the questions started again. The questions were always about Heydrich and when Henry kept refusing to confess to the killing, his legs were repeatedly rapped with a short black stick, on his kneecaps, his shin bones and his toes, each time the pain building. Still they got nothing from Henry.

***

Alfred, meanwhile, had returned to Fort Montluc after his three days in hospital. He was placed in a cell on the ground floor looking out over a courtyard with an armed sentry at the foot of his bed. The following morning, he was back at the Hôtel Terminus. The fact he was being taken back for more questioning so soon after leaving hospital confirmed in his own mind the Germans had got nothing out of Henry or the others. It was now his turn to stick to his guns and not betray them.

If asked why he had tried to escape, he had already prepared his answer. He would tell them he had become so fed up with the whole show and had just wanted to end it all.

This time it was Alfred's turn to meet Barbie. As he was led into the interrogation room, he could see a rubber truncheon and a belt on the desk. Barbie's opening words were to tell him that the others had told him everything, and it was now his turn to confirm their stories.

Unlike Henry's experience of constantly being accused of a link to Heydrich's assassination, Barbie's questions to Alfred were instead along the lines of the Twins being the leaders of a Resistance circuit carrying out spying and sabotage in France. There was no mention of Heydrich at all.

Barbie was on the right lines, of course, but Alfred was not going to let on. He denied having anything to do with a Resistance circuit, but Barbie simply responded by jerking on Alfred's fractured shoulder until he screamed in agony. The next thing Alfred remembered was being clubbed over the head by the rubber truncheon, and when Alfred repeatedly denied Barbie's claims, the truncheon crashed down again – and then again, until the room went dark.

Slowly Alfred came around. This time it was Larsen sat behind a desk. Then the questions started again. Those same tiring questions, along with some new ones about Alfred being a member of the British Intelligence Service. Larsen asked Alfred about the Racket and whether he knew Buckmaster. He even tried bluffing, saying that Henry had already confessed to them both going to Germany and then on to Czechoslovakia to kill Heydrich. But nothing came from Alfred's mouth.

When Alfred returned to Fort Montluc, he was put back into the same cell, still manacled and chained to the bed with only a German sentry for company. As Alfred's wounds started to heal, it became less painful to walk, although he still had a bad limp. His broken fingers were straightened by a German medical officer at the *Feldgendarmerie* in Place Carnot, with his hand dressed using toilet paper and then tied in a splint with a piece of string. It had not been pleasant, but at least it had made a welcome change from the routine interrogations at the Hôtel Terminus and the squalor of his cell at Fort Montluc.

The following day, Alfred was back at the hotel for more questioning. This time he was asked about the connection between crashed pilots and explosives. Alfred was shown a message from London, which the Germans had found in Joseph's office and included reference to Auguste and Artus. He was asked what he knew about Joseph and Gauthier.

While sticking to his overall story, Alfred offered the briefest explanation. He had been sent to France to work for Gauthier, specifically to check that any downed aircrew were British and not Germans posing as members of the RAF before sending them on to the Spanish border. However, because he and Gauthier had differing views, they had decided not to work together anymore. As for Joseph, he had fallen out with him because he had gone to France to save downed aircrew and not to play about with explosives, and so he had not seen Joseph again.

Either the Germans believed what Alfred had said, to some extent, or they chose to ignore his explanation altogether, but Larsen did not return to the same line of questioning again. Instead, he put other names to Alfred to try and get a reaction. Every time Alfred denied knowing who he was talking about, even when it meant another beating.

One of the names put to Alfred was Marie. Larsen even gave a description of her, telling Alfred she was a dangerous terrorist. Alfred denied knowing her but it only led to another beating before he was taken back to Fort Montluc.

Another technique used was to put Alfred and Henry, in turn, in front of another prisoner and ask if they knew who the man standing in front of them was. There were times when the Twins knew perfectly well who the other person was, but they dare not let on. It was quite upsetting to see a familiar face standing there, particularly when it was someone from Le Puy, but they could not show any emotion because it would let on to their German observers they were connected in some way.

When piecing the events together afterwards, it appears that word of the Twins' capture reached Le Puy the day after the arrests were made. The day after that, the Germans arrived in Le Puy and made four arrests, including the Joulians. But those arrested in Le Puy were not particularly close to the Twins, nor is it certain they were even members of GREENHEART at the time. However, they were part of Marie's network and had almost certainly been identified by the Bishop. Nonetheless, GREENHEART as a circuit was now dead, although most of its members escaped the snare. While some fled the commune to work with the Maquis elsewhere, others held their nerve and stayed put, including Marius and his wife, who decided against going into hiding or fleeing elsewhere.

Two days later, there were more names for Alfred to consider, one being Nicolas. Again, Alfred denied any knowledge of the name. There followed another beating. A piece of paper was then produced, which had been signed by Alfred and showed an uncoded message from Nicolas to London about a Lysander operation. Alfred was then shown a photo of Nicolas, followed by more photos of other men. Larsen asked about his special training, to which Alfred replied there had been no special training other than parachute jumps. Larsen went on to talk about the training establishment near Guildford, and the one near Loch Morar, and finally the SOE's Finishing School at Beaulieu.

Until now, Alfred had been convinced the Germans were guessing about almost everything, but the line of questioning was much closer to the mark. He was surprised to hear the names of these places coming from the mouth of a German. He felt he had to admit something and so he simply said that he had been sent to a training camp somewhere around Beaulieu. Larsen then started asking about the type of aircraft used when Alfred was dropped into France, how the crew navigated to the drop zone and about the reception committee that had been waiting for him on the ground. Alfred's answer was that he knew nothing of the aircraft type or about the route, and he could not know anything about the reception committee because he had been dropped blind and so there had been no one on the ground to meet him.

***

It had now been five days since the Twins were caught. Things started to settle into something of a routine, which went on for days and then ran into weeks. Each brother was interrogated on alternate days, with Barbie and Larsen taking it in turns to have a go.

Their interrogators had now seemingly become fixated on one discrepancy they had picked up between them. Alfred had said their parents were killed during the London Blitz while Henry had told them they had been killed in Manchester. What the Germans clearly did not know, though, was that this was a deliberate ploy by the Twins, which they had agreed when first formulating their story. They hoped that a minor discrepancy such as this would distract any interrogators by getting them to focus on one menial point rather than to pursue questioning about what they had really been up to, and with whom, during their time in France.

It worked. With typical pig-headedness, their interrogators had become determined to find out whether the parents were killed in London or Manchester, to the point that there were times when no other questions were being asked. It seems that Barbie and Larsen believed that if they could break the Twins on that one point in order to determine which of them was lying, they would then go on to tell them anything else they wanted to know.

Back and forth the Twins went, from their cells at Fort Montluc to the Hôtel Terminus for the same old questions and then back again to the prison. On one occasion after questioning, Alfred was bundled into the rear seat of a black Citroën car to be taken back to Fort Montluc. It was not very comfortable. His left arm was still in a sling, his hands were cuffed and he was squeezed between two Frenchmen – an army deserter caught by the Vichyites and given a long sentence at Montluc on his right, and on his left a former army officer who had joined the French Resistance and had been working with the SOE in Lyon under the code name Valentin.

Valentin was, in fact, André Devigny, who later became something of a legend in France. During his time at Montluc he made several attempts to escape, and unknown to Alfred at that time he was about to witness one of these. Soon after leaving the hotel, the car slowed down at the crossing of the Cours Charlemagne. It took no more than a second for Devigny to wrench the handle of the door, force it to open, jump out and bolt down the street.

The moment was later re-enacted as the opening scene of Robert Bresson's 1956 film, *A Man Escaped*, which is based on the memories of André Devigny, and although he eventually succeeded in escaping from Montluc just days before his execution was due to be carried out, on this occasion Devigny did not get very far. The driver and guard in the front of the car leapt out and went off in pursuit, and then the shooting started. Another car carrying German officers pulled up and its occupants joined in the chase. Alfred looked around, but the street was deserted. People had taken cover as soon as the first shots were fired. Besides, the whole incident was over in minutes. Devigny was soon recaptured and taken back to the car, where he was beaten by one of the guards before continuing their journey to Fort Montluc.

For Alfred, the whole episode was most frustrating. He had momentarily been in a stationary car with its engine running and no German guards, but there was little he could do. He was sat next to a Frenchman who was not prepared to try and escape, for fear of what would happen to him and, handcuffed and limping, he knew he would not get very far at all. He needed help but there was no one around. He could have wept with frustration.

After another couple of sessions at the Hôtel Terminus, there followed a period of ten days when no interrogations took place at all. Even to Barbie it must have become obvious they were getting nowhere with the Twins. Each was as obstinate as the other. Besides, as time marched on, any information they might squeeze out of them was getting staler by the day.

***

The Twins had survived their early weeks of captivity, but their ordeal was far from over. Alfred even had to suffer a mock execution one afternoon at Fort Montluc. A nasty Gestapo type made him stand up against a wall. As he cocked his sub-machine gun ready to shoot Alfred, he said that he wanted to satisfy his own curiosity and so he asked Alfred for one last time whether it really was London or Manchester. Alfred did not even bother to answer.

Then, early one morning before dawn, and completely without warning, Alfred was wakened by the sound of the cell door being unlocked. A German jack-booted and steel-helmeted officer ordered him out of his cell. There was no doubt in Alfred's mind that this was finally it. While the incident against the wall a few days before had been a bluff, this was certainly not. The Gestapo must have finally run out of patience and having got nothing out of him had now decided there was no longer any need to keep him alive.

While Alfred had long prepared himself to die, it was the unexpectedness of it all that had taken him by surprise. Most of all, though, he felt saddened at not having the chance to say goodbye to Henry. He stood outside in the courtyard with the four-man firing squad facing him.

As rifle bolts rattled, he suddenly felt shaken, very sad and anxious. He braced himself to go out with his chin up, as he had always intended to do. Apart from some faint noises in the distance, it was silent.

Suddenly, though, the execution was off. The officer said that it was too dark for the firing squad. Alfred would be shot later that morning, unless he had something more to say. There was nothing more to say. Another word of command followed, and the firing squad marched away. Alfred was led back to his cell, his ordeal over for now. He collapsed on the bed and drifted into a stupor.

15

FRESNES

The Twins had all but lost any comprehension of time. They had, in fact, been at Fort Montluc for just over six weeks, although to them it probably felt more like six months. As for the interrogations, the Germans were no further on than they had been at the start.

Then, on 21 May, and again without warning, a group of some thirty or forty prisoners were mustered in the yard, Alfred and Henry included, and herded into two coaches. From the stories they had heard about those who had gone before, the prisoners were almost certain their next stop would be a prison in Paris, and they knew it was not going to be a pleasant time. France had now been occupied for three years and there was a well-trodden path down which most resisters, like the Twins, had already gone.

At the Gare de Lyon-Perrache, the group were bundled onto a Paris-bound train. The Twins were in the same compartment and were reassured to know that wherever they were off to they were going together. They were also delighted to see that Thermogéne, Bohémienne and Fernande were boarding the same train. They were all still alive.

Although it was the height of spring, the Twins felt that Paris looked drab, its people miserable and it was not at all the vibrant capital it had once been. From the Gare de Lyon they were bundled into another coach and driven through the southern suburbs of Paris until they eventually pulled into a courtyard. They had arrived at the notorious Fresnes Prison.

Built in the late nineteenth century, Fresnes Prison is still in use today. With 1,200 cells for men and a smaller prison for women, it is the second largest prison in Paris behind Fleury-Mérogis, which also happens to be Europe's largest. Back in the Second World War, though, Fresnes was used by the Germans to house captured SOE agents and members of the French Resistance. Held in horrific conditions, many died there during the Nazi occupation of France.

The massive, forbidding prison had a grim appearance. As the new arrivals bundled off the coach, the guards were waiting for them. The prisoners were hustled through the sombre, underground passages.

From now on they were on their own. With a final glimpse of their friends, and a hopeful smile of encouragement here and there, they could not help but wonder whether they would ever see each other again.

The prisoners at Fresnes were held in one of its three divisions, or wings. Alfred was initially locked up in isolation somewhere in the basement, with just the glow of a dim bulb providing any light. He later described the feeling as being entombed and the silence oppressive, which was only broken by the sound of the footsteps of a guard walking up and down or the occasional scream of someone in pain coming from a cell elsewhere.

Although the prison was desperately overcrowded, being put in solitary confinement was a way of psychologically breaking down new prisoners. In the case of the Twins, it did not work, and Alfred was soon moved to cell 347 on the fourth floor of the second division, while Henry was put into cell 674 on the fifth floor of the third division.

However, the move was not particularly for the better. Where the cells had originally been intended for one man, they were now occupied by three or four prisoners at a time, as prisoners came and went. Each man was issued with two blankets and the beds were like those of an army barracks.

The walls were often decorated by previous occupants, with artwork ranging from signatures and salutations to lewd sketches, although those who had passed through before the war had obviously been better equipped than the prisoners now occupying the cells. Although the cell had a window, it was nailed shut and so when the sun beat down through the painted glass window it became a hothouse inside. Even breathing became difficult at times.

The prisoners had to exercise as best they could within the confines of their cell. Once a week, the guards brought razors from cell to cell, but the soap was bad, the brushes thin and the blades soon became blunt as they were passed from man to man. Coffee, if it could be classed as such, was brought round in the morning, but the daily highlight was at midday when the soup, usually cabbage, was served with bread and a minute piece of fat, a slice of liver sausage or a small piece of cheese.

The rations were barely enough to keep a man alive, yet liberal enough not to allow him to die. Hunger was all part of the horrible and inhumane game, but at least lunch provided an end to it. The evening came in on a relieved stomach, if not on a full one. Sleep depended upon eating, but the only thing to eat was the bread saved from lunch because to lie awake at night on an empty stomach was an ordeal best avoided.

Also being held on the same division as Alfred was Peter Churchill, with whom the Twins should have carried out the Sainte-Assise mission the year before, had it not have been cancelled at the last minute. Much had happened since then, but Churchill had been captured a couple of weeks after the Twins when he parachuted into the French Alps for what would have been his fourth mission.

Alfred knew Churchill was at Fresnes at that time because he occasionally heard his name being shouted by the German guards and because the prisoners passed word by shouting from cell to cell. There were other ways of communicating between the cells, too. The walls and pipes could be used for Morse tapping and the prison plumbing had been so arranged that there was a hollow between the adjoining corners of the cells, containing the pipes for the taps and toilets. By speaking through the hole that housed the taps, the prisoners could communicate. It was known as 'talking through the tap'.

There was little in the way of interrogations or beatings at Fresnes, although that was the only consolation, and the Twins knew that it could all start again at any time. However, gradually the weeks turned into months.

★★★

It was now November 1943. The Twins had been at Fresnes for six months. The autumn winds sweeping through the stone prison had taken the last of the warmth stored through the summer months with them. Somehow, the prisoners managed to help each other through it all – through their patriotism, faith and, at times, humour, but above all through their courage.

Sadly, not everyone got through it, as Alfred witnessed one evening when being led back to his cell having been photographed and finger-printed at a building in Rue des Saussaies. As his guard led him through the labyrinth of passages back at the prison, Alfred was made to wait with his face to a wall to let a group of men pass. They were marching proudly in step and it was clear from the patriotic song they were singing that they were all condemned men and were presumably off to their deaths.

The sound had a lasting impression on Alfred, but it typified the spirit of Fresnes. Even the Germans could not break that. Fresnes might have been built as a prison where silence reigned, but to keep hundreds of patriots quiet was all but impossible. The sound of 'V-for-Victory' would often be heard along the water pipes, echoing from the walls and ceilings, particularly when Allied bombers were heard overhead. When everyone joined in, it was a quite deafening sound and was often followed by the singing of the Marseillaise, sung at full voice by men determined to keep their souls.

★★★

Then, one bitterly cold morning, the Twins were bundled into a van, shackled together and driven to the notorious No. 84 Avenue Foch.

The Avenue Foch is a wide boulevard in the centre of Paris connecting the Arc de Triomphe with Port Dauphine. At the western end is No. 84, a rather ordinary-looking building that now contains a handful of privately owned flats. During the Nazi occupation of France, No. 84 Avenue Foch was used as the SD's headquarters in Paris and was where captured SOE agents, such as the Twins, were taken for further interrogation.

The building was under the overall command of Sturmbannführer Josef Kieffer, the senior German intelligence officer in Paris, but interrogations were carried out on the third floor under the authority of 33-year-old Standartenführer Helmut Knochen, the SD's senior commander whose jurisdiction stretched across northern France.

As well as being a headquarters and a place where interrogation took place, the building was used for other purposes. On the second floor, the SD's wireless unit transmitted bogus radio messages as a way of trying to flush out resistance groups and SOE agents. From here, the Germans were able to mimic SOE wireless operators using captured wireless sets, codes and security checks. It was all part of what became known as 'the radio game', or *Funkspiel* to the Germans, and was played out under the Gestapo's radio and coding expert, Doctor Josef Goetz.

When the Twins arrived at No. 84 Avenue Foch in November 1943, the radio game was at a peak. In fact, the Germans had gained the upper hand. Many SOE circuits had recently fallen, following the debacles of several large resistance networks, leading to the arrests of hundreds of French men and women. During those dark winter months, it is estimated that as many as eighteen SOE agents fell straight into the arms of the Gestapo, although the whole deception game was being cleverly played by both sides and it was not long before the tables were turned.

The Twins were dragged up the rather steep staircase to the fifth floor, which is the top floor of what is not a particularly spacious building. A narrow corridor now connects the rooms of the private flat, but at the time the fifth floor contained a guardroom and cell and an interpreter's office. It was where prisoners were first processed and then made to wait before being dragged back down the stairs for interrogation.

Alfred and Henry were left shackled together in the cell, guarded by a couple of armed troops. The thought of the interrogations resuming once again was sickening. While they were waiting, someone strolled in to greet them. It was someone they recognised, and this chance meeting took the Twins totally by surprise.

The man was another SOE agent called John Starr, although the Twins knew him at the time by his code name, Bob. They had all been on the same preliminary training course at Wanborough Manor. Starr had been captured a few months earlier during his second mission in France and was now at the Avenue Foch, but something did not seem right. He was clean-shaven and wearing a shirt, necktie and shoes.

When asked what he was doing there, Starr replied that he was a prisoner, just like the Twins, and went on to say that the Germans were not that bad. In fact, Starr said, he was keeping quite well, unlike some of the other boys around the place, but he had come to warn the Twins that they were about to be confronted by one of the German interrogators.

Nothing more was said between them at the time. For now, the Twins had other things on their minds than to give any further thought to what might have been going on. It was Henry who was called for initial questioning first, while Alfred was driven straight back to Fresnes, although his turn at Avenue Foch came soon enough.

The following morning, Alfred was back on the top floor of No. 84. This time, he was taken to the interpreter's office, where a tall, slim man in his late thirties, with curly black hair and dressed in civilian clothes and wearing an eye glass, was waiting for him. In perfect French, the soft-voiced man introduced himself as Ernest.

He was Sonderführer Ernst Vogt, a Swiss-German civilian attached to the SD as a senior interrogator and Kieffer's personal assistant and French interpreter. Vogt thumbed through Alfred's file and was clearly in no hurry to proceed with the interrogation. He had met many SOE agents before. He and Kieffer knew how to manipulate individuals and had even managed to negotiate with some of them, sparing their lives for information about others – a so-called 'pact', for want of a better word.

Ernest asked Alfred if he knew Captain Starr, at which point Starr walked in and greeted Alfred as if they had never met. However, when Ernest got up, supposedly to look for some papers, Alfred got the impression that the whole thing was staged so that he and Starr were left alone to have a few moments together.

This is exactly what happened. Starr spoke to Alfred in English, telling him not to lead the Germans up the garden path. It was quite useless, Starr said, the Germans knew everything. So much for the success of Orchard Court. Starr went on to say that he had seen some of the others while he had been at No. 84 Avenue Foch and he had another baby boy, although he had not seen him yet. Starr left the room, but Alfred could hear him talking and laughing with the Germans outside. It was all very strange.

Throughout Ernest's questioning, Alfred stuck to his story. And, like Larsen had done before, Ernest seemed keen to impress on Alfred just how much the Germans knew about the Racket, and Buckmaster in particular. However, it had no impact on Alfred; it was simply more German talk. Besides, it had been seven months since the Twins had been arrested and there was little or nothing either of them knew that would now be of any use to the Germans, so much would have changed during that time.

Ernest even asked Alfred if he thought he was going to be shot, to which Alfred replied that he thought he would be, only for Ernest to say that they, the Germans, were not as bad as London made them out to be. He would not be shot, Ernest said. Instead, he would be sent to a camp in Germany until the end of the war. Ernest then went on to say that it was a very nice camp, like a holiday camp with wonderful facilities including a cinema and baths.

Whatever Alfred might have been expecting at No. 84 Avenue Foch, he had certainly not expected to hear anything like that, although he was not naive enough to believe anything about the camp being a nice place. He was then taken back to Fresnes to find that the prisoners he had been sharing a cell with had gone. It was yet another rotation of people, something he had got used to over the months, although he could not help but wonder what would happen to them all.

***

It had been a similar experience for Henry. During his questioning, Ernest had over-elaborated his knowledge of the Racket and even claimed to have dined with Nicholas Bodington during his recent visit to Paris. Bodington had indeed been in Paris, but that had been more than three months earlier. It was yet another useless lie to try and impress Henry and trick him into co-operating. But, as with all that had gone on before, it was another trick that failed to work.

A week later, Alfred was taken to the prison office at Fresnes, where two Gestapo men were waiting. They had come for a prisoner by the name of Norman.

What followed next was a scene of utter confusion, during which the prison warders and the two men from the Gestapo seemed to argue. The confusion was about whether Alfred was the man they had come for as his first name did not tally with the one they had been given. They had come for a man called Gilbert Norman, who was to be taken off to be executed, and not Alfred Norman. They were clearly annoyed with the prison guards for bringing the wrong man.

Alfred was eventually taken back to his cell, but he was worried that it might have been Henry the Gestapo men had been after. Either that, or there really was a third prisoner being held at Fresnes with the surname of Norman.

There was, in fact, a third prisoner called Norman. This was 28-year-old Gilbert Norman, just as the Gestapo men had stated, and his story is as sad as many that have gone before. Sent into the field in late 1942 as a wireless operator for the PROSPER network in northern France, Norman was arrested in June 1943. But transmissions continued from his wireless set, although no one in London knew for certain whether they were being made by him under duress or even if it was Norman transmitting at all. It was all part of the radio game, and in one way or another Gilbert Norman was caught up in it all, although to what extent may never be known. From what is known, though, it seems Norman initially tried warning London that he was transmitting under duress by leaving out part of the security check. It was a safety check the Germans did not know about and had been devised for circumstances such as this, but on this occasion the security procedures in place did not work at all. Norman simply received a reply drawing his attention to the omission in the security check and telling him to be more careful next time. Norman was certainly seen at No. 84 Avenue Foch after his capture and so it is possible that he was working under Kieffer but, whatever the truth, the fact that Alfred had witnessed the arrival of the Gestapo at Fresnes to take Norman away merely confirms he had now outlived his usefulness to the Germans. Gilbert Norman's life came to an end in September 1944 at the Mauthausen concentration camp. It is yet another truly wretched tale.

***

Christmas 1943 came and went. Attempts by the Red Cross to send the prisoners a few home comforts merely added to the luxuries for the German guards at the prison, although some of the French prisoners are known to have received the occasional food parcel. It all depended on who the prisoner was and which guards were on duty at the time.

Then, in January 1944, Alfred was again taken to the prison office. This time he was given back his pipe and tobacco pouch that had been taken from him when he had first arrived at Fresnes, and then bundled into a large ground-floor cell with around thirty other prisoners. He could hear shouting outside. A convoy was being made ready in the courtyard.

The cell door opened, and they were all led outside to form up in the freezing cold. Hundreds of other prisoners were there as well. They were all herded onto the buses and were soon on their way, leaving Fresnes and its horrors behind.

16

BUCHENWALD

For many prisoners, it was the first time in several months they had seen the outside world. Those who had ventured out of their cells had only ever seen the walls of the courtyard or caught glimpses of the streets of Paris on their way to Rue des Saussaies or No. 84 Avenue Foch. Now there were open spaces once again and, even though it was the depth of a cold winter, the grey skies and brown fields were a beautiful sight.

Alfred could not help but wonder where Henry was. They had always been together, even since being captured, albeit they had been kept in different cells, and that had given them great moral strength. But it had also surprised them. The Germans must have considered separating them at some point as they were clearly getting nothing out of them. To separate them might just have broken the spirit of one or the other – although that would have been most unlikely. Now, though, it seemed that the Twins had finally been split up. And if that was to be the case, then Alfred felt quite sad.

As the bus made its way through the northern suburbs of Paris, Alfred started chatting to the young man sat next to him. They chatted openly but cautiously, and it soon became apparent that they had both been working for the SOE. The young man was 21-year-old Maurice Pertschuk, a wireless operator who had been working for Nicolas and had been arrested the week after the Twins. He was now travelling under the name of Martin Perkins.

Alfred was quite taken by the charm and maturity of such a young man and it was a classic case of two SOE agents who had both heard about each other yet had never met. They even spoke of John Starr, who had also confronted Pertschuk at No. 84 Avenue Foch, and of Ernest. They had both been through the same thing.

It was nearly dark by the time they approached the outskirts of Compiègne in northern France. The bus pulled up outside what was obviously a camp. As the prisoners were led in, Alfred could see that thousands of people were gathered there. But he suddenly felt alone.

They had arrived at the Royallieu-Compiègne internment and deportation camp. Originally built as an army barracks, it was the only fully German-run camp within France. Today, part of the camp has been preserved as the *Mémorial de l'internement et de la déportation (Camp de Royallieu)* to remember the 48,000 who passed through during the Second World War before the majority were deported elsewhere. Most were political prisoners or members of the Resistance, but thousands of Jews were deported as well.

The camp consisted of twenty-four low, one-storied buildings covering three sides of a square, all surrounded by miradors, or towers. On top of each was a searchlight and machine-gun post.

Alfred wandered through the crowded alleys separating each building, hoping that he might find Henry or at least someone who knew where he might be. Several times he thought he had spotted him, only to be disappointed. At the far end of the camp there was barbed wire separating the men from the women, many of whom were desperately calling out names in the hope of catching a glimpse of a loved one. It was all very depressing.

The new arrivals were crowded together in one of the buildings, where they spent the bitterly cold nights on the floor. No one knew what the following day would bring. The sight and sound of the heaped and jostling bodies was oppressive. It was all very different to the solitude and confinement of Fresnes. The silence and the privacy had gone.

At dawn the roll calls began. There seemed to be every age and class of Frenchman there. Prisoners were either tagged *Verbrecher*, meaning criminal, for those who had resisted the occupation, or *Indicateur* (informer), for those who had helped the Germans. Alfred could not help but feel sorry for this latter group. They were obviously of no further use to the Nazis and had now ended up in the same place to await their fate. They might just as well have resisted the occupation; it made no difference now which side they had been on.

On the morning of 27 January 1944, Alfred was one of 1,584 men, each clutching a ration of bread and a sausage, who were taken through the eastern outskirts of the town to a railway siding on the edge of the Forest of Compiègne where a long train of battered cattle trucks stood waiting. From there the single track ran eastwards, following the course of the River Aisne and what is today the N31 road, to the town of Soissons and ultimately to Germany. It was the third mass deportation from the camp that month. Another followed just two days later, this time women. Some 6,500 people were deported from Compiègne in January 1944 alone.

The prisoners were bundled into the trucks, as many as 150 per truck. They were packed so tightly that there was no room to move. The open windows that had once provided ventilation inside the trucks had all been boarded up with only a minimum amount of light passing through the gaps. The doors were shut and planks nailed across them, making it impossible for them to be opened from the inside. And, with every truck packed tight, the train eventually got under way.

One of the prisoners in Alfred's truck, a man known as Turk, immediately set to work on the boarded-up window with a saw and file he had smuggled on board. But the Germans soon found out and stopped the train. Threatening to shoot ten men unless the perpetrator owned up, Turk admitted what he had done; his reward for owning up was a beating, before he was stripped naked and bundled into another wagon.

Escape seemed impossible and no one knew where they were going or how long they would be locked up inside. It was hard to breathe, and the stench of filthy human bodies was unbearable. There was no water and only a bucket provided any sanitation, although it was impossible for most to get anywhere near it. They would have to do whatever they had to do wherever they were. It was inhumane.

The groans and prayers and the occasional scream of terror continued as the train kept going through the night. Many collapsed through lack of water, while some died of suffocation. In the dim light filtering through the boarded windows as daylight broke it was impossible to see who was alive and who was dead amongst the pile of bodies.

Eventually the train stopped at a small station. The doors were opened, but only for long enough to allow some food and water to be passed inside. From what the prisoners could gather, they had crossed into Germany. Other than that, they had no idea where they were. The planks were then put back in place across the doors and the train moved off once again.

The nightmare lasted for three days before the journey finally came to an end. The planks were ripped off and the doors slid open. In the dim light, the prisoners could make out that their truck was on a railway siding bordered by barbed-wire fences. A young soldier in the uniform of the SS waved them out on to the platform with his long black cane, shouting at them all the time. Those who could manage it scrambled over the pile of bodies and jumped out of the truck.

It was bitterly cold, with a layer of snow covering the ground. In a pitiful procession the prisoners filed past more SS men lining the way, some holding back dogs on chains, while the only light came from a row of lamps. The prisoners moved in an eerie silence. All that could be heard was the crunching sound of feet on the snow and the barking of the dogs. The prisoners simply followed the dimly lit road, but where it was leading no one knew.

After several minutes faint lights appeared in the distance. They started to become brighter. The shuffling came to a halt. Against the darkness of the night sky, Alfred could make out the shape of a large, square building with a watchtower and clock mounted centrally above, below which were iron gates and buildings on either side. So this was Ernest's 'holiday camp', he thought. They had arrived at the entrance to a Nazi concentration camp. It was Buchenwald.

Buchenwald was built just before the Second World War on the northern slope of the Ettersberg hill, a few miles to the north of Weimar, the city of Classicism in central Germany. It originally accommodated political opponents to the Nazi regime and others who had no place in the National Socialist so-called 'people's community', such as criminals, homosexuals, Jehovah's Witnesses, Jews, Sinti and Roma. Following the outbreak of war, the Nazis also sent people to Buchenwald from across occupied Europe, including the mentally ill and physically disabled to be used as guinea pigs for the sake of 'biological research'.

Buchenwald soon became the largest concentration camp on German soil. The total number ultimately imprisoned there and at its 139 sub-camps is estimated to be around 280,000, with most being used as forced labour. Everyone was ruthlessly exploited as the camp was run by some of the SS's most sadistic officers, and its guards consisted of the most brutal thugs.

The cocktail of miserable conditions, hard work, hunger and typhus, all made Buchenwald one of the worst camps. Some 56,000 died there.

Today, the site is preserved by the Buchenwald and Mittelbau-Dora Memorials Foundation as a permanent exhibition and museum and is financed by the Federal Republic of Germany and the Free State of Thuringia to counter the belittlement and denial of the crimes committed there with irrefutable evidence and to give the victims of persecution faces and voices.

When Alfred arrived at Buchenwald on 29 January 1944, the camp was being run by 58-year-old SS Oberführer Hermann Pister. There were around 45,000 prisoners being held there at that time, some three times the number who had been at the camp just a year before and nearly twenty times the pre-war figure. The number arriving at Buchenwald was rising so fast that by the end of the war the figure swelled to more than 86,000.

The dimly lit road Alfred had just walked up was the access road known as the Caracho Path, which connected the railway station at Buchenwald to the entrance to the camp. As he passed through the iron gateway, Alfred could see ahead of him the silhouetted shape of rows of long, low-built huts, while off to his right he could make out the shape of a building with a chimney towering above. Every now and then smoke belched from the chimney and as he got closer the air became sickly with the stench of death. This was the crematorium.

The prisoners were marched past the rows of huts. The ground was rough and sloped down towards a large building called the *Effektenkammer* (Effects Chamber), where the new arrivals handed in any personal belongings. They were then filed into a smaller adjoining building called the *Disenfektion* (Disinfection Station), where they passed through different rooms; first to remove their clothing, then to shower and have their heads shaved, and finally to be immersed in a disinfecting bath. They were then herded naked through an underground passageway to be issued with their prison clothing.

The arrivals process ran like clockwork and within a couple of hours of arriving at Buchenwald Alfred was standing in battle-scarred, moth-eaten green clothing and wooden-soled canvas shoes. The normal blue-and-white vertical-striped clothes of the prisoners had all been used up and so the new arrivals were issued with anything that was available at the time. There was certainly no question of sizing. They would have to wear whatever they had been given, no matter how it fitted. Men could only wonder what had happened to those who had worn the clothes before.

In addition to his greens, Alfred was given a strip of cloth printed with large numerals and a red inverted triangle bearing the initial 'E' for *Engländer* to sew onto his top clothing. Officially, he was simply *Häftling* (prisoner) 44437, Category: Enemy of the Reich.

Alfred was pleased to find there were two other British officers within his group, both of whom were members of the SOE. One was young Maurice Pertschuk, who Alfred had met on the coach journey to Compiègne, and the other was 25-year-old Christopher Burney, a tall, fair-haired former army officer and trained commando. The three were to become inseparable friends.

Sadly, there was still no sign of Henry, but Alfred would never give up hope of finding his brother. Prisoners were often moved around in groups, and he and Henry had always been part of a group so there was still hope that he might be at Buchenwald as well.

By the time processing was complete it was daybreak. It was bitterly cold, and it had started to rain. Their flimsy clothing provided no protection from such miserable conditions. Only now could they truly take in their new surroundings for the first time.

Having been built on the side of the hill, what was known as the Inmates' Camp, the *Häftlingslager*, sloped away from the main entrance. They could see several neat rows of wooden huts, which were called blocks and numbered more than sixty in total, with the gaps between them giving the appearance of narrow streets. The camp was essentially split in two with a barbed-wire fence separating the *Gross Lager* (Big Camp) from the *Kleines Lager* (Little Camp) on the lower part of the slope. It all seemed quite enormous and it was not a pleasant sight.

While Alfred's first glimpse of Buchenwald understandably gave him an impression of size, standing in the same spot today, in what is mostly an open space, the camp does not seem that large at all, particularly when considering the number of prisoners being held there at the time. The Inmates' Camp, in fact, covered more than 400,000 square yards, but the blocks were crammed into a relatively small space, measuring no more than 350 yards wide and 250 yards in depth, behind the workshops and main square.

As Alfred stood there looking across the camp it was starting to come to life and the new arrivals could see their fellow prisoners for the first time. It was a shocking sight.

The people wandering slowly and painfully around looked more like walking skeletons, or zombies from another planet. The majority were wearing the same red triangle as Alfred, but with a different letter to denote their nationality, such as 'F' for French, 'P' for Polish and 'T' for Czechoslovakian (*Tschechoslowakisch*), but he noticed there were no others with an 'E'. Those with a red triangle but no letter were German prisoners, many of whom had been at the camp since before the war. There were other coloured triangles as well, such as black or green to denote criminals who were condemned for common law offences, while a yellow triangle was for Jews, pink was for homosexuals and violet for Jehovah's Witnesses. It all looked most depressing. From now on it was all about survival, nothing more.

Some of the longer-serving prisoners helpfully pointed out to the new arrivals who they should be wary of, such as the *Kapos*. These were prisoners appointed by the SS to oversee the working parties. And then there were those who wore black armbands bearing '*Lagerschutz*' in white letters. These were effectively the camp police and were also recruited from the ranks of the prisoners. They were already busily taking up their positions to make sure that nobody escaped the roll call (the *Appell*), which was held on the main square, the *Appellplatz*, and which everyone was required to attend. Refusal to participate, the new arrivals were told, was punishable by death.

Roll calls were carried out systematically every morning at dawn and again at the end of the working day. Some lasted several hours, with no other purpose than to cause more misery for the prisoners. It was all part of the programme of humiliation.

Standing on the square facing the gate building, Alfred could see the iron gates bearing in forged letters the inscription *Jedem das Seine* (To each his own), a Roman legal maxim expressing the universal right to equality and justice but abused by the SS to justify the brutal ostracism of certain people from society. The inscription had been installed in such a way as to be read from within the camp.

The gate building was the only permissible entrance to and exit from the camp. It also served as the main watchtower. A machine gun had been positioned so that it could be aimed at any point on the main square. All SS announcements were made over loudspeakers installed on the gate building. The right wing of the building (when viewed from within the camp) housed the camp prison, known as the bunker, while the left wing was for the offices of Pister and his staff.

After the roll call, Alfred and the other new arrivals were taken to a block surrounded by barbed wire. They had been taken to the Little Camp, set up as a quarantine zone, where they would be required to stay for the first couple of weeks. The men were divided into the two wings of the block. Alfred was put in a dormitory containing tiers of long rows of bunks, with two men allocated to each bunk and only one dirty blanket between them, which was barely long enough to half cover a man.

The British prisoners were initially destined for one of the sub-camps, from where very few are known to have returned, and it was only the intervention of a Dutch prisoner, a naval officer called Peter Cool, married to an English woman and now working as a medical clerk at Buchenwald, that prevented it from happening. Being sympathetic to the British, Cool was twice able to recover their prisoner cards from the SS prior to mass camp transfers taking place and so they were not moved.

Buchenwald was surrounded by electric barbed wire and overlooked by twenty-three watchtowers. Escape was clearly not an option, certainly not at this early stage. First and foremost, Alfred needed to know how to survive in the camp. Hunger dominated everyday life and the shortage of food created a situation of constant rivalry. Rations consisted of bread and soup, again usually cabbage, with the amount received depending on the prisoner's duties.

Those in the Little Camp were allocated half the rations because they were not assigned to working parties.

Food depravation was one of the severest punishments imposed at Buchenwald. The SS deliberately used hunger as a way of fuelling rivalry amongst the prisoners and keeping the camp under their control. Alfred soon saw for himself just how desperate the situation was. When the rations were distributed prisoners lunged at the food cauldrons and the bread. For the last in line there was never anything left and any prisoner not possessing a spoon or bowl was doomed. The law of the jungle ruled, and that was not all – diseases, primarily tuberculosis, quickly spread.

During the days that followed, Alfred learned more about the camp and how it was run. The daily routine was organised by block seniors. These were prisoners selected by the SS to carry out the administrative functions within the block, such as distributing the scant rations, assigning sleeping places and controlling their fellow prisoners' privileges.

It was clear from the outset that there was a huge communist presence and influence within the camp. If it had been the Nazis who had been his enemies before, then his new enemies were the communists; not because Alfred had done anything wrong, simply because he represented a world where freedom of thought and speech was the accepted right of the human being. Because the forced order of the camp was aimed at destroying the prisoners' personalities, to survive meant preserving personal habits and convictions, and upholding beliefs and culture. It was all about self-preservation, although fear and lack of familiarity with other cultures meant that it was difficult to build trust within the camp. Solidarity could only come about in groups that were formed on common political convictions, religious beliefs or origins.

The prisoners had soon learned to undermine the system at Buchenwald. They had already set up the International Camp Committee, which was organised by the German communists, many of whom had been in the camp since before the war and included like-minded individuals from other countries. The committee had many purposes, such as helping to prevent conflicts between the different national groups, secretly documenting the crimes that were being committed at Buchenwald and obtaining news on the course of the war, while also doing everything within its power to sabotage armaments production and hide people who were doomed to death.

With so many nationalities and factions at Buchenwald, there would always be problems inside the camp. Leaving the German communists to one side, the French were not all patriots. Some had been Nazi collaborators or black marketeers who had fallen out of favour with the Boche, while others had volunteered to work as slave labourers simply to protect their families back in France. Then there were the Russian prisoners, a mix of military and civilians, the Poles, the Yugoslavs and the Czechs, the Republican Spaniards, the Hungarians and Rumanians, the Greeks, the Belgians and the Dutch.

Not everyone inside the camp got on and not everyone could be trusted. There were even differences amongst the guards at Buchenwald, the worst being the Russian SS guards who had volunteered for the German forces. They were even more merciless than the Germans. It is difficult to sum up the peculiarity of how the camp was being run but, simply put, Buchenwald was a Nazi concentration camp, run by German communists, in which thousands of Russians slaved and died under the guns of Russian SS guards.

It took time for Alfred to learn who was who, and to find out who could be trusted, but he had to learn fast and he also had to know who were in the jobs that could one day be useful to him.

***

One day, Alfred was standing in front of the block thinking things through when he noticed a man staring at him. The man was wearing the same red triangle with the letter 'E' and the number 43984. The man spoke in clear English, 'Alfred?' It was Henry! Against all the odds, the Twins had been reunited. Although they had not realised it at the time, they had been deported on the same train from Compiègne. Neither of them knew whether to laugh or cry.

With their period of quarantine over, the Twins, Burney and Pertschuk were moved to the Big Camp and put to work in the limestone quarry on the western side of the hill. It supplied the material for the construction of buildings, roads and paths, and had been one of the prerequisites for the choice of the Ettersberg as the site of the camp.

The weather was awful during the early months of 1944 with heavy snow, bitter winds and freezing cold temperatures. The quarry was just a few hundred yards outside the main gate and although it initially felt good to get outside the camp after the months spent locked up at Fresnes, they soon discovered that this was a site of despotic shootings, cruel physical exploitation and abuse by the prison guards. The day was spent humping and dumping heavy stones. The work and cold were extremely painful.

Exhausted by the hard labour and lack of food, they were slowly, but surely, physically worn down to the lowest point of their lives. Yet, night after night, they returned to camp with the tenacity and stubbornness of the British before collapsing fully clothed and caked in mud on the bare planks that served as beds.

The Twins were then put on to night work, moving machine tools from one part of a factory to another. However, Alfred was soon put onto trench-digging duties. He was back out in the snowstorms in freezing temperatures for twelve hours a day and, working on an empty stomach, he soon became ill. For three days he continued to work with a fever, but his condition was clearly getting worse.

One evening they were all formed up on the main square with the other walking skeletons waiting for the roll call. Alfred was in a terrible state. Without the support of his brother's arm he would have collapsed. Pertschuk was ill too, and without the help of Burney he would never have survived. Mercifully, the roll call lasted just two hours, after which Henry helped his brother back to their hut. Alfred could barely breathe. He was convinced he would be dead in the morning, but he no longer cared.

The following morning the mortuary cart was doing its rounds as usual. As it pulled up outside each block, more bodies were piled on. Anyone who died after the cart had gone had to be put on a stretcher and taken to the roll call. One body was already on a stretcher and so Henry piled Alfred on top to save him having to walk or stand.

The morning roll calls were always soon over. The SS guards counted those on the square as quickly as they could to avoid keeping the prisoners from their work. With the roll call over, and as the thousands of men were forming up into their working groups, Henry quickly whisked Alfred away to the inmates' infirmary.

The infirmary was a separate compound situated on the lower slope of the camp, at its western extremity and surrounded by barbed wire. The camp initially had two huts used as the sick quarters, but because of epidemics and overcrowding, the compound now consisted of seven large huts; four were used as wards for the prisoners, one was a surgical ward, another was used for quarantine, and the seventh doubled up for X-rays and an operating room at one end while the other end was the morgue.

The infirmary was not just there to provide healthcare in the camp, it was also where medical experiments were being carried out on prisoners as part of a much larger programme. This included Blocks 46 and 50, where Sturmbannführer Doctor Erwin Ding-Schuler carried out typhus experiments on prisoners in search of new anti-typhus serums.

It was only because of Henry's persuasive powers and the help of a Dutch prisoner called Piek, who seemed to have some influence over the German running the ward, that Alfred's life was saved. He was taken to a ward and laid down on a bunk where a prisoner-nurse called Heinrich, another communist, took Alfred's temperature.

Alfred was very ill with double pneumonia and for the next three nights Heinrich tended to him as if he were his own brother. He stayed at Alfred's side, keeping him wrapped from head to toe in ice-cold wet blankets, and eventually Alfred's temperature started to come down. A few days later he was able to stand.

Pertschuk was also in the infirmary with pneumonia. Burney and Henry, meanwhile, worked like Titans, Henry having been sent back to the quarry. Burney even proved to be quite the diplomat and managed to convince the most influential communist prisoners that the four British officers should not be messed with. The reason was quite simple, he said. When the camp was liberated by the Anglo-Americans, as it surely would be one day, and not by the Russian Army as the communist prisoners had hoped, the British Government would want to know all about those inside the camp and how it was run. Like their Nazi over-lords, the members of the Communist Party Committee, as the International Camp Committee was known, would have to account for their behaviour. And so, it made sense to treat the British officers well should it ever come to the communists needing friends in court.

It was potentially a dangerous game that Burney was playing, but it worked. He and Henry were transferred to another block, where they were joined by Pertschuk and Alfred as soon as they were released from the infirmary.

★★★

It was now the beginning of June 1944 and through their influential contacts all four were given decent indoor jobs away from the brutal hard labour. Burney worked in the *Disenfektion* and Pertschuk the *Effektenkammer*, while Henry became an orderly in Block 10, which was mostly French prisoners, dishing up soup and bread to the new arrivals, and Alfred worked in an administration office run by SS Scharführer Winkler, a man Alfred later reported as 'one of the most wicked and cold-blooded murderers of Buchenwald'.

Night after night, Alfred typed up the long list of names as thousands more forlorn creatures of all nationalities arrived at the camp, as well as keeping a record of those who were sent to one of the many sub-camps elsewhere. Only by farming off thousands to the sub-camps could the number of prisoners at Buchenwald be maintained at what was considered a manageable level.

Life had settled into something of a routine, although there were still hardships along the way. After roll call the Twins would gather in the *Effektenkammer* with Pertschuk and Burney to discuss anything that had recently come to light.

Word had now filtered through of the Allied landings in Normandy as well as the push northwards through Italy and the Soviet advance on Germany from the east. Then came news that Paris was about to be liberated. But even as the Allies were advancing on the French capital, prisoners were still being deported to Germany. Another 1,250 men left Compiègne for Buchenwald on 17 August. They could not possibly have been of any further use to their captors and many would not live to see the freedom they had fought so gallantly for.

The Second World War had entered its final phase, but the daily struggle for survival at Buchenwald went on. Still the cattle trucks arrived and every time a train arrived at Buchenwald station, Alfred checked through the list of names of the new arrivals.

While checking through one list, he noticed that several names were British, quite possibly members of the SOE, while others were French and Belgian. They could also be agents, or at least members of the Resistance. There were thirty-seven names in all.

As Alfred had correctly guessed, the thirty-seven were all members of the SOE and Resistance. They had also trodden the well-worn path to Buchenwald. But, while it was sad to see that so many others had undergone the same brutal and miserable existence they had all been through, the arrival of the thirty-seven was a great morale booster for the Twins, Pertschuk and Burney. Until now, they had been the only SOE officers at the camp.

The senior British officer amongst the newcomers was 42-year-old Wing Commander 'Tommy' Yeo-Thomas, the legendary SOE agent known to the Gestapo as the 'White Rabbit'. He had been betrayed in Paris during his third mission with the SOE while operating under the cover of being a downed pilot called Kenneth Dodkin.

There were other RAF officers in the group too, including 31-year-old Squadron Leader Maurice Southgate. He was on his second mission when he had been captured three months earlier in a Gestapo trap in Montluçon. Another RAF officer was Flight Lieutenant Denis Barrett, a wireless operator, who had also been arrested on his second mission after going to the aid of a special forces operation in the forest of Fontainebleau.

Alfred even recognised one of the new arrivals. He had been at Germaine's flat the night the Twins had met the Bishop. This was Marcel Leccia and he was one of a trio caught up in the same maelstrom that had brought Maurice Southgate's war to an end. Now he and his two colleagues, Élisée Allard and Pierre Geelen, a Belgian, faced an uncertain future at Buchenwald.

There were two Canadians in the group, John Macalister and Frank Pickersgill. They had been dropped in the Cher valley the year before to set up a new circuit in the Ardennes called ARCHDEACON. Briefed to first go to Paris, they had been stopped and arrested at a vehicle checkpoint, and so theirs was another mission to be over before it had even started. Not only that, their arrests then triggered the chain of events leading to the PROSPER debacle, after which the Germans were able to use their captured wireless set to operate ARCHDEACON as a bogus circuit from the Avenue Foch. This, in turn, led to reception committees being set up, using unsuspecting members of the French Resistance, with supplies then driven away by collaborators. It was all yet another part of the catastrophic radio game.

Another new arrival was Desmond Hubble, an intelligence officer attached to the SOE, who had been captured soon after parachuting into the Ardennes ahead of the D-Day landings. He was to have organised and trained resistance groups in the area. The list went on, and behind every name there was a story of courage. Gradually, the Twins, Pertschuk and Burney met them all.

***

Then, around noon on 24 August, the war came to Buchenwald.

First, the air-raid siren wailed. The prisoners were confined to their blocks and as the first bombs fell on the camp, Alfred and Henry instantly dived for cover. For the next thirty minutes there was utter confusion as more bombs fell on the camp and its surroundings, while black

clouds of smoke darkened the sky above. Buchenwald
was shaking but, seeing a potential opportunity to escape,
many of the prisoners watched from their huts in the hope
that the barbed wire might be cut. Sadly, though, it was
not and the jubilation of seeing the aircraft soon turned to
sorrow when it was realised that so many prisoners were
lying dead.

More than 100 American bombers had been sent to
attack the armaments factory bordering the perimeter
of the camp. Their facilities were being used for the
manufacture of control parts for the A4 rocket project,
one of Germany's so-called 'wonder weapons', soon to
become better known as the V2. Nearly 400 prisoners
were killed during the raid, many of whom died when
the factory received a direct hit. A further 2,000 were
injured because they had not been allowed to leave the
factory during the attack. There were German casualties
as well, more than 100, when bombs fell on the SS barracks outside the main gate.

For the next couple of days, Buchenwald was in disar-
ray. While the members of the SS killed during the raid
were given heroes' burials with full military honours at the
Weimar main cemetery, the corpses of the prisoners killed
during the attack were incinerated in the camp crematorium and their ashes simply thrown away. Some of the
German guards even sought revenge by taking out their
hatred of the Allies on the prisoners, and there was no rush
to repair the damage inside the camp. Even the damaged
water pipes were left untended.

Things had just started to settle down again when, suddenly, on 9 September, an order was heard over the camp
loudspeakers for sixteen of the thirty-seven new arrivals to

report to the main gate at once. Amongst the names read out were Hubble, Macalister and Pickersgill. Leccia's name had been read out too.

At first, there was no great reason to be alarmed. Prisoners were often summoned to the camp gate for all sorts of reasons. As the rest of the group gathered to watch, the sixteen formed up outside Block 17 and marched smartly off in columns of four. But they were never seen again.

The following morning the rumours started. Someone said the sixteen had been thrown into the bunker after being beaten up, although they were all said to still be alive. In the evening, the rumours were more encouraging. Someone even said they had been seen out walking.

While there may well have been some truth in these rumours, it is more likely the sixteen had all been executed the previous night. They would have made the short walk to the far side of the crematorium and down the steps to the morgue, where they were each hanged from a hook, after which their bodies would have been burned in the furnaces. Some 1,100 are known to have been executed in this way during the latter years of the war, and there were enough hooks to have them all executed in one go. However, the exact date of death for each of the sixteen is not certain as the dates recorded by the Commonwealth War Graves Commission vary. Hubble, for example, is recorded as having died on 11 September whereas the deaths of Macalister and Pickersgill are recorded as 14 September. Sadly, it makes no difference. The outcome was the same.

Word of the deaths of the sixteen filtered through to Yeo-Thomas the following day, 11 September, after which he immediately informed the others. The thirty-seven had been reduced to twenty-one, and it was now perfectly clear what lay in store for them as well.

Desperate to save as many of the remaining members of his group as possible, Yeo-Thomas became involved in an audacious and collaborative plan, which resulted in a proposal being put to Erwin Ding-Schuler, the doctor leading the typhus experiments in Block 46. With the war all but over, the proposal put to him was that if he agreed to help the twenty-one remaining prisoners by allowing them to switch identities with other prisoners as they died from typhus then, in return, Yeo-Thomas, as the senior British officer in the camp, would testify on Ding-Schuler's behalf at any war crimes trial after the war.

Ding-Schuler initially agreed to help all twenty-one, but then changed his mind. Because a corpse had to be taken from the block bearing the identity of the deceased, prisoners could only be switched one at a time as someone died. And because he only had three Frenchman on the point of death, Ding-Schuler agreed to save just three men, one of whom had to be Yeo-Thomas as it was only him who could be of use to Ding-Schuler after the war.

Yeo-Thomas tried to argue against the change of plan, but he was in no position to set any conditions. To keep the plan secret, he then had to choose who to save without notifying the others. It was the hardest decision for anyone to have to make but, for the record, he chose Harry Peulevé and Stéphane Hessel, although Yeo-Thomas feared it would be a death sentence for the rest.

And so, in his own words, Yeo-Thomas 'conveniently died of typhus on 13 October 1944' to spend the rest of the war as Maurice Choquet, the dead Frenchman whose identity he had taken on. Within a month he had been transferred to another camp, which was all part of the plan to make sure his real identity was never exposed. By then, though, only five others (including Peulevé and Hessel) from the thirty-seven were still alive; the rest having gone to their deaths in the same gruesome way.

***

One who had yet to be called for execution was Maurice Southgate. Henry had managed to find him a job in the tailoring department, generally accepted to be one of the best jobs in the camp. Southgate, Burney, Pertschuk and the Twins were now the only five British officers left at Buchenwald. They could not help but wonder who would be called next. Perhaps they would all be called together.

Meanwhile, more trainloads of prisoners continued to arrive. Even with the executions and deaths, Buchenwald was at bursting point. Every now and then Alfred recognised a name on his lists or a face in the block. The stories he heard from captured members of the French Resistance filled him with envy. The Allies were advancing across Europe and there were plenty of weapons for the resisters, who were now freely opposing the Nazis. It was all a very different situation to the one he had been a part of just a couple of years before.

Christmas came, not that there was anything to celebrate, and it was freezing cold but there was hope the war would be over before too long. Then it was 1945. Slowly, the weeks passed. It had now been nearly two years since the Twins had been caught. Against all the odds they had somehow managed to survive.

From the sound of aircraft overhead and the noise of guns nearby, it was obvious the Allies were getting close. Confirmation of the Allied advance was reinforced by the arrival of thousands of prisoners from other camps. Buchenwald would be liberated, that was for sure, but for some prisoners it meant the tide was about to turn. Men who had decided the fate of others now faced an uncertain future themselves. Some who realised they might one day have to answer to their Anglo-American liberators decided they no longer wanted to be hard-line communists, while others believed, or at least hoped, the Russians would be the first to arrive.

All this created tension inside the camp and often split loyalties amongst the prisoners. Even the SS guards seemed to be treading more carefully for fear of what the prisoners might one day have to say about them. But while the Twins should have been able to relax and look forward to their freedom, they could do nothing of the kind. The killings inside the camp still went on. Now, as much as ever, they had to look after themselves and they just hoped the camp would be liberated before their call for execution came.

It was now coming to the end of March 1945. Not that those inside the camp knew it at the time, but Buchenwald would be liberated within two weeks, and less than a month after that the war in Europe would be over. They were nearly through it.

Then, out of nowhere, came the biggest blow of them all. Maurice Pertschuk was told to report to the main gate. Only Burney was with him when the call over the loudspeakers came. The two walked together as far as the square, after which the young Pertschuk was left to make the rest of the walk alone. Burney could only watch in silence, the tears unashamedly streaming down his face as the slim, boyish figure went striding into the distance, his shoulders squared, and his head still held magnificently high.

17

LIBERATION

It is most likely that Maurice Pertschuk suffered the same miserable fate as the others. His date of death is officially recorded as 29 March 1945. He was just 23 years old. How anyone could order the execution of someone at such a late stage of the war is beyond comprehension.

For the four surviving British officers at Buchenwald it was the bitterest of blows and left Burney, Southgate and the Twins in no doubt as to what also lay in store for them. And with the war obviously nearing its end, their executions would almost certainly come quite soon.

Burney had already arranged hiding places within the camp should the need ever arise, and it was now time for them all to disappear. But it was not to be as simple as that. Burney's contact suddenly got cold feet, declaring there was only a hiding place for two and the others would have to find somewhere else.

Agreeing that no one would shed any tears for them back home, the Twins told Southgate and Burney to go ahead and hide. They would make their own arrangements. However, Southgate and Burney disagreed. There was a time when it looked like they would all have to argue it out but, in the end, their contact said he had found space for all four.

They were first taken to a coal shed behind one of the blocks, where they were told to remain in silence until they could be moved across to the Little Camp. It was dark and cramped inside the shed and the time spent waiting was tense.

It was dark by the time their contact returned. Without a word, they all followed him through the barbed wire. Where they had once been pleased to leave the squalor of the Little Camp behind, it was now their only chance of survival. The four were led into one of the squalid huts, where one of its occupants took them to a couple of spare bunks. They could sleep there, but if the hut was ever to be searched the board under the lower bunks was loose and there was enough space for them all to hide under the floor. For the next forty-eight hours they stayed in the squalid hut, listening to their names being called out over the camp loudspeakers.

Conditions inside the Little Camp were as bad as at any time during the war. It was in the infamous Block 61, known to the prisoners as the 'Block of Death', that the SS deliberately killed the sick, weak and dying by lethal injection. In the final three months before liberation more than 6,000 died there.

On the third night of their disappearance, a dozen more prisoners came to the hut, mostly Germans who had been at the camp since before the war. After being tipped off that their time was up, they had also gone into hiding.

Until now, Burney, Southgate and the Twins had felt relatively comfortable in their hiding place, but they felt the arrival of this new group put their own chances of survival at risk. The decision to leave the hut was a difficult one to make, but after a couple of days the four decided to take their chances mingling amongst the tens of thousands of other prisoners in the main camp. However, before they did, they first stitched false numbers over their own and exchanged their red triangles for ones with the letter 'F'.

As they returned to the main camp, they could see there was even more turmoil than there had been before. Prisoners being called to the main gate were clearly not going, and so there were SS guards roaming around the camp in pairs trying to find them. As the Twins later wrote, 'Buchenwald had become a ghastly game of hide-and-seek, in which the penalty for losing was death.'

At curfew they slipped into the *Effektenkammer* and hid in the loft, from where they had a commanding view across the whole camp. The loudspeakers continued to bark out orders. This time it was the Jews that were being called. They could only watch helplessly as people were being rounded up, while others could be seen running from block to block in a desperate bid to find somewhere to hide. It was all a pitiful sight; such memories would never go away.

The war was all but over, yet these were extremely tense days for the prisoners at Buchenwald. The SS had accelerated the evacuation process from the camp, inciting even more fear amongst those still inside. The prisoners feared a massacre, but they were not strong enough to liberate the camp on their own.

On their sixth day in the loft, they were joined by four German prisoners. From the sound of guns nearby a battle was being fought just a few hundred yards away. Then, as they looked down on the scene below, they could not believe their eyes. The SS guards were fleeing the camp. They were running for the woods, some discarding their uniforms in a desperate bid to hide their identities as they went. The once mighty SS were now on the run. It was a most wonderful sight. The loudspeakers again burst into life. All SS personnel were to leave the camp immediately.

After fifteen months of hell, Alfred and Henry were witnessing the final moments of Buchenwald. American tanks of the 37th Tank Battalion, 4th Armoured Division, had reached the outer part of the camp and, soon after, a reconnaissance troop of the 9th Infantry Battalion, 6th Armoured Division, entered the camp. Buchenwald had been liberated. It was 3.15 p.m. on 11 April 1945.

***

To their liberators, the four British officers looked more like skeletons than the strong human beings they had once been. They could barely walk, for their strength was ebbing and suppressed emotion was choking them. That night was spent in one of the camp's bungalows that had been home to an SS officer and his family. It was all very different to the blocks inside the camp. Then, the following day, they returned inside the camp to say emotional farewells to the prisoners who had become their friends. They were all survivors, but the mental scars of their ordeal would never go away.

Although the camp had been liberated, the prisoners were still far from home and the American soldiers could do little to help. There were still battles to be fought.

For a while, the Twins wondered what to do next. But then Burney and Southgate came to the rescue. They had been chatting to a British officer and a BBC correspondent, Bob Reid, who had been covering the Allied advance. Reid had a jeep and although its trailer was packed with recording equipment, he would get them on their way home.

With Alfred, Southgate and Burney crammed inside the jeep, and Henry sprawled across the equipment in the trailer as best he could, Reid set off west.

Three days later, the four were back in England. Reid had driven them to General Patton's US Army Headquarters in Gotha, where they were looked after by the Americans before being flown home. As they stepped back on British soil, they were greeted by Red Cross women dishing out cups of tea and cake. There was even a banner that simply read, 'Welcome Home'. This was the Britain they had all fought so gallantly for.

They reported to an office where Southgate passed a note to the RAF officer on duty, telling him to ring the number that he had written down and inform the person answering the phone that Hector, César, Artus and Auguste had landed back in England. The officer looked at them all, not knowing who they were or whether it was a joke, but as the four made perfectly clear, it was certainly not a joke.

The four were soon piling into a lorry. While there was obvious relief at their ordeal finally being over, there were also questions starting to circulate in their own minds. Why were they returning home and not Maurice Pertschuk, or any of the others for that matter? Why them? There would never be a satisfactory answer.

The lorry eventually pulled up outside the old Berners Hotel in central London. Maurice Buckmaster and Vera Atkins were there to greet them. Walking through the lounges, there were men drinking whisky and smoking cigars. It was all too much. The Twins stopped, almost in unison, and stared. The laughter and chatter of the people turned to the screams of the insane and the dying. They were suddenly back in the cattle truck on the way to Buchenwald.

Alfred did not sleep in his bed that night. It was too soft, too comfortable and too unreal. He slept on the floor, wrapped in a blanket and using his shoes for a pillow. The following morning, he went into Henry's room. Henry was sat on the floor with his back to the wall, just as he had done in prison. His bed, too, remained untouched.

After breakfast a car took the Twins to Baker Street. There were new people there; faces they had never seen. But everybody seemed to have heard about the Twins. F Section, they were told, had done its job, but with the war in Europe over its people were of no further use.

However, that was not all. The Twins soon discovered that the personal belongings they had left behind three years ago, just as they were about to go into France, had gone missing, and nothing had been paid into their bank accounts for the past year. It was as if London had given up on the Twins long ago and no one had expected them to return.

If the Twins had been forgotten – and it certainly seems as if they had – the reason for this probably goes back to 1943. News of their arrests had officially been reported on 19 April with an unconfirmed report saying they had been shot. Then, on 24 July, more than three months after their arrest, a Battle Casualty Form was raised for each of them reporting 'Probably Shot', although it is not clear why this form was raised at that time, unless it was procedural. However, a later entry on their files, dated 28 December 1944, reports that a Monsieur Gouill, the proprietor of the Café du Commerce in Le Mans, had seen the Twins while he had been at Fresnes, although when he had seen them is not recorded (the Twins were at Fresnes for more than seven months). But as Gouill had made his report four months after Paris had been liberated, and as nothing had been heard of the Twins during the previous twenty months, it is quite possible that his observation might have been questioned at the time as to whether it had really been the Twins he had seen. As nothing had been known of their whereabouts since, it is quite likely that those in Baker Street genuinely believed the Twins were no longer alive.

For now, though, the Twins were required to compile their official report. Dated 26 April 1945, it was written by Alfred, as he had the better grasp of writing English, and is completed in three parts: the first detailing their activity after being dropped in the field; the second covering their arrest and period in captivity in France; and the third recording their time at Buchenwald.

For a while, Alfred and Henry moved into a house in Nottingham Place, Marylebone, just off Regent's Park, which was being used by the SOE to accommodate stragglers like them. During the days that followed there were further questions about what had happened to others who had been at Buchenwald at the same time, particularly the thirty-seven. Alfred and Henry even bumped into John Starr, who they had last seen at No. 84 Avenue Foch a couple of years before. Since arriving back in England, they had been advised not to talk to Starr should they ever meet up with him, but their chance meeting occurred in Piccadilly Circus while he was on his way to the Aperitif Bar, a popular haunt of agents prior to going into the field. They were all very happy to see each other alive and although they had been advised not to talk to him, the brothers took the opportunity to ask Starr about what had been going on at No. 84 Avenue Foch.

For the next hour, Starr gave his version of events and how he even tried to escape the building with two others before he ended up surviving the concentration camps at Sachsenhausen and Mauthausen. Rightly or wrongly, the Twins accepted Starr's version of what had happened and were satisfied he had not told the Germans anything about them. Starr had known, for example, that their family had been killed at sea and not during the Blitz as they had said during their interrogations, and so he could easily have disclosed that, although the fact that the three had been friends before going to France may well have been the reason the Twins were saved.

John Starr's time at No. 84 Avenue Foch is full of controversy, with some of his fellow prisoners suspecting him of collaborating with the enemy. In the Government Official History Series book, *SOE in France*, the SOE's official historian, M.R.D. Foot, states that John Starr:

> … took a liberal – from the official viewpoint, a far too liberal – interpretation of the advice he had been given at Beaulieu: that if he fell into enemy hands, it would be

as well to play along a bit with his captors, to save himself from torture. For several months, he made himself thoroughly agreeable at the Avenue Foch.

During the following weeks, word gradually filtered through about the others. Brian Stonehouse (Célestin) had also survived the horrors of the concentration camps, the last being Dachau, from where he was liberated at the end of the war. Alan Jickell (Gustave), who the Twins were to have escaped France with, had arrived at the flat in Lyon a day too late, although he had safely made his way back to England via Gibraltar, arriving in London in June 1943. His mission in France was not considered a success and so he did not return to operations with the SOE, but instead ended the war as an interpreter at a prisoner-of-war camp in rural Cumberland.

Virginia Hall (Marie) had also successfully crossed the Pyrenees and after transferring to the American Office of Strategic Services, she returned to occupied France. With the war now over, she joined the Central Intelligence Agency as an intelligence analyst on French parliamentary affairs. Robert Boiteux (Nicolas) also survived the war and later moved to Australia, where he changed his name to Burdett.

There was also news about those with whom the Twins had worked so closely during their time in France. Marie-Fortunée Besson (Bohémienne) had survived the women's concentration camp at Ravensbrück, but sadly her husband, Alphonse, the gallant and loyal Thermogéne, had been executed in 1944. Eugénie Catin (Fernande) had also been deported to Germany but survived the hardships of forced labour before returning home at the end of the war.

Another to survive the horrors of Ravensbrück was Germaine Guérin. She later gave evidence against Robert Alesch, the Bishop, during his trial in Paris; he was executed in 1949. Doctor Jean Rousset (Pépin), Virginia Hall's closest ally in Lyon, like the Twins, had also survived the horrors of Buchenwald and later gave evidence against Alesch as well. Philippe de Vomécourt (Gauthier) had also been arrested but had escaped from prison and, after making his way to England, had returned to France in 1944 for another mission.

And of those in Le Puy, Hubert did not survive the war. The Joulians, however, did; Jean being deported to Germany to work as forced labour while Marie-Louise had been released a few weeks after capture. Eugène Labourier (Marius), meanwhile, was never captured and he had managed to carry on the fight. But it had come at a personal cost. Several months after the Twins were arrested, the Germans swooped on his home. Having been pre-warned of their arrival, he had fled by the time the Germans arrived, but they arrested his wife and 16-year-old son instead. She ultimately returned from Ravensbrück, but his son, Marcel, did not survive the war.

***

The Twins had now been told they were to be officially discharged from duty on 4 September 1945. However, a dispute about their substantive rank, and therefore their pay, went on for many years. It all hinged on whether their field promotion to the rank of captain, which they had been told about while in France, was valid as nothing had officially been promulgated back in London at the time.

The SOE was never the most thorough when it came to administration, and there was clearly some degree of carelessness in the treatment of its records at the end of the war. As the organisation was wound up, there were simply not the staff nor, it would seem, the appetite, to work through the bundles of paperwork to retain records of everything that had gone on. Much of the material simply disappeared, either intentionally or otherwise. As far as the SOE's official records are concerned, the Twins were only ever shown with the substantive rank of lieutenant. As it was put to them, there had been a slip-up somewhere and it was now too late to do anything about it.

With their wartime days over, the Twins moved to Spring Street in Paddington. Then, one morning in mid-September, a letter arrived addressed to them both. It was dated 13 September and was from Vera Atkins. It simply read, 'I am very pleased indeed to forward you the enclosed notifications that you have been awarded the M.B.E. (Mil.) for your good work in FRANCE. We are all delighted and send you both heartiest congratulations.'

There was another letter for each of them, this time from Maurice Buckmaster offering his congratulations. The news left the Twins stunned. They had not expected any reward. There were others, they felt, who were far more deserving. They had done more, and they had given more – they had given their lives.

For the record, their citation, promulgated in the *Supplement to the London Gazette* dated 30 August 1945, reads as follows:

This officer parachuted into France with his brother on 30 June 1942 as a saboteur instructor to a circuit in the unoccupied zone. In this capacity he worked for a period of nine months, throughout which period he showed outstanding courage and devotion to duty. He travelled continuously and organised and trained sabotage cells in various regions, in particular Lyon, St Etienne and Le Puy. These groups subsequently carried out effective sabotage on enemy industrial installations and railway communications. Newton was arrested in April 1943 with his brother and incarcerated at Fresnes, where he spent over a year in solitary confinement. He was later transferred to Buchenwald concentration camp where he suffered grave hardships. He was liberated in April 1945 when American forces occupied the camp. For his courageous work in the French Resistance and his remarkable endurance during his two years in captivity, it is recommended that he be appointed a Member of the Order of the British Empire (Military Division).

★★★

General Dwight D. Eisenhower, the Supreme Commander of the Allied Expeditionary Forces in Europe, said after the war that the operations carried out by the SOE, together with those of the French Resistance with whom they had been so closely associated, had shortened the war by nine months. Nine months is a long time in war, particularly in terms of lives saved. And if it is true that the war in Europe was shortened by nine months, then the SOE needs no further testimonial. The Twins had served through its most difficult years and they had certainly played their part.

Alfred and Henry did what they always did in such moments. They went for a drink. London was still full of joy and celebration, and together they shared each other's happiness for having received an award. But they could not help thinking of others and of their sacrifice.

And what now? The war was over, but what did the future have in store for them? They remembered how they had felt when they first joined the SOE. They had known then that as soon as the war was over, they would be of no further use. Worse still, they would probably be anti-social misfits – and that was exactly what they had become.

Above all, though, their thoughts were of their family and what had happened to them nearly four years ago – their parents, their wives and the smiling faces of Gigi, Jimmy and Coco. The memories and the pain came flooding back. They suddenly shared an overpowering sense of sadness and loneliness, as they had done so many years before after their show had ended and the audience had gone home.

BIBLIOGRAPHY AND REFERENCES

Published Sources

Bourne-Paterson, Robert, *SOE in France 1941–1945* (Barnsley: Frontline Books, 2016).

Bower, Tom, *Klaus Barbie: Butcher of Lyons* (London: Michael Joseph, 1984).

Braeuer, Lue, *German U-Boat Ace: Rolf Mützelburg* (Atglen, PA, USA: Schiffer Publishing Ltd, 2015).

Buckmaster, Maurice, *They Fought Alone: The True Story of SOE's Agents in Wartime France* (London: Odhams Press Ltd, 1958).

Burney, Christopher, *The Dungeon Democracy* (London: William Heinemann Ltd, 1945).

—*Solitary Confinement* (London: MacMillan & Co. Ltd, 1961).

Churchill, Peter, *Duel of Wits* (London: Hodder & Stoughton, 1953).

Cookridge, E.H., *Inside SOE: The First Full Story of SOE in Western Europe 1940–45* (London: Arthur Barker Ltd, 1966).

Cowburn, Benjamin, *No Cloak, No Dagger: Allied Spycraft in Occupied France* (London: Adventurers Club, Brown, Watson and Jarrolds, 1960).

Creighton, Rear Admiral Sir Kenelm, *Convoy Commodore* (London: Futura Publications Ltd, 1956).

Crowdy, Terry, *SOE Agent: Churchill's Secret Warriors* (Oxford: Osprey, 2008).

Escott, Squadron Leader Beryl E., *The Heroines of SOE: Britain's Secret Women in France* (Stroud: The History Press, 2010).

Foot, M.R.D., *SOE in France* (London: HMSO, 1966).

Fuller, Jean Overton, *The Starr Affair* (London: Victor Gollancz Ltd, 1954).

Helm, Sarah, *A Life in Secrets: The Story of Vera Atkins and the Lost Agents of SOE* (London: Little Brown, 2005).

Howarth, Patrick, *Undercover: The Men and Women of the SOE* (London: Routledge & Keegan Paul Books, 1980).

Hudson, Sydney, *Undercover Operator: An SOE Agent's Experiences in France & the Far East* (Barnsley: Leo Cooper, 2003).

Jacobs, Peter, *Setting France Ablaze: The SOE in France During WWII* (Barnsley: Pen & Sword, 2015).

Knigge, Volkhard, *Buchenwald: Ostracism & Violence 1937–45* (Göttingen, Germany: Wallstein Verlag, 2017).

Le Chêne, Evelyn, *Watch for Me by Moonlight: A British Agent with the French Resistance* (London: Corgi, 1974).

Marshall, Bruce, *The White Rabbit: The Secret Agent the Gestapo Could Not Crack* (London: Cassell, 1952).

Pearson, Judith L., *The Wolves at the Door: The True Story of America's Greatest Female Spy* (Guilford, CT, USA: The Lyons Press, 2005).

Purnell, Sonia, *A Woman of No Importance: The Untold Story of Virginia Hall, WW2's Most Dangerous Spy* (London: Virago Press, 2019).

Ruby, Marcel, *F Section SOE: The Story of the Buckmaster Network* (London: Leo Cooper, 1988).

Thomas, Jack, *No Banners: The Fabulous Story of the Legendary Newton 'Twins' Who Waged a 'Private' War Against the Nazis* (London: W.H. Allen, 1955).

Vomécourt, Philippe de, *Who Lived to See the Day: France in Arms 1940–45* (London: Hutchinson & Co. Ltd, 1961).

Yarnold, Patrick, *Wanborough Manor: School for Secret Agents* (Guildford: Hopfield Publications, 2009).

The National Archives – File and Document References

FO 950/1388	Nazi Persecution Claim: Captain Alfred Newton & Henry Newton.
HS 7/135	SOE Activities in France 1941–44.
HS 7/244	France F Section Diary, July–September 1942.
HS 7/245	France F Section Diary, October–December 1942.
HS 8/1002	British Circuits in France by Major Bourne-Patterson.
HS 9/314	Personnel File – Peter Morland Churchill (Vol. 1).
HS 9/315	Personnel File – Peter Morland Churchill (Vol. 2).
HS 9/797/3	Personnel File – Alan William Jickell.
HS 9/1096/8	Personnel File – Alfred Willie Oscar Newton.

HS 9/1097/1	Personnel File – Henry George Rodolfo Newton.
HS 9/1110/5	Personnel File – Gilbert Maurice Norman.
HS 9/1395/3	Personnel File – Maurice Southgate.
HS 9/1419/8	Personnel File – Brian Julian Warry Stonehouse.
HS 9/1458	Personnel File – Forest Frederick Edward Yeo-Thomas.
WO 373/98/306	Recommendations for Honours and Awards.

Imperial War Museum

Doc.26220	Private Papers of Captain A.W.O. Newton M.B.E.
Doc.8470	Private Papers of Captain H.G.R. Newton M.B.E.

INDEX